THE NEW F
SHAK

Designed to make Shakespeare's great plays available to all readers, the New Folger Library edition of Shakespeare's plays provides accurate texts in modern spelling and punctuation, as well as scene-by-scene action summaries, full explanatory notes, many pictures clarifying Shakespeare's language, and notes recording all significant departures from the early printed versions. Each play is prefaced by a brief introduction, by a guide to reading Shakespeare's language, and by accounts of his life and theater. Each play is followed by an annotated list of further readings and by a "Modern Perspective" written by an expert on that particular play.

Barbara A. Mowat is Director of Research *emerita* at the Folger Shakespeare Library, Consulting Editor of *Shakespeare Quarterly*, and author of *The Dramaturgy of Shakespeare's Romances* and of essays on Shakespeare's plays and their editing.

Paul Werstine is Professor of English in the Graduate School and at King's University College at Western University. He is a general editor of the New Variorum Shakespeare and author of *Early Modern Playhouse Manuscripts and the Editing of Shakespeare*, as well as many papers and essays on the printing and editing of Shakespeare's plays.

The Folger Shakespeare Library

The Folger Shakespeare Library in Washington, D.C., is a privately funded research library dedicated to Shakespeare and the civilization of early modern Europe. It was founded in 1932 by Henry Clay and Emily Jordan Folger, and incorporated as part of Amherst College in Amherst, Massachusetts, one of the nation's oldest liberal arts colleges, from which Henry Folger had graduated in 1879. In addition to its role as the world's preeminent Shakespeare collection and its emergence as a leading center for Renaissance studies, the Folger Shakespeare Library offers a wide array of cultural and educational programs and services for the general public.

EDITORS

BARBARA A. MOWAT
Director of Research emerita
Folger Shakespeare Library

PAUL WERSTINE
Professor of English
King's University College at Western University, Canada

Folger SHAKESPEARE LIBRARY

The Tragedy of

Richard III

By
WILLIAM SHAKESPEARE

An Updated Edition

Edited by Barbara A. Mowat
and Paul Werstine

Simon & Schuster Paperbacks
New York London Toronto Sydney New Delhi

Simon & Schuster Paperbacks
An Imprint of Simon & Schuster, Inc.
1230 Avenue of the Americas
New York, NY 10020

This Simon & Schuster trade paperback edition February 2018

For information about special discounts for bulk purchases,
please contact Simon & Schuster Special Sales at 1-866-506-1949
or business@simonandschuster.com.

The Simon & Schuster Speakers Bureau can bring authors
to your live event. For more information or to book an event,
contact the Simon & Schuster Speakers Bureau at 1-866-248-3049
or visit our website at www.simonspeakers.com.

Manufactured in the United States of America

10   9   8

ISBN 978-0-7434-8284-4
ISBN 978-1-4767-8692-6 (pbk)
ISBN 978-1-4767-8850-0 (ebook)

From the Director of the Folger Shakespeare Library

It is hard to imagine a world without Shakespeare. Since their composition four hundred years ago, Shakespeare's plays and poems have traveled the globe, inviting those who see and read his works to make them their own.

Readers of the New Folger Editions are part of this ongoing process of "taking up Shakespeare," finding our own thoughts and feelings in language that strikes us as old or unusual and, for that very reason, new. We still struggle to keep up with a writer who could think a mile a minute, whose words paint pictures that shift like clouds. These expertly edited texts, presented here with accompanying explanatory notes and up-to-date critical essays, are distinctive because of what they do: they allow readers not simply to keep up, but to engage deeply with a writer whose works invite us to think, and think again.

These New Folger Editions of Shakespeare's plays are also special because of where they come from. The Folger Shakespeare Library in Washington, DC, where the Editions are produced, is the single greatest documentary source of Shakespeare's works. An unparalleled collection of early modern books, manuscripts, and artwork connected to Shakespeare, the Folger's holdings have been consulted extensively in the preparation of these texts. The Editions also reflect the expertise gained through the regular performance of Shakespeare's works in the Folger's Elizabethan Theater.

I want to express my deep thanks to editors Barbara Mowat and Paul Werstine for creating these indispensable editions of Shakespeare's works, which incorporate the best of textual scholarship with a richness of commentary that is both inspired and engaging. Readers who want to know more about Shakespeare and his plays can follow the paths these distinguished scholars have tread by visiting the Folger itself, where a range of physical and digital resources (available online) exist to supplement the material in these texts. I commend to you these words, and hope that they inspire.

Michael Witmore
Director, Folger Shakespeare Library

Contents

Editors' Preface — *ix*

Shakespeare's *Richard III* — *xiii*

Reading Shakespeare's Language:
Richard III — *xvii*

Shakespeare's Life — *xxix*

Shakespeare's Theater — *xxxix*

The Publication of Shakespeare's Plays — *xlix*

An Introduction to This Text — *liii*

The Tragedy of Richard III
Text of the Play with Commentary — *1*

Longer Notes — *305*

Textual Notes — *309*

Richard III: A Modern
Perspective by Phyllis Rackin — *339*

Further Reading — *353*

Key to Famous Lines and Phrases — *380*

Editors' Preface

In recent years, ways of dealing with Shakespeare's texts and with the interpretation of his plays have been undergoing significant change. This edition, while retaining many of the features that have always made the Folger Shakespeare so attractive to the general reader, at the same time reflects these current ways of thinking about Shakespeare. For example, modern readers, actors, and teachers have become interested in the differences between, on the one hand, the early forms in which Shakespeare's plays were first published and, on the other hand, the forms in which editors through the centuries have presented them. In response to this interest, we have based our edition on what we consider the best early printed version of a particular play (explaining our rationale in a section called "An Introduction to This Text") and have marked our changes in the text—unobtrusively, we hope, but in such a way that the curious reader can be aware that a change has been made and can consult the "Textual Notes" to discover what appeared in the early printed version.

Current ways of looking at the plays are reflected in our brief introductions, in many of the commentary notes, in the annotated lists of "Further Reading," and especially in each play's "Modern Perspective," an essay written by an outstanding scholar who brings to the reader his or her fresh assessment of the play in the light of today's interests and concerns.

As in the Folger Library General Reader's Shakespeare, which the New Folger Library Shakespeare replaces, we include explanatory notes designed to help make Shakespeare's language clearer to a modern reader, and we place the notes on the page facing the text that they explain. We also follow the earlier edition in including illustrations—of objects, of clothing, of mythological figures—from books and manuscripts in the Folger Shakespeare Library collection. We provide fresh accounts of the life of Shakespeare, of the publishing of his plays, and of the theaters in which his plays were performed, as well as an introduction to the text itself. We also include a section called "Reading Shakespeare's Language," in which we try to help readers learn to "break the code" of Elizabethan poetic language.

For each section of each volume, we are indebted to a host of generous experts and fellow scholars. The "Reading Shakespeare's Language" sections, for example, could not have been written had not Arthur King, of Brigham Young University, and Randal Robinson, author of *Unlocking Shakespeare's Language,* led the way in untangling Shakespearean language puzzles and shared their insights and methodologies generously with us. "Shakespeare's Life" profited by the careful reading given it by S. Schoenbaum; "Shakespeare's Theater" was read and strengthened by Andrew Gurr, John Astington, and William Ingram; and "The Publication of Shakespeare's Plays" is indebted to the comments of Peter W. M. Blayney. We, as editors, take sole responsibility for any errors in our editions.

We are grateful to the authors of the "Modern Perspectives"; to Leeds Barroll and David Bevington for their generous encouragement; to the Huntington and Newberry Libraries for fellowship support; to King's University College for the grants it has provided to Paul Werstine; to the Social Sciences and Humanities Research Council of Canada, which has provided him with Research Time Stipends; to R. J. Shroyer of Western University for essential computer support;

and to the Folger Institute's Center for Shakespeare Studies for its fortuitous sponsorship of a workshop on "Shakespeare's Texts for Students and Teachers" (funded by the National Endowment for the Humanities and led by Richard Knowles of the University of Wisconsin), a workshop from which we learned an enormous amount about what is wanted by college and high-school teachers of Shakespeare today.

In preparing this preface for the publication of *Richard III* in 1996, we wrote: "Our biggest debt is to the Folger Shakespeare Library: to Werner Gundersheimer, Director of the Library, who made possible our edition; to Deborah Curren-Aquino, who provides extensive editorial and production support; to Jean Miller, the Library's Art Curator, who combs the Library holdings for illustrations, and to Julie Ainsworth, Head of the Photography Department, who carefully photographs them; to Peggy O'Brien, former Director of Education at the Folger and now Director of Education Programs at the Corporation for Public Broadcasting, and her assistant at the Folger, Molly Haws, who gave us expert advice about the needs being expressed by Shakespeare teachers and students (and to Martha Christian and other "master teachers" who used our texts in manuscript in their classrooms); to Jessica Hymowitz, who provides expert computer support; to the staff of the Academic Programs Division, especially Mary Tonkinson, Lena Cowen Orlin, Amy Adler, Kathleen Lynch, and Carol Brobeck; and, finally, to the staff of the Library Reading Room, whose patience and support are invaluable."

As we revise the play for publication in 2014, we add to the above our gratitude to Michael Witmore, Director of the Folger Shakespeare Library, who brings to our work a gratifying enthusiasm and vision; to Gail Kern Paster, Director of the Library from 2002 until

July 2011, whose interest and support have been unfailing and whose scholarly expertise continues to be an invaluable resource; to Stephen Llano, Jonathan Evans, and Alysha Bullock, our production editors at Simon & Schuster, whose expertise, attention to detail, and wisdom are essential to this project; to the Folger's Photography Department; to Deborah Curren-Aquino, for continuing superb editorial assistance; to Alice Falk for her expert copyediting; to Michael Poston for unfailing computer support; to Anna Levine; and to Rebecca Niles (whose help is crucial). Among the editions we consulted, we found James R. Siemon's 2009 Arden edition especially useful. Finally, we once again express our thanks to the late Jean Miller for the wonderful images she unearthed, and to the ever-supportive staff of the Library Reading Room.

Barbara A. Mowat and Paul Werstine
2014

Shakespeare's *Richard III*

In *Richard III*, Shakespeare invites us on a moral holiday. The early part of the play draws its readers to identify with Richard and thereby to participate in a fantasy
of total control of self and domination of others. We
begin to be pulled into the fantasy in the play's opening
speech, where Richard presents himself as an enter-
prising, self-made villain and offers an elaborate justi-
fication for this self-renovation. He then confides to us
his plans to dispose of his first victim, his brother Clarence, who is already being taken to prison as a result
of Richard's plots. Clarence's imprisonment serves as
immediate confirmation of Richard's sure power over
others. Richard deceives Clarence into believing that
Richard is his staunchest ally; in case we were mis-
led along with Clarence, Shakespeare gives Richard
another soliloquy as soon as Clarence has left. Richard achieves similar success in conquering the woman
with whom he chooses to ally himself in marriage. His
utter mastery of the political arena continues long into
the play as he carves a way to the throne through assas-
sination and summary execution of his rivals.

But Richard's advance is not wholly without resis-
tance, which appears most threateningly in the person
of Queen Margaret, widow of Henry VI, the king whom
Richard killed before this play begins. With a will as
strong as Richard's and a keen appetite for vengeance,
Margaret issues a stream of curses, and manages, in
spite of Richard's efforts, to curse him too. The further we proceed into the play, the greater the number
of characters who recall how Margaret cursed them as
they go to their deaths at Richard's hands. As this pattern builds, it begins to seem more and more inevitable

Richard III.
From John Taylor, *All the workes of . . .* (1630).

that all curses may come true—including her curse against Richard himself.

The more clear this pattern becomes, the more the play works to direct our sympathies away from Richard. His supporters desert him; his victims pile up. His fantasy of utter control of himself and domination of others crumbles. In this world of moral holiday, audience fantasy may begin to share in the desire for vengeance voiced by Margaret as Richard is presented increasingly as the monstrous and hideous villain that Sir Thomas More created in his early sixteenth-century narrative of Richard III's reign. More had spent his youth in the household of Cardinal Morton, the lord chancellor of England under Henry VII. (Both Cardinal Morton, in his earlier position as bishop of Ely, and Henry VII, as the earl of Richmond, appear as characters in Shakespeare's *Richard III*.) Morton, who had himself suffered under Richard III, may well have provided More with the highly prejudicial account of Richard's person and reign that More worked up into a brilliantly satirical and sometimes even comical tale of horror. More's history was so highly regarded in the sixteenth century that it became a standard part of compilations of British history throughout that century. In Shakespeare's play we can enjoy in dramatic form what so many of his immediate contemporaries and predecessors read and loved as a narrative.

After you have read the play, we invite you to turn to the essay printed after it, *"Richard III:* A Modern Perspective," by Phyllis Rackin, Professor of English *emerita* at the University of Pennsylvania.

Reading Shakespeare's Language: *Richard III*

For many people today, reading Shakespeare's language can be a problem—but it is a problem that can be solved. Those who have studied Latin (or even French or German or Spanish) and those who are used to reading poetry will have little difficulty understanding the language of Shakespeare's poetic drama. Others, however, need to develop the skills of untangling unusual sentence structures and of recognizing and understanding poetic compressions, omissions, and wordplay. And even those skilled in reading unusual sentence structures may have occasional trouble with Shakespeare's words. More than four hundred years of "static," caused by changes in language and in life, intervene between his speaking and our hearing. Most of his vocabulary is still in use, but a few of his words are no longer used, and many of his words now have meanings quite different from those they had in the sixteenth and seventeenth centuries. In the theater, most of these difficulties are solved for us by actors who study the language and articulate it for us so that the essential meaning is heard—or, when combined with stage action, is at least *felt*. When we are reading on our own, we must do what each actor does: go over the lines (often with a dictionary close at hand) until the puzzles are solved and the lines yield up their poetry and the characters speak in words and phrases that are, suddenly, rewarding and wonderfully memorable.

Shakespeare's Words

As you begin to read the opening scenes of a Shakespeare play, you may notice occasional unfamiliar words. Some are unfamiliar simply because we no longer use them. In the opening scenes of *Richard III*, for example, you will find the words *alarums* ("calls to arms"), *crossrow* ("alphabet"), *belike* ("perhaps"), and *naught* ("nothing," but also "wickedness"). Words of this kind are explained in notes to the text and will become familiar the more of Shakespeare's plays you read.

In *Richard III*, as in all of Shakespeare's writing, more problematic are the words that are still in use but that now have different meanings. In the opening scene of *Richard III*, for example, the word *measures* has the meaning of "dances"; *front* is used where we would say "forehead," *halt* where we would say "limp," and *tempers* where we would say "guides" or "directs." Again, such words will be explained in the notes to the text, but they, too, will become familiar as you continue to read Shakespeare's language.

Some words are strange not because of the "static" introduced by changes in language over the past centuries but because these are words that Shakespeare is using to build a dramatic world that has its own space, time, and history. The play's physical setting is concentrated, for the most part, in London, the seat of English royal power, until in Act 5 the play moves off to the battlefield. The London location is constructed for us by frequent reference to "the Tower" (i.e., the Tower of London), "Paul's" (usually St. Paul's Cathedral, sometimes Paul's Cross in the yard of the cathedral, where proclamations were issued), Whitefriars, and Crosby House (one of Richard's residences). The play's temporal and historical setting is more varied. The play opens at a moment that its language presents as doubly transitional. The first transition is from the Wars of the Roses to the peaceful reign of Edward IV, "son of York" and ultimate victor in these wars against Henry VI of the Lancasters. These wars are made vivid in a number of ways: with colorful references to implements, sounds, and events common to late medieval warfare: "bruisèd arms," "stern alarums," "dreadful marches," and "barbèd steeds"; with the names of the battlefields of those wars, such as "Tewkesbury" and "St. Albans," and of some of the notable victims—"virtuous Lancaster" (Henry VI), his son "Edward," Richard's brother "Rutland," their father "York," and Queen Elizabeth's first husband, "Grey." The second transition is from the peace imposed by Edward IV, who is now "sickly, weak, and melancholy," to an atmosphere of murderous intrigue. This transition is effected by means of the "plots" and "inductions dangerous" of the self-styled "subtle, false, and treacherous" Richard against the family of Edward's queen, whose brothers and sons Richard terms "silken, sly, insinuating Jacks." The political climate of the play's opening is created through such language as "envious slanders of . . . false accusers," "dissentious rumors," "lewd complaints," "interior hatred," "shameful injury," "vile suspects," and "deadly web." However strange these expressions and proper names appear at first, the words and phrases that create this language world will become increasingly familiar to you as you read further into the play.

Shakespeare's Sentences

In an English sentence, meaning is quite dependent on the place given each word. "The dog bit the boy" and "The boy bit the dog" mean very different things, even though the individual words are the same. Because English places such importance on the positions of words in sentences, on the way words are arranged, unusual arrangements can puzzle a reader. Shakespeare frequently shifts his sentences away from "normal" English arrangements—often to create the rhythm he seeks, sometimes to use a line's poetic rhythm to emphasize a particular word, sometimes to give a character his or her own speech patterns or to allow the character to speak in a special way. When we attend a good performance of the play, the actors will have worked out the sentence structures and will articulate the sentences so that the meaning is clear. When reading the play, we need to do as the actor does: that is, when puzzled by a character's speech, check to see if the words are being presented in an unusual sequence.

Shakespeare often places the verb before the subject (e.g., instead of "he goes" we find "goes he") or places the subject between the two parts of a verb (e.g., instead of "we will go" we find "will we go.") In the opening lines of *Richard III*, we find an inverted subject-verb construction in Richard's words "Now is the winter of our discontent / Made glorious summer," a construction repeated immediately in his "Now are our brows bound." Such inversions rarely cause much confusion. More problematic is Shakespeare's frequent placing of the object before the subject and verb (e.g., instead of "I hit him" we might find "him I hit"). Lady Anne's assertion "His soul thou canst not have" is an example of such an inversion (the normal order would be "Thou canst not have his soul"). Another example is Richard's "plots have I laid," where normally one would say "I have laid plots."

Inversions are not the only unusual sentence structures in Shakespeare's language. Often in his sentences words that would normally appear together are separated from each other. (Again, this is often done to create a particular rhythm or to stress a particular word.) Take, for example, Clarence's "*His Majesty, / Tend'ring my person's safety, hath appointed* / This conduct"; here the phrase "Tend'ring my person's safety" separates the subject ("His Majesty") from its verb ("hath appointed"). Or take Richard's lines "*The jealous o'erworn widow and herself, / Since that our brother dubbed them gentlewomen, / Are mighty gossips,*" where the normal construction "The . . . widow and herself are" is interrupted by the clause "Since that our brother dubbed them gentlewomen." In order to create for yourself sentences that seem more like the English of everyday speech, you may wish to rearrange the words, putting together the word clusters ("His Majesty hath appointed," "The widow and herself are mighty gossips"). You will usually find that the sentences will gain in clarity but will lose their rhythm or shift their emphases.

Locating and if necessary rearranging words that "belong together" is especially helpful in passages that separate subjects from verbs by long delaying or expanding interruptions—a structure that is sometimes used in *Richard III*. When Richard is rationalizing his villainy in the play's opening speech, he uses such an interrupted construction in a particularly extravagant way:

But *I*, that am not shaped for sportive tricks,
Nor made to court an amorous looking glass;
I, that am rudely stamped and want love's majesty
To strut before a wanton ambling nymph;
I, that am curtailed of this fair proportion,
Cheated of feature by dissembling nature,
Deformed, unfinished, sent before my time
Into this breathing world scarce half made up,

And that so lamely and unfashionable
That dogs bark at me as I halt by them—
Why, *I*, in this weak piping time of peace,
Have no delight to pass away the time,
Unless to see my shadow in the sun
And descant on mine own deformity.   (1.1.14–27)

Here the conjunction of the basic sentence elements, the subject "I" and its verb "have," is interrupted no fewer than four times, making it necessary to repeat the subject "I" three times and thereby making the speech markedly self-referential. In *Richard III*, as in many other of Shakespeare's plays (*Hamlet*, for instance), long interrupted sentences are used frequently, sometimes to catch the audience up in the narrative and sometimes as a characterizing device.

Occasionally, rather than separating basic sentence elements, Shakespeare simply holds them back, delaying them until subordinate material to which he wants to give greater emphasis has been presented. This kind of delaying structure is sometimes used in the speeches of *Richard III*, though usually not by Richard, who tends to assert himself more forcefully than such a delaying construction would allow. Queen Elizabeth, for example, uses such a construction in asserting her innocence of any conspiracy against her brother-in-law Clarence:

By Him that raised me to this careful height
From that contented hap which I enjoyed,
I never did incense his Majesty
Against the Duke of Clarence. . . . (1.3.87–90)

Here the subject and verb ("I never did incense") are delayed until the completion of a mighty oath ("By Him . . . enjoyed").

Shakespeare's sentences are sometimes complicated

not because of unusual structures or interruptions or delays but because he omits words and parts of words that English sentences normally require. (In conversation, we, too, often omit words. We say "Heard from him yet?" and our hearer supplies the missing "Have you.") Frequent reading of Shakespeare—and of other poets—trains us to supply such missing words. In his later plays, Shakespeare uses omissions both of verbs and of nouns to great dramatic effect. In the opening scenes of *Richard III*, one of Shakespeare's early plays, omissions seem to be used to affect the tone of the speech or for the sake of speech rhythm. Take, for example, the illusion of natural conversation between Richard and Hastings that is created by the omission of just three or four words in the blank verse:

RICHARD What news abroad?
HASTINGS
   No news so bad abroad as this at home:
   The King is sickly, weak, and melancholy,
   And his physicians fear him mightily.
                      (1.1.138–41)

Had this elliptical exchange been filled out with the inclusion of all the words appropriate to formal speech, Richard would have asked woodenly "What news *is* abroad?" and Hastings would have replied, to the destruction of the tone and the verse: "*There is* no news so bad abroad as *is* this *news* at home: the King is sickly, weak, and melancholy, and his physicians fear *for* him mightily."

Shakespearean Wordplay

Shakespeare plays with language so often and so variously that entire books are written on the topic. Here we will mention only two kinds of wordplay, puns and metaphors. A pun is a play on words that sound the same but have different meanings, or—as is sometimes the case in *Richard III*—on a single word that has more than one meaning. There is an example of the first kind of pun in the first lines of the play: "Now is the winter of our discontent / Made glorious summer by this son of York." Here Richard actually uses only one of the two words that make up the pun, namely the word *son*, with reference to the first son of the duke of York, King Edward IV. But because the word *son* appears in the context of "glorious summer," the audience itself supplies the second part of the pun in the word *sun*. The second kind of pun is evident a few lines later in the same speech when Richard suggests that he is so ugly there is nothing for him to do but "see my shadow in the sun / And descant on mine own deformity." The single word *descant* means both "comment" and "sing harmoniously."

A metaphor is a play on words in which one object or idea is expressed as if it were something else, something with which it is said to share common features. Again the opening lines of Richard's first speech supply an excellent example of such wordplay:

> Now is the winter of our discontent
> Made glorious summer by this son of York,
> And all the clouds that loured upon our house
> In the deep bosom of the ocean buried.

In this metaphor, Richard describes the adversity suffered by the family of York during the Wars of the Roses as if the adversity had been a cloudy winter sky threatening a house. The comparison continues as the peace achieved through Edward IV's victory is likened to a "glorious summer." In this speech, Richard demonstrates his linguistic powers, his control over language—his most attractive and engaging feature.

Implied Stage Action

Finally, in reading Shakespeare's plays we should always remember that what we are reading is a performance script. The dialogue is written to be spoken by actors who, at the same time, are moving, gesturing, picking up objects, weeping, shaking their fists. Some stage action is described in what are called "stage directions"; some is suggested within the dialogue itself. We must learn to be alert to such signals as we stage the play in our imaginations. Sometimes these signals are unambiguous. For example, when Richard says to Lady Anne "Lo, here I lend thee this sharp-pointed sword, . . . And humbly beg the death upon my knee" (1.2.191–95), it is pretty clear that the words are to be accompanied by his offering his sword to Lady Anne and his kneeling before her. And so, like other editors, we expand the Folio's stage direction *"He lays his breast open; she offers at ⌈it⌉ with his sword"* to include the direction that he kneel.

However, in other respects, the stage action that may be required by the dialogue is not nearly so clear. Having knelt, Richard must later rise, but the early printed texts give no indication, in either their stage directions or dialogue, when Richard is to stand. Nor do the early printed texts prescribe when Richard is to draw the sword that he offers to Lady Anne. Like other recent editors who include fairly complete stage directions indicating the action that may accompany the dialogue, we feel obliged to add a stage direction for Richard to rise after he has knelt; he is hardly to be imagined to exit from the stage on his knees. Yet we recognize that our choice of where to place this direction and other directions that we add has no authority beyond our own judgment based upon our reading of the early printed text. (This is one of the reasons we always mark such additions to the text with brackets.)

The question of when Richard should unsheathe his sword is even more challenging. Does he bring it onstage already drawn, using it to threaten a halberdier guarding the corpse of Henry VI: "Advance thy halberd higher than my breast, / Or by Saint Paul I'll strike thee to my foot" (1.2.41–42)? Or does he simply stare down the halberdier and not draw his sword until later? The scene can be played any number of ways, and there is nothing in the dialogue of the scene to mandate editorial intrusion of stage directions at any one place rather than another. We therefore do not print a stage direction for Richard either to enter with his sword drawn or to draw it at any particular point, since how extensively Richard may use his sword in this scene, beyond offering it to Anne, is, in our judgment, a matter to be left entirely to the imagination of readers, directors, and actors.

Learning to read the language of stage action repays one many times over when one reaches a crucial scene like that in Act 5 in which action takes place variously in tents pitched side by side on the stage and in which the ghosts of Richard's victims address in turn the sleeping Richard and Richmond. In such scenes, implied stage action vitally affects our response to the play.

It is immensely rewarding to work carefully with Shakespeare's language so that the words, the sentences, the wordplay, and the implied stage action all become clear—as readers for the past four centuries have discovered. It may be more pleasurable to attend a good performance of a play—though not everyone has thought so. But the joy of being able to stage one of Shakespeare's plays in one's imagination, to return to passages that continue to yield further meanings (or further questions) the more one reads them—these are pleasures that, for many, rival (or at least augment) those of the performed text, and certainly make it worth considerable effort to "break the code" of Elizabethan poetic drama and let free the remarkable language that makes up a Shakespeare text.

Shakespeare's Life

Surviving documents that give us glimpses into the life of William Shakespeare show us a playwright, poet, and actor who grew up in the market town of Stratford-upon-Avon, spent his professional life in London, and returned to Stratford a wealthy landowner. He was born in April 1564, died in April 1616, and is buried inside the chancel of Holy Trinity Church in Stratford.

We wish we could know more about the life of the world's greatest dramatist. His plays and poems are testaments to his wide reading—especially to his knowledge of Virgil, Ovid, Plutarch, Holinshed's *Chronicles*, and the Bible—and to his mastery of the English language, but we can only speculate about his education. We know that the King's New School in Stratford-upon-Avon was considered excellent. The school was one of the English "grammar schools" established to educate young men, primarily in Latin grammar and literature. As in other schools of the time, students began their studies at the age of four or five in the attached "petty school," and there learned to read and write in English, studying primarily the catechism from the Book of Common Prayer. After two years in the petty school, students entered the lower form (grade) of the grammar school, where they began the serious study of Latin grammar and Latin texts that would occupy most of the remainder of their school days. (Several Latin texts that Shakespeare used repeatedly in writing his plays and poems were texts that schoolboys memorized and recited.) Latin comedies were introduced early in the lower form; in the upper form, which the boys entered at age ten or eleven, students wrote their

Title page of a 1573 Latin and Greek catechism for children.
From Alexander Nowell, *Catechismus paruus pueris
primum Latine . . .* (1573).

own Latin orations and declamations, studied Latin historians and rhetoricians, and began the study of Greek using the Greek New Testament.

Since the records of the Stratford "grammar school" do not survive, we cannot prove that William Shakespeare attended the school; however, every indication (his father's position as an alderman and bailiff of Stratford, the playwright's own knowledge of the Latin classics, scenes in the plays that recall grammar-school experiences—for example, *The Merry Wives of Windsor*, 4.1) suggests that he did. We also lack generally accepted documentation about Shakespeare's life after his schooling ended and his professional life in London began. His marriage in 1582 (at age eighteen) to Anne Hathaway and the subsequent births of his daughter Susanna (1583) and the twins Judith and Hamnet (1585) are recorded, but how he supported himself and where he lived are not known. Nor do we know when and why he left Stratford for the London theatrical world, nor how he rose to be the important figure in that world that he had become by the early 1590s.

We do know that by 1592 he had achieved some prominence in London as both an actor and a playwright. In that year was published a book by the playwright Robert Greene attacking an actor who had the audacity to write blank-verse drama and who was "in his own conceit [i.e., opinion] the only Shake-scene in a country." Since Greene's attack includes a parody of a line from one of Shakespeare's early plays, there is little doubt that it is Shakespeare to whom he refers, a "Shake-scene" who had aroused Greene's fury by successfully competing with university-educated dramatists like Greene himself. It was in 1593 that Shakespeare became a published poet. In that year he published his long narrative poem *Venus and Adonis*; in 1594, he followed it with *The Rape of Lucrece*. Both poems were dedicated to the young earl of South-ampton (Henry Wriothesley), who may have become Shakespeare's patron.

It seems no coincidence that Shakespeare wrote these narrative poems at a time when the theaters were closed because of the plague, a contagious epidemic dis-ease that devastated the population of London. When the theaters reopened in 1594, Shakespeare apparently resumed his double career of actor and playwright and began his long (and seemingly profitable) service as an acting-company shareholder. Records for December of 1594 show him to be a leading member of the Lord Chamberlain's Men. It was this company of actors, later named the King's Men, for whom he would be a principal actor, dramatist, and shareholder for the rest of his career.

So far as we can tell, that career spanned about twenty years. In the 1590s, he wrote his plays on English history as well as several comedies and at least two tragedies (*Titus Andronicus* and *Romeo and Juliet*). These histories, comedies, and tragedies are the plays credited to him in 1598 in a work, *Palladis Tamia*, that in one chapter compares English writers with "Greek, Latin, and Italian Poets." There the author, Francis Meres, claims that Shakespeare is comparable to the Latin dramatists Seneca for tragedy and Plautus for comedy, and calls him "the most excellent in both kinds for the stage." He also names him "Mellifluous and honey-tongued Shakespeare": "I say," writes Meres, "that the Muses would speak with Shakespeare's fine filed phrase, if they would speak English." Since Meres also mentions Shakespeare's "sugared sonnets among his private friends," it is assumed that many of Shake-speare's sonnets (not published until 1609) were also written in the 1590s.

In 1599, Shakespeare's company built a theater

for themselves across the river from London, naming it the Globe. The plays that are considered by many to be Shakespeare's major tragedies (*Hamlet, Othello, King Lear,* and *Macbeth*) were written while the company was resident in this theater, as were such comedies as *Twelfth Night* and *Measure for Measure.* Many of Shakespeare's plays were performed at court (both for Queen Elizabeth I and, after her death in 1603, for King James I), some were presented at the Inns of Court (the residences of London's legal societies), and some were doubtless performed in other towns, at the universities, and at great houses when the King's Men went on tour; otherwise, his plays from 1599 to 1608 were, so far as we know, performed only at the Globe. Between 1608 and 1612, Shakespeare wrote several plays—among them *The Winter's Tale* and *The Tempest*—presumably for the company's new indoor Blackfriars theater, though the plays were performed also at the Globe and at court. Surviving documents describe a performance of *The Winter's Tale* in 1611 at the Globe, for example, and performances of *The Tempest* in 1611 and 1613 at the royal palace of Whitehall.

Shakespeare seems to have written very little after 1612, the year in which he probably wrote *King Henry VIII.* (It was at a performance of *Henry VIII* in 1613 that the Globe caught fire and burned to the ground.) Sometime between 1610 and 1613, according to many biographers, he returned to live in Stratford-upon-Avon, where he owned a large house and considerable property, and where his wife and his two daughters lived. (His son Hamnet had died in 1596.) However, other biographers suggest that Shakespeare did not leave London for good until much closer to the time of his death. During his professional years in London, Shakespeare had presumably derived income from the acting company's profits as well as from his

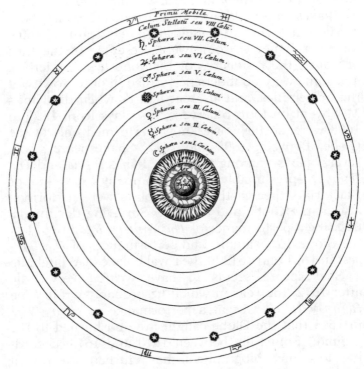

Ptolemaic universe.
From Marcus Manilius, *The sphere of* . . . (1675).

own career as an actor, from the sale of his play manuscripts to the acting company, and, after 1599, from his
shares as an owner of the Globe. It was presumably that
income, carefully invested in land and other property,
that made him the wealthy man that surviving documents show him to have become. It is also assumed
that William Shakespeare's growing wealth and reputation played some part in inclining the Crown, in 1596,
to grant John Shakespeare, William's father, the coat
of arms that he had so long sought. William Shakespeare died in Stratford on April 23, 1616 (according
to the epitaph carved under his bust in Holy Trinity
Church) and was buried on April 25. Seven years after
his death, his collected plays were published as *Mr. William Shakespeares Comedies, Histories, & Tragedies* (the
work now known as the First Folio).

The years in which Shakespeare wrote were among
the most exciting in English history. Intellectually,
the discovery, translation, and printing of Greek and
Roman classics were making available a set of works
and worldviews that interacted complexly with Christian texts and beliefs. The result was a questioning, a
vital intellectual ferment, that provided energy for the
period's amazing dramatic and literary output and
that fed directly into Shakespeare's plays. The Ghost
in *Hamlet*, for example, is wonderfully complicated
in part because he is a figure from Roman tragedy—
the spirit of the dead returning to seek revenge—who
at the same time inhabits a Christian hell (or purgatory); Hamlet's description of humankind reflects at
one moment the Neoplatonic wonderment at mankind
("What a piece of work is a man!") and, at the next, the
Christian attitude toward sinful humanity ("And yet, to
me, what is this quintessence of dust?").

As intellectual horizons expanded, so also did geo-
graphical and cosmological horizons. New worlds—

both North and South America—were explored, and in them were found human beings who lived and worshiped in ways radically different from those of Renaissance Europeans and Englishmen. The universe during these years also seemed to shift and expand. Copernicus had earlier theorized that the earth was not the center of the cosmos but revolved as a planet around the sun. Galileo's telescope, created in 1609, allowed scientists to see that Copernicus had been correct: the universe was not organized with the earth at the center, nor was it so nicely circumscribed as people had, until that time, thought. In terms of expanding horizons, the impact of these discoveries on people's beliefs—religious, scientific, and philosophical—cannot be overstated.

London, too, rapidly expanded and changed during the years (from the early 1590s to around 1610) that Shakespeare lived there. London—the center of England's government, its economy, its royal court, its overseas trade—was, during these years, becoming an exciting metropolis, drawing to it thousands of new citizens every year. Troubled by overcrowding, by poverty, by recurring epidemics of the plague, London was also a mecca for the wealthy and the aristocratic, and for those who sought advancement at court, or power in government or finance or trade. One hears in Shakespeare's plays the voices of London—the struggles for power, the fear of venereal disease, the language of buying and selling. One hears as well the voices of Stratford-upon-Avon—references to the nearby Forest of Arden, to sheepherding, to small-town gossip, to village fairs and markets. Part of the richness of Shakespeare's work is the influence felt there of the various worlds in which he lived: the world of metropolitan London, the world of small-town and rural England, the world of the theater, and the worlds of craftsmen and shepherds.

That Shakespeare inhabited such worlds we know from surviving London and Stratford documents, as well as from the evidence of the plays and poems themselves. From such records we can sketch the dramatist's life. We know from his works that he was a voracious reader. We know from legal and business documents that he was a multifaceted theater man who became a wealthy landowner. We know a bit about his family life and a fair amount about his legal and financial dealings. Most scholars today depend upon such evidence as they draw their picture of the world's greatest playwright. Such, however, has not always been the case. Until the late eighteenth century, the William Shakespeare who lived in most biographies was the creation of legend and tradition. This was the Shakespeare who was supposedly caught poaching deer at Charlecote, the estate of Sir Thomas Lucy close by Stratford; this was the Shakespeare who fled from Sir Thomas's vengeance and made his way in London by taking care of horses outside a playhouse; this was the Shakespeare who reportedly could barely read, but whose natural gifts were extraordinary, whose father was a butcher who allowed his gifted son sometimes to help in the butcher shop, where William supposedly killed calves "in a high style," making a speech for the occasion. It was this legendary William Shakespeare whose Falstaff (in *1* and *2 Henry IV*) so pleased Queen Elizabeth that she demanded a play about Falstaff in love, and demanded that it be written in fourteen days (hence the existence of *The Merry Wives of Windsor*). It was this legendary Shakespeare who reached the top of his acting career in the roles of the Ghost in *Hamlet* and old Adam in *As You Like It*—and who died of a fever contracted by drinking too hard at "a merry meeting" with the poets Michael Drayton and Ben Jonson. This legendary Shakespeare is a rambunctious, undisciplined man, as attractively "wild" as his plays were seen by earlier generations to be. Unfortunately, there is no trace of evidence to support these wonderful stories.

Perhaps in response to the disreputable Shakespeare of legend—or perhaps in response to the fragmentary and, for some, all-too-ordinary Shakespeare documented by surviving records—some people since the mid-nineteenth century have argued that William Shakespeare could not have written the plays that bear his name. These persons have put forward some dozen names as more likely authors, among them Queen Elizabeth, Sir Francis Bacon, Edward de Vere (earl of Oxford), and Christopher Marlowe. Such attempts to find what for these people is a more believable author of the plays is a tribute to the regard in which the plays are held. Unfortunately for their claims, the documents that exist that provide evidence for the facts of Shakespeare's life tie him inextricably to the body of plays and poems that bear his name. Unlikely as it seems to those who want the works to have been written by an aristocrat, a university graduate, or an "important" person, the plays and poems seem clearly to have been produced by a man from Stratford-upon-Avon with a very good "grammar-school" education and a life of experience in London and in the world of the London theater. How this particular man produced the works that dominate the cultures of much of the world four centuries after his death is one of life's mysteries—and one that will continue to tease our imaginations as we continue to delight in his plays and poems.

Shakespeare's Theater

The actors of Shakespeare's time are known to have performed plays in a great variety of locations. They played at court (that is, in the great halls of such royal residences as Whitehall, Hampton Court, and Greenwich); they played in halls at the universities of Oxford and Cambridge, and at the Inns of Court (the residences in London of the legal societies); and they also played in the private houses of great lords and civic officials. Sometimes acting companies went on tour from London into the provinces, often (but not only) when outbreaks of bubonic plague in the capital forced the closing of theaters to reduce the possibility of contagion in crowded audiences. In the provinces the actors usually staged their plays in churches (until around 1600) or in guildhalls. While surviving records show only a handful of occasions when actors played at inns while on tour, London inns were important playing places up until the 1590s.

The building of theaters in London had begun only shortly before Shakespeare wrote his first plays in the 1590s. These theaters were of two kinds: outdoor or public playhouses that could accommodate large numbers of playgoers, and indoor or private theaters for much smaller audiences. What is usually regarded as the first London outdoor public playhouse was called simply the Theatre. James Burbage—the father of Richard Burbage, who was perhaps the most famous actor in Shakespeare's company—built it in 1576 in an area north of the city of London called Shoreditch. Among the more famous of the other public playhouses that capitalized on the new fashion were the Curtain and the Fortune (both also built north of the city), the Rose,

A stylized representation of the Globe theater.
From Claes Jansz Visscher, *Londinum florentissima Britanniae urbs* . . . [c. 1625].

the Swan, the Globe, and the Hope (all located on the Bankside, a region just across the Thames south of the city of London). All these playhouses had to be built outside the jurisdiction of the city of London because many civic officials were hostile to the performance of drama and repeatedly petitioned the royal council to abolish it.

The theaters erected on the Bankside (a region under the authority of the Church of England, whose head was the monarch) shared the neighborhood with houses of prostitution and with the Paris Garden, where the blood sports of bearbaiting and bullbaiting were carried on. There may have been no clear distinction between playhouses and buildings for such sports, for we know that the Hope was used for both plays and baiting and that Philip Henslowe, owner of the Rose and, later, partner in the ownership of the Fortune, was also a partner in a monopoly on baiting. All these forms of entertainment were easily accessible to Londoners by boat across the Thames or over London Bridge.

Evidently Shakespeare's company prospered on the Bankside. They moved there in 1599. Threatened by difficulties in renewing the lease on the land where their first theater (the Theatre) had been built, Shakespeare's company took advantage of the Christmas holiday in 1598 to dismantle the Theatre and transport its timbers across the Thames to the Bankside, where, in 1599, these timbers were used in the building of the Globe. The weather in late December 1598 is recorded as having been especially harsh. It was so cold that the Thames was "nigh [nearly] frozen," and there was heavy snow. Perhaps the weather aided Shakespeare's company in eluding their landlord, the snow hiding their activity and the freezing of the Thames allowing them to slide the timbers across to the Bankside without paying tolls for repeated trips over London

Bridge. Attractive as this narrative is, it remains just as likely that the heavy snow hampered transport of the timbers in wagons through the London streets to the river. It also must be remembered that the Thames was, according to report, only "nigh frozen," and therefore did not necessarily provide solid footing. Whatever the precise circumstances of this fascinating event in English theater history, Shakespeare's company was able to begin playing at their new Globe theater on the Bankside in 1599. After this theater burned down in 1613 during the staging of Shakespeare's *Henry VIII* (its thatch roof was set alight by cannon fire called for in performance), Shakespeare's company immediately rebuilt on the same location. The second Globe seems to have been a grander structure than its predecessor. It remained in use until the beginning of the English Civil War in 1642, when Parliament officially closed the theaters. Soon thereafter it was pulled down.

The public theaters of Shakespeare's time were very different buildings from our theaters today. First of all, they were open-air playhouses. As recent excavations of the Rose and the Globe confirm, some were polygonal or roughly circular in shape; the Fortune, however, was square. The most recent estimates of their size put the diameter of these buildings at 72 feet (the Rose) to 100 feet (the Globe), but we know that they held vast audiences of two or three thousand, who must have been squeezed together quite tightly. Some of these spectators paid extra to sit or stand in the two or three levels of roofed galleries that extended, on the upper levels, all the way around the theater and surrounded an open space. In this space were the stage and, perhaps, the tiring house (what we would call dressing rooms), as well as the so-called yard. In the yard stood the spectators who chose to pay less, the ones whom Hamlet contemptuously called "groundlings." For a roof they had only the sky, and so they were exposed to all kinds of weather. They stood on a floor that was sometimes made of mortar and sometimes of ash mixed with the shells of hazelnuts, which, it has recently been discovered, were standard flooring material in the period.

Unlike the yard, the stage itself was covered by a roof. Its ceiling, called "the heavens," is thought to have been elaborately painted to depict the sun, moon, stars, and planets. The exact size of the stage remains hard to determine. We have a single sketch of part of the interior of the Swan. A Dutchman named Johannes de Witt visited this theater around 1596 and sent a sketch of it back to his friend, Arend van Buchel. Because van Buchel found de Witt's letter and sketch of interest, he copied both into a book. It is van Buchel's copy, adapted, it seems, to the shape and size of the page in his book, that survives. In this sketch, the stage appears to be a large rectangular platform that thrusts far out into the yard, perhaps even as far as the center of the circle formed by the surrounding galleries. This drawing, combined with the specifications for the size of the stage in the building contract for the Fortune, has led scholars to conjecture that the stage on which Shakespeare's plays were performed must have measured approximately 43 feet in width and 27 feet in depth, a vast acting area. But the digging up of a large part of the Rose by late-twentieth-century archaeologists has provided evidence of a quite different stage design. The Rose stage was a platform tapered at the corners and much shallower than what seems to be depicted in the van Buchel sketch. Indeed, its measurements seem to be about 37.5 feet across at its widest point and only 15.5 feet deep. Because the surviving indications of stage size and design differ from each other so much, it is possible that the stages in other theaters, like the Theatre, the Curtain, and the Globe (the outdoor playhouses where we know that Shake-speare's plays were performed), were different from those at both the Swan and the Rose.

After about 1608 Shakespeare's plays were staged not only at the Globe but also at an indoor or private playhouse in Blackfriars. This theater had been constructed in 1596 by James Burbage in an upper hall of a former Dominican priory or monastic house. Although Henry VIII had dissolved all English monasteries in the 1530s (shortly after he had founded the Church of England), the area remained under church, rather than hostile civic, control. The hall that Burbage had purchased and renovated was a large one in which Parliament had once met. In the private theater that he constructed, the stage, lit by candles, was built across the narrow end of the hall, with boxes flanking it. The rest of the hall offered seating room only. Because there was no provision for standing room, the largest audience it could hold was less than a thousand, or about a quarter of what the Globe could accommodate. Admission to Blackfriars was correspondingly more expensive. Instead of a penny to stand in the yard at the Globe, it cost a minimum of sixpence to get into Blackfriars. The best seats at the Globe (in the Lords' Room in the gallery above and behind the stage) cost sixpence; but the boxes flanking the stage at Blackfriars were half a crown, or five times sixpence. Some spectators who were particularly interested in displaying themselves paid even more to sit on stools on the Blackfriars stage.

Whether in the outdoor or indoor playhouses, the stages of Shakespeare's time were different from ours. They were not separated from the audience by the dropping of a curtain between acts and scenes. Therefore the playwrights of the time had to find other ways of signaling to the audience that one scene (to be imagined as occurring in one location at a given time) had ended and the next (to be imagined at perhaps a different location at a later time) had begun. The customary way used by Shakespeare and many of his contemporaries was to have everyone on stage exit at the end of one scene and have one or more different characters enter to begin the next. In a few cases, where characters remain onstage from one scene to another, the dialogue or stage action makes the change of location clear, and the characters are generally to be imagined as having moved from one place to another. For example, in *Romeo and Juliet,* Romeo and his friends remain onstage in Act 1 from scene 4 to scene 5, but they are represented as having moved between scenes from the street that leads to Capulet's house into Capulet's house itself. The new location is signaled in part by the appearance onstage of Capulet's servingmen carrying table napkins, something they would not take into the streets. Playwrights had to be quite resourceful in the use of hand properties, like the napkin, or in the use of dialogue to specify where the action was taking place in their plays because, in contrast to most of today's theaters, the playhouses of Shakespeare's time did not fill the stage with scenery to make the setting precise. A consequence of this difference was that the playwrights of Shakespeare's time did not have to specify exactly where the action of their plays was set when they did not choose to do so, and much of the action of their plays is tied to no specific place.

Usually Shakespeare's stage is referred to as a "bare stage," to distinguish it from the stages of the last two or three centuries with their elaborate sets. But the stage in Shakespeare's time was not completely bare. Philip Henslowe, owner of the Rose, lists in his inventory of stage properties a rock, three tombs, and two mossy banks. Stage directions in plays of the time also call for such things as thrones (or "states"), banquets (presumably tables with plaster replicas of food on them), and beds and tombs to be pushed onto the stage. Thus the stage often held more than the actors.

The actors did not limit their performing to the stage alone. Occasionally they went beneath the stage, as the Ghost appears to do in the first act of *Hamlet*. From there they could emerge onto the stage through a trapdoor. They could retire behind the hangings across the back of the stage, as, for example, the actor playing Polonius does when he hides behind the arras. Sometimes the hangings could be drawn back during a performance to "discover" one or more actors behind them. When performance required that an actor appear "above," as when Juliet is imagined to stand at the window of her chamber in the famous and misnamed "balcony scene," then the actor probably climbed the stairs to the gallery over the back of the stage and temporarily shared it with some of the spectators. The stage was also provided with ropes and winches so that actors could descend from, and reascend to, the "heavens."

Perhaps the greatest difference between dramatic performances in Shakespeare's time and ours was that in Shakespeare's England the roles of women were played by boys. (Some of these boys grew up to take male roles in their maturity.) There were no women in the acting companies. It was not so in Europe, and had not always been so in the history of the English stage. There are records of women on English stages in the thirteenth and fourteenth centuries, two hundred years before Shakespeare's plays were performed. After the accession of James I in 1603, the queen of England and her ladies took part in entertainments at court called masques, and with the reopening of the theaters in 1660 at the restoration of Charles II, women again took their place on the public stage.

The chief competitors of such acting companies as the one to which Shakespeare belonged and for which he wrote were companies of exclusively boy actors. The competition was most intense in the early 1600s. There were then two principal children's companies: the Children of Paul's (the choirboys from St. Paul's Cathedral, whose private playhouse was near the cathedral); and the Children of the Chapel Royal (the choirboys from the monarch's private chapel, who performed at the Blackfriars theater built by Burbage in 1596). In *Hamlet* Shakespeare writes of "an aerie [nest] of children, little eyases [hawks], that cry out on the top of question and are most tyrannically clapped for 't. These are now the fashion and . . . berattle the common stages [attack the public theaters]." In the long run, the adult actors prevailed. The Children of Paul's dissolved around 1606. By about 1608 the Children of the Chapel Royal had been forced to stop playing at the Blackfriars theater, which was then taken over by the King's Men, Shakespeare's own troupe.

Acting companies and theaters of Shakespeare's time seem to have been organized in various ways. For example, with the building of the Globe, Shakespeare's company apparently managed itself, with the principal actors, Shakespeare among them, having the status of "sharers" and the right to a share in the takings, as well as the responsibility for a part of the expenses. Five of the sharers, including Shakespeare, owned the Globe. As actor, as sharer in an acting company and in ownership of theaters, and as playwright, Shakespeare was about as involved in the theatrical industry as one could imagine. Although Shakespeare and his fellows prospered, their status under the law was conditional upon the protection of powerful patrons. "Common players"—those who did not have patrons or masters—were classed in the language of the law with "vagabonds and sturdy beggars." So the actors had to secure for themselves the official rank of servants of patrons. Among the patrons under whose protection Shakespeare's company worked were the lord chamberlain and, after the accession of King James in 1603, the king himself.

In the early 1990s we began to learn a great deal more about the theaters in which Shakespeare and his contemporaries performed—or, at least, began to open up new questions about them. At that time about 70 percent of the Rose had been excavated, as had about 10 percent of the second Globe, the one built in 1614. Excavation was halted at that point, but London has come to value the sites of its early playhouses, and takes what opportunities it can to explore them more deeply, both on the Bankside and in Shoreditch. Information about the playhouses of Shakespeare's London is therefore a constantly changing resource.

The Publication of Shakespeare's Plays

Eighteen of Shakespeare's plays found their way into print during the playwright's lifetime, but there is nothing to suggest that he took any interest in their publication. These eighteen appeared separately in editions in quarto or, in the case of *Henry VI, Part 3*, octavo format. The quarto pages are not much larger than a modern mass-market paperback book, and the octavo pages are even smaller; these little books were sold unbound for a few pence. The earliest of the quartos that still survive were printed in 1594, the year that both *Titus Andronicus* and a version of the play now called *Henry VI, Part 2* became available. While almost every one of these early quartos displays on its title page the name of the acting company that performed the play, only about half provide the name of the playwright, Shakespeare. The first quarto edition to bear the name Shakespeare on its title page is *Love's Labor's Lost* of 1598. A few of the quartos were popular with the book-buying public of Shakespeare's lifetime; for example, quarto *Richard II* went through five editions between 1597 and 1615. But most of the quartos were far from best sellers; *Love's Labor's Lost* (1598), for instance, was not reprinted in quarto until 1631. After Shakespeare's death, two more of his plays appeared in quarto format: *Othello* in 1622 and *The Two Noble Kinsmen*, coauthored with John Fletcher, in 1634.

In 1623, seven years after Shakespeare's death, *Mr. William Shakespeares Comedies, Histories, & Tragedies* was published. This printing offered readers in a single book thirty-six of the thirty-eight plays now thought to have been written by Shakespeare, including eighteen that had never been printed before. And it offered them in a style that was then reserved for serious literature and scholarship. The plays were arranged in double columns on pages nearly a foot high. This large page size is called "folio," as opposed to the smaller "quarto," and the 1623 volume is usually called the Shakespeare First Folio. It is reputed to have sold for the lordly price of a pound. (One copy at the Folger Shakespeare Library is marked fifteen shillings—that is, three-quarters of a pound.)

In a preface to the First Folio entitled "To the great Variety of Readers," two of Shakespeare's former fellow actors in the King's Men, John Heminge and Henry Condell, wrote that they themselves had collected their dead companion's plays. They suggested that they had seen his own papers: "we have scarce received from him a blot in his papers." The title page of the Folio declared that the plays within it had been printed "according to the True Original Copies." Comparing the Folio to the quartos, Heminge and Condell disparaged the quartos, advising their readers that "before you were abused with divers stolen and surreptitious copies, maimed, and deformed by the frauds and stealths of injurious impostors." Many Shakespeareans of the eighteenth and nineteenth centuries believed Heminge and Condell and regarded the Folio plays as superior to anything in the quartos.

Once we begin to examine the Folio plays in detail, it becomes less easy to take at face value the word of Heminge and Condell about the superiority of the Folio texts. For example, of the first nine plays in the Folio (one-quarter of the entire collection), four were essentially reprinted from earlier quarto printings that Heminge and Condell had disparaged, and four have now been identified as printed from copies written in the hand of a professional scribe of the 1620s named Ralph Crane; the ninth, *The Comedy of Errors,* was apparently also printed from a manuscript, but one whose origin cannot be readily identified. Evidently, then, eight of the first nine plays in the First Folio were not printed, in spite of what the Folio title page announces, "according to the True Original Copies," or Shakespeare's own papers, and the source of the ninth is unknown. Since today's editors have been forced to treat Heminge and Condell's pronouncements with skepticism, they must choose whether to base their own editions upon quartos or the Folio on grounds other than Heminge and Condell's story of where the quarto and Folio versions originated.

Editors have often fashioned their own narratives to explain what lies behind the quartos and Folio. They have said that Heminge and Condell meant to criticize only a few of the early quartos, the ones that offer much shorter and sometimes quite different, often garbled, versions of plays. Among the examples of these are the 1600 quarto of *Henry V* (the Folio offers a much fuller version) or the 1603 *Hamlet* quarto. (In 1604 a different, much longer form of the play got into print as a quarto.) Early twentieth-century editors speculated that these questionable texts were produced when someone in the audience took notes from the plays' dialogue during performances and then employed "hack poets" to fill out the notes. The poor results were then sold to a publisher and presented in print as Shakespeare's plays. More recently this story has given way to another in which the shorter versions are said to be re-creations from memory of Shakespeare's plays by actors who wanted to stage them in the provinces but lacked manuscript copies. Most of the quartos offer much better texts than these so-called bad quartos. Indeed, in most of the quartos we find texts that are at least equal to or better than what is printed in the Folio. Many Shakespeare enthusiasts persuaded themselves that most of the quartos were set into type directly from Shakespeare's own papers, although there is nothing on which to base this conclusion except the desire for it to be true. Thus speculation continues about how the Shakespeare plays got to be printed. All that we have are the printed texts.

The book collector who was most successful in bringing together copies of the quartos and the First Folio was Henry Clay Folger, founder of the Folger Shakespeare Library in Washington, D.C. While it is estimated that there survive around the world only about 230 copies of the First Folio, Mr. Folger was able to acquire more than seventy-five copies, as well as a large number of fragments, for the library that bears his name. He also amassed a substantial number of quartos. For example, only fourteen copies of the First Quarto of *Love's Labor's Lost* are known to exist, and three are at the Folger Shakespeare Library. As a consequence of Mr. Folger's labors, scholars visiting the Folger Shakespeare Library have been able to learn a great deal about sixteenth- and seventeenth-century printing and, particularly, about the printing of Shakespeare's plays. And Mr. Folger did not stop at the First Folio, but collected many copies of later editions of Shakespeare, beginning with the Second Folio (1632), the Third (1663–64), and the Fourth (1685). Each of these later folios was based on its immediate predecessor and was edited anonymously. The first editor of Shakespeare whose name we know was Nicholas Rowe, whose first edition came out in 1709. Mr. Folger collected this edition and many, many more by Rowe's successors, and the collecting and scholarship continues.

An Introduction to This Text

The early printing history of *Richard III* is a fascinating study. It testifies to the enduring popularity of the play among readers. Furthermore, although several other Shakespeare plays are like *Richard III* in that they survive in more than one printed version, *Richard III* is unique among even these plays for the degree of complexity in the relations between the two quite different versions of it printed in the period 1597–1623. The complexity arises from the evidence that the first version to see print in 1597 is very likely a later version of the play than the second version that was printed in 1623. But the complexity does not end there. The 1597 printed version was reprinted over and over again. More than one of the reprinted texts of this version also appear to have influenced what was printed in the second version of 1623. And so the versions of *Richard III* crisscross: the first printed version, almost all scholars agree, provides a second state of the play, and later printings of this second state, in turn, influenced the printing of the play in its first state. It is possible (and necessary) then to write a quite detailed account of what lies behind the extant printed versions— and possible to do so with reference only to extant printed texts, without resorting to questionable narratives about Shakespeare's own manuscripts or about memorial reconstructions of plays by actors in the provinces.

This account begins by identifying and briefly describing the seven earliest printings of *Richard III* in the order of their printing. The play first appeared as *The Tragedy of King Richard the third. Containing, His treacherous Plots against his brother Clarence: the pittiefull murther of his iunocent [sic] nephews: his tyrannicall vsurpation: with the whole course of his detested life, and most deserued death. As it hath beene lately Acted by the Right honourable the Lord Chamberlaine his seruants . . . 1597.* This printing was a quarto or pocket-size book known today as "Q" for "(First) Quarto." Since it offers one of the two basic versions of the play, we need to pause to remark on its differences from and probable relation to the other basic version, which was not printed until 1623, the version usually called simply "F" by editors because it is found in the so-called First Folio of Shakespeare. The Quarto (Q) version is the shorter one: gone from Q are about 200 lines of the Folio (F) version. The passages unique to F range all the way from single words and phrases to one stretch of over fifty lines. But Q also has nearly forty lines that are not in F, including one passage of about twenty lines. In total the individual verbal variants between F and Q—for example, substitution in one text of a word (say, "evils" Q) that is often nearly synonymous to the word found in the other ("crimes" F), or transpositions of the same words ("may you" Q; "you may" F)—run into the hundreds.

Ordinarily when such a textual situation presents itself, there is no way to determine the priority of either text. In the case of *Richard III*, however, there is a kind of variation between the texts that has enabled editors to arrive at a convincing judgment about the priority of the F text to the Q text. Certain characters appear in Q engaging in dialogue unsuited to them in scenes where they evidently do not belong; their inappropriateness to these situations seems all the more striking in comparison to the appropriateness of their counterparts in the same scenes in F. It therefore appears that in these cases it is Q, rather than F, that is substituting one character for another, and that therefore Q is the later

version than F. (It is impossible now to determine just
who introduced these changes into the text printed as
Q, but since the substitutions affect roles, many have
thought that the changes were made in the playhouse.)
While there are quite a few examples of this pattern,
two instances will suffice to outline it.

The first occurs in 2.4. There in F an anonymous
messenger enters to deliver some very bad news to,
among others, the Duchess of York, Queen Elizabeth,
and the Duke of York, who is the Queen's young son.
The messenger announces that the Queen's brother
Lord Rivers, her son Lord Grey, and Sir Thomas
Vaughan have been captured by their political opponents Richard and Buckingham. Once the Queen
has heard the messenger's news—which he delivers
baldly, as is appropriate for a mere messenger who can
scarcely intrude on the Queen's grief to offer comfort
in her distress—she entirely ignores him and instead
laments the ensuing "ruin of [her] house [i.e., family]"
and flees with her son to the protection of sanctuary.
No one says farewell to the messenger, nor does he say
farewell to anyone. He, like other messengers in this
play and many others, just exits.

In Q, F's anonymous messenger is, instead, the Marquess of Dorset, another of the Queen's sons. Yet he
delivers virtually the same lines as F's anonymous messenger; like the messenger, then, he fails to comfort
his grieving mother; like the messenger, he is ignored
by his grieving mother, who is so intent on preserving
her other son, the young Duke of York, that she fails
to remark on the danger of death also confronting her
son Dorset; treated as the anonymous messenger into
whose role Dorset has been somehow miscast in Q,
Dorset leaves the stage without even a single farewell
being spoken. The parallel between this scene (2.4) and
another later in the play (4.1) only serves to highlight

how misplaced Dorset is in 2.4. In the later scene, Dorset is onstage in both Q and F when it is announced by Stanley that, in another obviously threatening move against the Queen's family, Richard has seized the throne from the Queen's son Prince Edward. Then, in both texts, Dorset attempts to comfort his mother; then in both texts she voices her anxiety about Dorset's survival by bidding him "hie thee from this slaughter-house, / Lest thou increase the number of the dead." Before he exits, in both texts, Dorset formally takes his leave of the new queen, Anne, and is wished "good fortune" by the Duchess of York. While a few critics and editors have attempted ingenious defenses of Q's substitution in 2.4 of Dorset for F's anonymous messenger, there is little question that the F messenger is the character who is wanted, and that Dorset has somehow been put in a place made for a messenger.

A similar substitution appears in Q's version of 3.4, where Catesby evidently takes the place of F's Lovell and Ratcliffe, and leads Hastings off to execution. In both Q and F, Hastings and his escort address each other as strangers. Such a conversational style is appropriate in F's version because in neither F nor Q has Hastings ever claimed either Lovell or Ratcliffe as a friend—but utterly inappropriate in Q, because Catesby is no stranger to Hastings. Both versions of the play have earlier presented Hastings's great trust in Catesby; depending on his "good friend Catesby," Hastings boasts that "nothing can proceed that toucheth us / Whereof I shall not have intelligence." Both versions also present Catesby's deception and betrayal of Hastings, something that would need to be remarked if Catesby were later to lead Hastings to the block. Again it seems that the substitution has been made in Q; again substitution marks Q as a version derivative from the F version. There are a number of other instances: substitution of Brakenbury for the Keeper in Q's 1.4; of the Cardinal for the Archbishop in Q's 2.4; of Catesby for Lovell and Ratcliffe in Q's 3.5; of Catesby for Ratcliffe alone in 4.3; of Ratcliffe for the Sheriff in Q's 5.1; of Catesby for F's Surrey in 5.3. In addition, now and again Q appears to eliminate characters from scenes—and sometimes awkwardness is the result. See, for example, Q's 2.2, from which Rivers and Dorset have seemingly been cut. Or see Q's 4.1, where, with the removal of Clarence's daughter, Q's "my niece Plantagenet" (in the first line) can refer to nobody then onstage. It has been argued that the Q version, even with these questionable substitutions and cuts, could still be performed onstage. No editor would deny such a possibility; the resourcefulness and imagination of theatrical personnel are equal to almost anything. Nevertheless, there is a strong case that the F version of *Richard III* represents, in large part, the earlier state of the play and Q a later state in which some roles have been disturbed.

Q, the First Quarto of 1597, was reprinted five times before the F version saw print in 1623. In each reprinting of the quarto version, the typesetters occasionally recognized usually obvious errors in the printed copy in front of them, and then corrected these, as, for example, did the typesetter(s) of the Second Quarto (Q2, 1598) in resetting the text of Q; more often, however, the typesetter(s) miscorrected their copy or made mistakes. Thus each subsequent quarto that derives directly or indirectly from Q, the First Quarto, has an identifiable pattern of errors in it. There is no good evidence that any printers of these derivative quartos had recourse to manuscripts of the play. Instead, the pattern of errors in each quarto allows scholars to discover exactly which earlier quarto each printer used as his copy for a subsequent quarto. Long ago schol-

ars concluded that, as already mentioned, the Second
Quarto reprints the First, the Third (Q3, 1602) reprints
the Second, the Fourth (Q4, 1605) reprints the Third,
the Fifth (Q5, 1612) reprints in part Q3 and in part Q4,
and the Sixth (Q6, 1622) reprints the Fifth.

None of these quartos differs very much from the
others in comparison to the great difference already
described between the Q version and the F version
printed in 1623. No doubt the printers of F, unlike the
printers of Q2–6, had access to a manuscript of the
play, a manuscript very different from the one behind
Q. But, as has already been suggested, the F version
is by no means wholly independent of the tradition of
quartos. The dependence of part of F upon a quarto
becomes strikingly evident to anyone who is comparing Q and F (or anyone who consults the textual notes
at the back of this book) as soon as one arrives at Act 3.
In the first two acts, one encounters hundreds of variants between Q and F; but in the first 169 lines of dialogue in Act 3, there are only thirteen verbal differences
between Q (1597) and F. Ten of these differences are
also found in one or more of the five derivative quartos
(Q2–6); part way through these first 169 lines of Act 3,
F even begins to reproduce Q's distinctive speech prefix for Richard, Duke of Gloucester (*Glo.*), rather than
Rich., which is invariable in F until this point, and to
which F returns at line 184 of Act 3. Q3 is the only one
of the quartos that has all ten of the verbal differences
from Q found in the F printing of the first 169 lines of
Act 3. Thus scholars have concluded that this portion
of F was printed directly from a copy of Q3. Closely
similar circumstances begin to present themselves
again at 5.3.52 and are in force until the end of the
play. And so scholars conclude that for the end of the
play the printers of F also employed Q3 as copy.

While it is hard to deny that a copy of Q3 served as

the basis for these two parts of F (3.1.1–169; 5.3.52–
end), the relationship of F to the quartos is fraught with
additional complexity. Consider the rest of F, i.e., the
five-sixths of its text outside of the two parts just discussed; there one finds that F prints about four dozen
or so readings that had already appeared in the derivative quartos (Q2–6). Some of these readings are corrections; some are obvious errors. Coincidence may be the
explanation for these readings common to F and to the
derivative quartos, but it is hard to trust to a belief in
coincidence in the face of F's demonstrable dependence
on Q3 in the two stretches of text already discussed.
Thus no editors, including ourselves, have been able
to eliminate the possibility that F may have picked up
these readings from the derivative quartos. For a long
time, scholars have held the opinion that the F typesetters must have had in hand a derivative quarto *after that
quarto had been for the most part very thoroughly annotated with reference to a manuscript from which so many
of the differences between Q and F must be presumed to
arise.* The difficulty with this hypothesis is that scholars have not been able to demonstrate which derivative
quarto served as printer's copy for the five-sixths of F
that are not demonstrably dependent on Q3. One scholar
argues that Q3 alone was used throughout the printing
of F; others argue that Q6 was used in combination with
Q3, and some have proposed intricate patterns of alter-
nation between Q3 and Q6 by the F printers. Such dis-
agreement among advocates of the use of printed copy
for F weakens their case that printed copy *must* have
been used to print the five-sixths of F still in question.
In spite of the difficulties attending arguments that the
F printers had Q3 or Q6 or both actually in hand during
the typesetting of F, we as editors still cannot afford to
ignore the possible influence of the derivative quartos
on F at any point in its text.

Throughout the editorial tradition, editors have disagreed on the much larger issue of which of the two versions to select as the basis for an edition of the play. For much of the late nineteenth century and the early twentieth century, Q was given precedence over F. More recently the choice has been made in terms of the narratives that scholars have written about the origins of the manuscripts behind Q and F. The preferred narrative about Q has been that it is based on a memorial reconstruction of the play by an entire company of actors (with Shakespeare perhaps among them); the preferred narrative about F is that the manuscript behind it is directly related to what Shakespeare first wrote. In light of such narratives, recent editors, in their quest to decide and present to their readers what Shakespeare wrote, have chosen F as the basis for editions. More recently, however, editors, while still on the whole preferring F to Q, have been admitting more readings from Q into editions, sometimes on the grounds that Q may contain Shakespeare's revisions (which these editors claim to have winnowed from the "corruptions" in Q), or sometimes in the belief that Q, allegedly a memorial reconstruction by actors, offers access to the play as it was originally performed. Since all that we have are the early printed texts, these narratives of origin are mere speculation and provide no reasonable basis for a choice between Q and F.

The present edition is based upon a fresh examination of the early printed texts, rather than upon any modern edition.* This examination has been conducted in light of the needs of today's readers, and not under the influence of the ungrounded narratives just

---

*We have also consulted a computerized text of the First Folio provided by the Text Archive of the Oxford University Computing Centre, to which we are grateful.

recounted. We have preferred F to Q on the following grounds: (1) F has fewer errors in need of emendation; (2) its role assignments are to be preferred (as has been exemplified above); (3) it has fewer gaps that require the addition of lines. While the present edition offers its readers the Folio printing of *Richard III*, it is far from slavish in following F. It prints such editorial changes and such readings from other early printed versions as are, in the editors' judgments, needed to repair what may be errors and deficiencies in the Folio. One major deficiency in F is, of course, its dependence upon Q3 in the two portions (3.1.1–169; 5.3.52–end) already discussed. For those portions our edition is based on Q (from which, of course, Q3 derives). Indeed, every time elsewhere in the play that F prints a reading that first appears in a derivative quarto, we scrutinize the reading; only if it is a necessary correction of Q do we print it; otherwise we adopt the reading of Q. (This policy allows for the possibility discussed above of bibliographical or textual influence from Q3 and/or Q6 upon the five-sixths of the F text not based on Q3.) In spite of our caution about possible influence on F by derivative quartos, it is also our policy to resist some of the more ingenious arguments advanced by editors on their presumption that the F printers must have had a particular quarto in hand when setting a particular reading in the F text.* Since the present edition is an edition of a single version of *Richard III*, the F version, we do not include Q-only lines unless they are needed to fill what

---

*For example, at 3.5.67, where Q reads "cause," Q6 "ease," and F "case," editors who are strongly persuaded that the F printers used Q6 at this juncture argue that the F reading (quite unobjectionable in itself) is a careless and unauthoritative alteration of the reading "ease" offered by Q6 alone among the derivative quartos. Here, rather than accept such an ingenious argument, we follow F.

we judge to be gaps in F; thus while we at one point print a stretch of twenty lines from Q in order to fill what we believe is a gap in F's 4.2, we do not include a number of lines that many editors have imported into F from Q in their attempts to fashion from the F and Q versions a purely ideal Shakespearean work that transcends F and Q. However, when there has been some measure of recent editorial agreement about incorporating lines from Q into the F version, these lines are printed and discussed for the reader in the explanatory notes.

Whenever we change the wording of the Folio (or of the Quarto in the two long passages for which we must rely on it) or add anything to stage directions, we mark the change by enclosing it in brackets. We use three different kinds of brackets:

(1) superior half-brackets (⌜ ⌝) enclose all readings that do not derive from either F or Q;
(2) pointed brackets (⟨ ⟩) enclose all readings taken from Q in the five-sixths of the play for which our edition is based on F; and
(3) full square brackets ([ ]) enclose all readings taken from F in the two substantial passages (3.1.1–169 and 5.3.52–end) for which our edition is based on Q.

We want our readers to be immediately aware when we have intervened. (Only when we correct an obvious typographical error in the Quarto or Folio does the change not get marked.) Whenever we change a word in the Folio or Quarto or change punctuation so that the meaning changes, we list the change in the textual notes at the back of the book, even if all we have done is fix an obvious error.

For the convenience of the reader, we have modernized the punctuation and the spelling of both the Folio and the Quarto. Sometimes we go so far as to modernize certain old forms of words; for example, when *a* means "he," we change it to *he;* we change *mo* to *more* and *ye* to *you.* But it is not our practice in editing any of the plays to modernize forms of words that sound distinctly different from modern forms. For example, when the early printed texts read *sith* or *apricocks* or *porpentine,* we have not modernized to *since, apricots, porcupine.* When the forms *an, and,* or *and if* appear instead of the modern form *if,* we have reduced *and* to *an* but have not changed any of these forms to their modern equivalent, *if.*

We correct or regularize a number of proper names, as is the usual practice in editions of the play. For example, the proper name of the Lieutenant of the Tower usually appears in F as "Brakenbury"; however, in the passage at the end of the play where F is dependent on Q3 and this edition follows Q, we find the Q spelling "Brookenbury," which we regularize to "Brakenbury."

This edition differs from many earlier ones in its efforts to aid the reader in imagining the play as a performance, rather than as a series of historical events. Thus stage directions are written with reference to the stage. For example, in the fiction of the play at 5.3.43, Richmond hands his "good Captain Blunt" a letter for Lord Stanley, and so many editors add a stage direction that reads *"He gives a letter."* However, when the play is staged, one actor hands another not a letter but a paper prop that stands for a letter. Thus we print the stage direction *"He gives a paper."*

Whenever it is reasonably certain, in our view, that a speech is accompanied by a particular action, we provide a stage direction describing the action. (Occasional exceptions to this rule occur when the action is

so obvious that to add a stage direction would insult
the reader.) Stage directions for the entrance of characters in mid-scene are, with rare exceptions, placed
so that they immediately precede the characters' par-
ticipation in the scene, even though these entrances
may appear somewhat earlier in the early printed texts.
Whenever we move a stage direction, we record this
change in the textual notes. Latin stage directions (e.g.,
Exeunt) are translated into English (e.g., *They exit*).

We expand the often severely abbreviated forms of
names used as speech headings in early printed texts
into the full names of the characters. We also regularize the speakers' names in speech headings, using only
a single designation for each character, even though
the early printed texts sometimes use a variety of desig-
nations. Variations in the speech headings of the early
printed texts are recorded in the textual notes.

In the present edition, as well, we mark with a dash
any change of address within a speech, unless a stage
direction intervenes. When the *-ed* ending of a word
is to be pronounced, we mark it with an accent. Like
editors for the last two centuries, we print metrically
linked lines in the following way:

RICHARD
  Bid me farewell.
ANNE   'Tis more than you deserve.

However, when there are a number of short verse-lines
that can be linked in more than one way, we do not,
with rare exceptions, indent any of them.

The Explanatory Notes

The notes that appear on the pages facing the text are designed to provide readers with the help that they may need to enjoy the play. Whenever the meaning of a word in the text is not readily accessible in a good contemporary dictionary, we offer the meaning in a note. Sometimes we provide a note even when the relevant meaning is to be found in the dictionary but when the word has acquired since Shakespeare's time other potentially confusing meanings. In our notes, we try to offer modern synonyms for Shakespeare's words. We also try to indicate to the reader the connection between the word in the play and the modern synonym. For example, Shakespeare sometimes uses the word *head* to mean "source," but, for modern readers, there may be no connection evident between these two words. We provide the connection by explaining Shakespeare's usage as follows: "**head:** fountainhead, source." On some occasions, a whole phrase or clause needs explanation. Then, if space allows, we rephrase in our own words the difficult passage, and add at the end synonyms for individual words in the passage. When scholars have been unable to determine the meaning of a word or phrase, we acknowledge the uncertainty. Biblical quotations are from the Geneva Bible (1560), with spelling modernized.

The Tragedy of
RICHARD III

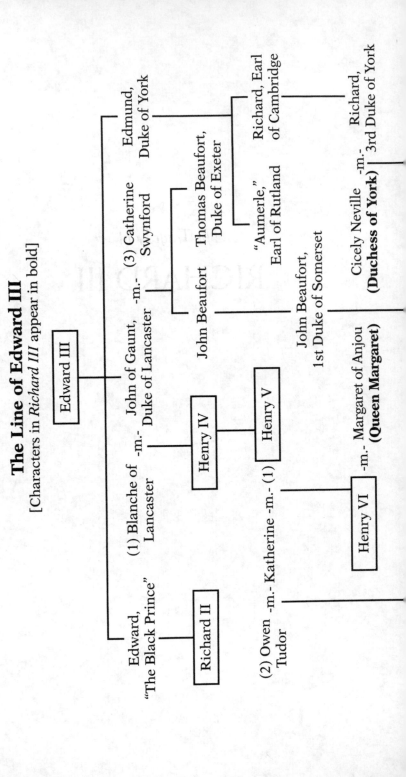

The Line of Edward III
[Characters in *Richard III* appear in bold]

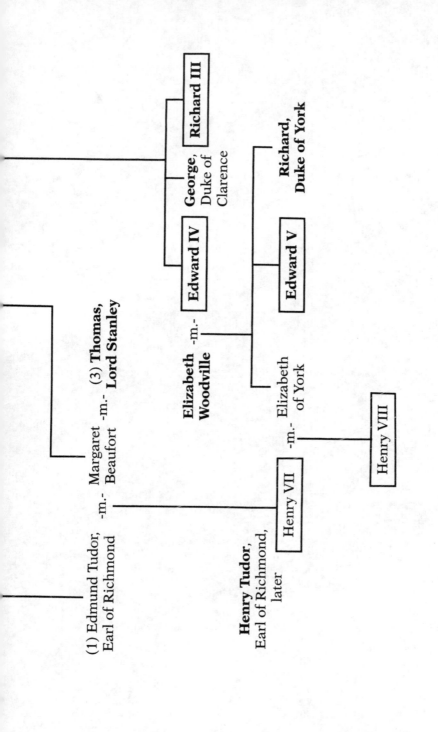

Characters in the Play

RICHARD, Duke of Gloucester, later King Richard III

LADY ANNE, widow of Edward, son to the late King Henry VI; later wife to Richard

KING EDWARD IV, brother to Richard

QUEEN ELIZABETH, Edward's wife, formerly the Lady Grey

PRINCE EDWARD
RICHARD, DUKE OF YORK } *their sons*

GEORGE, DUKE OF CLARENCE, brother to Edward and Richard

Clarence's BOY

Clarence's DAUGHTER

DUCHESS OF YORK, mother of Richard, Edward, and Clarence

QUEEN MARGARET, widow of King Henry VI

DUKE OF BUCKINGHAM

WILLIAM, LORD HASTINGS, Lord Chamberlain

LORD STANLEY, Earl of Derby

EARL RIVERS, brother to Queen Elizabeth
LORD GREY } *sons of Queen Elizabeth by her*
MARQUESS OF DORSET } *former marriage*

SIR THOMAS VAUGHAN

SIR WILLIAM CATESBY
SIR RICHARD RATCLIFFE
LORD LOVELL   } *Richard's supporters*
DUKE OF NORFOLK
EARL OF SURREY

5

EARL OF RICHMOND, Henry Tudor, later King Henry VII

EARL OF OXFORD
SIR JAMES BLUNT
SIR WALTER HERBERT   *Richmond's supporters*
SIR WILLIAM BRANDON
SIR CHRISTOPHER, a priest

ARCHBISHOP
CARDINAL

JOHN MORTON, BISHOP OF ELY

SIR ROBERT BRAKENBURY, Lieutenant of the Tower of London
JAMES TYRREL, gentleman
GENTLEMAN, attending Lady Anne
Two MURDERERS
KEEPER in the Tower
Three CITIZENS
LORD MAYOR of London
PURSUIVANT
SIR JOHN, a priest
SCRIVENER
PAGE
SHERIFF
Seven MESSENGERS
GHOSTS of King Henry VI, his son Prince Edward, Clarence, Rivers, Grey, Vaughan, the two Princes, Hastings, Lady Anne, and Buckingham

Guards, Tressel, Berkeley, Halberds, Gentlemen, Anthony Woodeville and Lord Scales (brothers to Queen Elizabeth), Two Bishops, Sir William Brandon, Lords, Attendants, Citizens, Aldermen, Councillors, Soldiers

The Tragedy of

RICHARD III

ACT 1

1.1   Richard, alone onstage, reveals his intention to play the villain. He then pretends to console Clarence, the first victim of this villainy. After Clarence is led off toward prison, Richard greets Hastings, who tells him that King Edward is very ill. Richard, once again alone onstage, outlines his plan to have Clarence killed and to marry Lady Anne.

---

2. **son:** Spelled "Son" in the Folio and "sonne" in the quarto, this pun could be properly modernized as either "son" or "sun." The **son of York** is Richard's brother, King Edward IV, whose emblem, according to Shakespeare's play *Henry VI, Part 3*, was "three . . . shining suns" (2.1.40).

3. **loured:** frowned, looked dark and threatening; **house:** the family of York

6. **bruisèd arms:** i.e., battered armor; **monuments:** memorials

7. **alarums:** calls to arms

8. **dreadful:** terrible, formidable; **measures:** dances

9. **front:** forehead

10. **barbèd steeds:** horses armed with a protective covering over breast and flanks

11. **fright:** frighten; **fearful:** (1) frightening; (2) frightened

13. **pleasing:** pleasingness

14. **sportive:** amorous

16. **rudely stamped:** i.e., clumsily fashioned **rudely:** roughly, irregularly **stamped:** formed by impressing a figure upon a substance, as a coin is fashioned from metal; **want:** lack   *(continued)*

ACT 1

Scene 1
Enter Richard, Duke of Gloucester, alone.

RICHARD
Now is the winter of our discontent
Made glorious summer by this son of York,
And all the clouds that loured upon our house
In the deep bosom of the ocean buried.
Now are our brows bound with victorious wreaths,   5
Our bruisèd arms hung up for monuments,
Our stern alarums changed to merry meetings,
Our dreadful marches to delightful measures.
Grim-visaged war hath smoothed his wrinkled front;
And now, instead of mounting barbèd steeds   10
To fright the souls of fearful adversaries,
He capers nimbly in a lady's chamber
To the lascivious pleasing of a lute.
But I, that am not shaped for sportive tricks,
Nor made to court an amorous looking glass;   15
I, that am rudely stamped and want love's majesty
To strut before a wanton ambling nymph;
I, that am curtailed of this fair proportion,
Cheated of feature by dissembling nature,
Deformed, unfinished, sent before my time   20
Into this breathing world scarce half made up,
And that so lamely and unfashionable
That dogs bark at me as I halt by them—

9

17. **wanton ambling:** i.e., provocatively dancing or walking

18. **fair proportion:** attractive shape

19. **feature:** handsome form

21. **made up:** i.e., created, formed

22. **unfashionable:** badly shaped

23. **halt:** limp

24. **piping time:** i.e., time marked by the music of pipes rather than martial fifes and drums (Pipes are associated with shepherds and with the dance.)

27. **descant on:** (1) comment on; (2) warble, or sing harmoniously about

28, 30. **prove:** i.e., prove to be; turn out to be

32. **inductions:** initial steps

33. **By:** i.e., by means of

38. **mewed up:** caged

39. **About:** i.e., because of

40. **Of Edward's . . . shall be:** i.e., **shall be the murderer of** Edward IV's **heirs** (namely, Prince Edward and Richard, Duke of York)

44. **waits upon:** attends, accompanies

46. **Tend'ring:** holding dear, caring for

47. **conduct:** escort; **the Tower:** the Tower of London (See page 130.)

52. **godfathers:** i.e., those who sponsored you when you were named at your christening

53. **belike:** perhaps

54. **new:** i.e., newly

55. **matter:** cause, reason

Why, I, in this weak piping time of peace,
Have no delight to pass away the time,   25
Unless to see my shadow in the sun
And descant on mine own deformity.
And therefore, since I cannot prove a lover
To entertain these fair well-spoken days,
I am determinèd to prove a villain   30
And hate the idle pleasures of these days.
Plots have I laid, inductions dangerous,
By drunken prophecies, libels, and dreams,
To set my brother Clarence and the King
In deadly hate, the one against the other;   35
And if King Edward be as true and just
As I am subtle, false, and treacherous,
This day should Clarence closely be mewed up
About a prophecy which says that "G"
Of Edward's heirs the murderer shall be.   40
Dive, thoughts, down to my soul. Here Clarence
    comes.

Enter Clarence, guarded, and Brakenbury.

Brother, good day. What means this armèd guard
That waits upon your Grace?
CLARENCE   His Majesty,   45
Tend'ring my person's safety, hath appointed
This conduct to convey me to the Tower.
RICHARD   Upon what cause?
CLARENCE   Because my name is
    George.   50
RICHARD
Alack, my lord, that fault is none of yours.
He should, for that, commit your godfathers.
O, belike his Majesty hath some intent
That you should be new christened in the Tower.
But what's the matter, Clarence? May I know?   55

59. **crossrow:** alphabet (Children learned the alphabet from a hornbook—a leaf of paper mounted on a small board and covered with translucent horn—where the letters of the alphabet were preceded by a cross. Hence the name **crossrow.** See page 250.)

61. **issue:** offspring, progeny

62. **for:** because

64. **These:** i.e., these considerations; **toys:** trifles

65. **commit me:** send me to prison

68. **My Lady Grey:** Richard's demeaning name for King Edward's queen, Elizabeth Grey, who had previously been married to Sir John Grey (Richard consistently refers to her in denigrating terms.)

69. **tempers:** guides, directs

70. **worship:** honor

77. **Mistress Shore:** Edward IV's mistress (**Mistress,** as in **Mistress Shore,** was equivalent to the modern "Ms.")

79. **her:** Mistress Shore

80. **her Deity:** a mock title for Mistress Shore

81. **Lord Chamberlain:** Hastings

84. **men:** servants

85. **jealous o'erworn widow:** i.e., Queen Elizabeth, who was a widow when she married Edward IV; **herself:** Mistress Shore (whom Richard also consistently demeans)

86. **dubbed:** a parodic use of the word, since only knights were dubbed; **gentlewomen:** Richard again slurs both women by suggesting that they are no more than gentry. While Mistress Shore was not perhaps by birth even a gentlewoman, she became, as Edward's mistress, the most powerful woman

(continued)

CLARENCE
Yea, Richard, when I know, ⟨for⟩ I protest
As yet I do not. But, as I can learn,
He hearkens after prophecies and dreams,
And from the crossrow plucks the letter *G*,
And says a wizard told him that by "G" 60
His issue disinherited should be.
And for my name of George begins with *G*,
It follows in his thought that I am he.
These, as I learn, and such like toys as these
Hath moved his Highness to commit me now. 65
RICHARD
Why, this it is when men are ruled by women.
'Tis not the King that sends you to the Tower.
My Lady Grey his wife, Clarence, 'tis she
That ⟨tempers⟩ him to this extremity.
Was it not she and that good man of worship, 70
Anthony Woodeville, her brother there,
That made him send Lord Hastings to the Tower,
From whence this present day he is delivered?
We are not safe, Clarence; we are not safe.
CLARENCE
By heaven, I think there is no man secure 75
But the Queen's kindred and night-walking heralds
That trudge betwixt the King and Mistress Shore.
Heard you not what an humble suppliant
Lord Hastings was ⟨to her⟩ for ⟨his⟩ delivery?
RICHARD
Humbly complaining to her Deity 80
Got my Lord Chamberlain his liberty.
I'll tell you what: I think it is our way,
If we will keep in favor with the King,
To be her men and wear her livery.
The jealous o'erworn widow and herself, 85
Since that our brother dubbed them gentlewomen,
Are mighty gossips in our monarchy.

in England and had great wealth; in history Queen Elizabeth was born a gentlewoman, the daughter of a knight and a duchess, and had a claim to the higher rank of noblewoman when her father was created a baron before she ever met Edward IV.

87. gossips: busybodies, or women friends (For Richard's claim that the women act in concert, see 3.4.71–73.)

89. straitly . . . charge: strictly commanded

90–91. no man . . . soever: no man, no matter what his rank, may have private conversation

92. An . . . Worship: i.e., if it please your Honor

96. Well . . . years: i.e., well advanced in age; **fair:** attractive

98. passing: surpassingly

101. naught: nothing

104. naught: wickedness

105. alone: In the Second Quarto, a text that seems, in all other respects, simply a reprint of the First Quarto, there appear at this point the following lines: "*Bro.* What one my Lord? | *Glo.* Her husband knaue, wouldst thou betray me?" (See longer note, page 305.)

106. withal: at the same time

107. Forbear your conference: cease your conversation

108. thy charge: i.e., the command you have been given

109. abjects: degraded people (with wordplay on *subjects*)

112. widow: i.e., the widow whom Edward married, Richard's sister-in-law

BRAKENBURY
  I beseech your Graces both to pardon me.
  His Majesty hath straitly given in charge
  That no man shall have private conference,   90
  Of what degree soever, with your brother.
RICHARD
  Even so. An please your Worship, Brakenbury,
  You may partake of anything we say.
  We speak no treason, man. We say the King
  Is wise and virtuous, and his noble queen   95
  Well struck in years, fair, and not jealous.
  We say that Shore's wife hath a pretty foot,
  A cherry lip, a bonny eye, a passing pleasing tongue,
  And that the Queen's kindred are made gentlefolks.
  How say you, sir? Can you deny all this?   100
BRAKENBURY
  With this, my lord, myself have naught to do.
RICHARD
  Naught to do with Mistress Shore? I tell thee,
    fellow,
  He that doth naught with her, excepting one,
  Were best to do it secretly, alone.   105
BRAKENBURY
  I do beseech your Grace to pardon me, and withal
  Forbear your conference with the noble duke.
CLARENCE
  We know thy charge, Brakenbury, and will obey.
RICHARD
  We are the Queen's abjects and must obey.—
  Brother, farewell. I will unto the King,   110
  And whatsoe'er you will employ me in,
  Were it to call King Edward's widow "sister,"
  I will perform it to enfranchise you.
  Meantime, this deep disgrace in brotherhood
  Touches me deeper than you can imagine.   115

118. **lie for you:** i.e., lie in prison in your place (with a possible second meaning, "tell lies for you")

120. **perforce:** of necessity ("Patience perforce" was a proverbial phrase.)

137. **kites:** Like **buzzards, kites** are vicious predatory birds. (See picture, page 18.)

CLARENCE
  I know it pleaseth neither of us well.
RICHARD
  Well, your imprisonment shall not be long.
  I will deliver you or else lie for you.
  Meantime, have patience.
CLARENCE   I must, perforce. Farewell.   120
         Exit Clarence, ⌜*Brakenbury, and guard.*⌝
RICHARD
  Go tread the path that thou shalt ne'er return.
  Simple, plain Clarence, I do love thee so
  That I will shortly send thy soul to heaven,
  If heaven will take the present at our hands.
  But who comes here? The new-delivered Hastings?   125

         Enter Lord Hastings.

HASTINGS
  Good time of day unto my gracious lord.
RICHARD
  As much unto my good Lord Chamberlain.
  Well are you welcome to ⟨the⟩ open air.
  How hath your Lordship brooked imprisonment?
HASTINGS
  With patience, noble lord, as prisoners must.   130
  But I shall live, my lord, to give them thanks
  That were the cause of my imprisonment.
RICHARD
  No doubt, no doubt; and so shall Clarence too,
  For they that were your enemies are his
  And have prevailed as much on him as you.   135
HASTINGS
  More pity that the eagles should be mewed,
  Whiles kites and buzzards ⟨prey⟩ at liberty.
RICHARD   What news abroad?
HASTINGS
  No news so bad abroad as this at home:

141. **fear:** i.e., fear for

143. **diet:** way of living

150. **with post-horse:** i.e., in the fastest way possible (Post-horses were ridden by express messengers.)

157. **Warwick's youngest daughter:** Anne, daughter of the earl of Warwick, known as "Warwick the Kingmaker" for his often decisive intervention in the fifteenth-century Wars of the Roses to put first Edward IV and then his opponent Henry VI on the throne

158. **husband:** i.e., Prince Edward, son of Henry VI, to whom, in history, Anne was engaged but perhaps not married; **father:** i.e., father-in-law, Henry VI

162. **close:** private

164. **run . . . market:** i.e., am getting ahead of myself (proverbial)

A kite. (1.1.137)
From Konrad Gesner, . . . *Historiae animalium* . . . (1585–1604).

The King is sickly, weak, and melancholy,   140
And his physicians fear him mightily.
RICHARD
Now, by Saint John, that news is bad indeed.
O, he hath kept an evil diet long,
And overmuch consumed his royal person.
'Tis very grievous to be thought upon.   145
Where is he, in his bed?
HASTINGS   He is.
RICHARD
Go you before, and I will follow you.

                                        Exit Hastings.
He cannot live, I hope, and must not die
Till George be packed with post-horse up to heaven.   150
I'll in to urge his hatred more to Clarence
With lies well steeled with weighty arguments,
And, if I fail not in my deep intent,
Clarence hath not another day to live;
Which done, God take King Edward to His mercy,   155
And leave the world for me to bustle in.
For then I'll marry Warwick's youngest daughter.
What though I killed her husband and her father?
The readiest way to make the wench amends
Is to become her husband and her father;   160
The which will I, not all so much for love
As for another secret close intent
By marrying her which I must reach unto.
But yet I run before my horse to market.
Clarence still breathes; Edward still lives and reigns.   165
When they are gone, then must I count my gains.
                                        He exits.

1.2 Richard woos Lady Anne over the corpse of King Henry VI, Anne's father-in-law, whom Richard murdered.

---

0 SD. **corse:** corpse; **Halberds:** i.e., halberdiers, guards armed with weapons that combined features of the spear and the ax (See page 284.)

2. **shrouded:** (1) wrapped in a shroud; (2) hidden, given refuge; **hearse:** (1) funeral pall or cloth; (2) wooden frame supporting the pall over the body

3. **obsequiously:** in the manner of a mourner

4. **Lancaster:** i.e., Henry VI, of the house of Lancaster, the enemies of the house of York in the Wars of the Roses

5. **key-cold:** i.e., as cold as the metal of a key

8. **invocate:** conjure

14. **helpless:** unavailing, unprofitable

18. **direful:** dire or terrible; **hap:** fortune or chance

21. **venomed thing:** i.e., insect or reptile endowed with venom

22. **abortive:** born prematurely

23. **Prodigious:** abnormal, monstrous

24. **aspect:** look, appearance

26. **that:** i.e., the newly born child; **unhappiness:** misfortune; evil

Scene 2

*Enter the corse of Henry the Sixth ⌈on a bier,⌉ with
Halberds to guard it, Lady Anne being the mourner,
⌈accompanied by Gentlemen.⌉*

ANNE
Set down, set down your honorable load,
If honor may be shrouded in a hearse,
Whilst I awhile obsequiously lament
Th' untimely fall of virtuous Lancaster.

⌈*They set down the bier.*⌉

Poor key-cold figure of a holy king,   5
Pale ashes of the house of Lancaster,
Thou bloodless remnant of that royal blood,
Be it lawful that I invocate thy ghost
To hear the lamentations of poor Anne,
Wife to thy Edward, to thy slaughtered son,   10
Stabbed by the selfsame hand that made these
    wounds.
Lo, in these windows that let forth thy life
I pour the helpless balm of my poor eyes.
O, cursèd be the hand that made these holes;   15
Cursèd the heart that had the heart to do it;
Cursèd the blood that let this blood from hence.
More direful hap betide that hated wretch
That makes us wretched by the death of thee
Than I can wish to wolves, to spiders, toads,   20
Or any creeping venomed thing that lives.
If ever he have child, abortive be it,
Prodigious, and untimely brought to light,
Whose ugly and unnatural aspect
May fright the hopeful mother at the view,   25
And that be heir to his unhappiness.
If ever he have wife, let her be made
More miserable by the death of him
Than I am made by my young lord and thee.—

30. **Chertsey:** site of a famous abbey on the Thames River west of London

31. **Paul's:** St. Paul's Cathedral in London (See page 24.)

35. **black magician:** i.e., evil conjurer who can summon fiends from hell

36. **devoted:** consecrated

37. **Villains:** baseborn men (French *villeins*)

40. **stand:** halt

41. **Advance ... breast:** i.e., hold your halberd upright

43. **spurn:** trample

44. **What:** an interjection introducing a question

47. **Avaunt:** begone (used to send away witches and devils)

48–49. **Thou hadst ... canst not have:** See Matthew 10.28: "And fear ye not them which kill the body, but are not able to kill the soul; but rather fear him which is able to destroy both soul and body in hell." **his:** i.e., Henry VI's

50. **curst:** angry, bad-tempered

Come now towards Chertsey with your holy load,   30
Taken from Paul's to be interrèd there.
⌜*They take up the bier.*⌝
And still, as you are weary of this weight,
Rest you, whiles I lament King Henry's corse.

Enter Richard, Duke of Gloucester.

RICHARD
Stay, you that bear the corse, and set it down.
ANNE
What black magician conjures up this fiend   35
To stop devoted charitable deeds?
RICHARD
Villains, set down the corse or, by Saint Paul,
I'll make a corse of him that disobeys.
GENTLEMAN
My lord, stand back and let the coffin pass.
RICHARD
Unmannered dog, ⟨stand⟩ thou when I command!—   40
Advance thy halberd higher than my breast,
Or by Saint Paul I'll strike thee to my foot
And spurn upon thee, beggar, for thy boldness.
⌜*They set down the bier.*⌝
ANNE, ⌜*to the Gentlemen and Halberds*⌝
What, do you tremble? Are you all afraid?
Alas, I blame you not, for you are mortal,   45
And mortal eyes cannot endure the devil.—
Avaunt, thou dreadful minister of hell.
Thou hadst but power over his mortal body;
His soul thou canst not have. Therefore begone.
RICHARD
Sweet saint, for charity, be not so curst.   50
ANNE
Foul devil, for God's sake, hence, and trouble us
    not,
For thou hast made the happy Earth thy hell,

54. **exclaims:** exclamations
56. **pattern:** notable example
60. **exhales:** draws forth
63. **Provokes:** i.e., provoke
69. **quick:** alive
73. **for . . . for:** i.e., in return for
74. **nor . . . nor:** neither . . . nor
75. **No . . . knows:** i.e., no animal is so fierce as to be without
77. **devils . . . truth:** Proverbial: "The devil sometimes speaks the truth."
79. **Vouchsafe:** grant
80–81. **Of . . . myself:** i.e., the opportunity to acquit myself of these alleged crimes **By circumstance:** i.e., in full detail
82. **defused:** widely dispersed; disordered

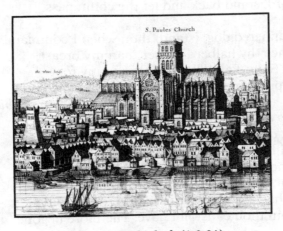

St. Paul's Cathedral. (1.2.31)
From Claes Jansz Visscher, *Londinum florentissima Britanniae urbs* . . . [c. 1625].

Filled it with cursing cries and deep exclaims.
If thou delight to view thy heinous deeds,   55
Behold this pattern of thy butcheries.

⌐*She points to the corpse.*¬

O, gentlemen, see, see dead Henry's wounds
Open their congealed mouths and bleed afresh!—
Blush, blush, thou lump of foul deformity,
For 'tis thy presence that exhales this blood   60
From cold and empty veins where no blood dwells.
Thy deeds, inhuman and unnatural,
Provokes this deluge most unnatural.—
O God, which this blood mad'st, revenge his death!
O Earth, which this blood drink'st, revenge his   65
    death!
Either heaven with lightning strike the murderer
    dead,
Or Earth gape open wide and eat him quick,
As thou dost swallow up this good king's blood,   70
Which his hell-governed arm hath butcherèd.

RICHARD
Lady, you know no rules of charity,
    Which renders good for bad, blessings for curses.

ANNE
Villain, thou know'st nor law of God nor man.
    No beast so fierce but knows some touch of pity.   75

RICHARD
But I know none, and therefore am no beast.

ANNE
O, wonderful, when devils tell the truth!

RICHARD
More wonderful, when angels are so angry.
    Vouchsafe, divine perfection of a woman,
    Of these supposèd crimes to give me leave   80
    By circumstance but to acquit myself.

ANNE
Vouchsafe, defused infection of ⟨a⟩ man,

86. **patient:** calm
88. **current:** genuine, authentic (like currency)
91. **worthy:** deserved
99. **In . . . liest:** "To lie in one's throat" was proverbial.
100. **falchion:** sword; **smoking in:** i.e., steaming
with
101. **The which:** i.e., the same sword; **bend:** turn
104. **their:** i.e., my brothers'
106. **aught:** anything
109. **hedgehog:** perhaps a mocking reference to
Richard's emblem, the boar (See page 56.)

Of these known evils but to give me leave
By circumstance to curse thy cursèd self.

RICHARD

Fairer than tongue can name thee, let me have   85
Some patient leisure to excuse myself.

ANNE

Fouler than heart can think thee, thou canst make
No excuse current but to hang thyself.

RICHARD

By such despair I should accuse myself.

ANNE

And by despairing shalt thou stand excused   90
For doing worthy vengeance on thyself
That didst unworthy slaughter upon others.

RICHARD   Say that I slew them not.

ANNE   Then say they were not slain.
But dead they are, and, devilish slave, by thee.   95

RICHARD   I did not kill your husband.

ANNE   Why then, he is alive.

RICHARD

Nay, he is dead, and slain by Edward's hands.

ANNE

In thy foul throat thou liest. Queen Margaret saw
Thy murd'rous falchion smoking in his blood,   100
The which thou once didst bend against her breast,
But that thy brothers beat aside the point.

RICHARD

I was provokèd by her sland'rous tongue,
That laid their guilt upon my guiltless shoulders.

ANNE

Thou wast provokèd by thy bloody mind,   105
That never dream'st on aught but butcheries.
Didst thou not kill this king?

RICHARD   I grant you.

ANNE

Dost grant me, hedgehog? Then, God grant me too

114. **holp:** helped
115. **fitter:** better fitted
117. **one place else:** one other place
120. **Ill:** miserable; **betide:** befall
125. **something:** somewhat
126. **timeless:** untimely, premature
129. **Thou . . . effect:** i.e., all the responsibility was yours
130. **effect:** result, consequence
133. **So:** i.e., so that

Richard III.
From John Speed, *The theatre of the empire of Great Britaine . . .* (1627 [i.e., 1631]).

Thou mayst be damnèd for that wicked deed. 110
O, he was gentle, mild, and virtuous.

RICHARD
The better for the King of heaven that hath him.

ANNE
He is in heaven, where thou shalt never come.

RICHARD
Let him thank me, that holp to send him thither,
For he was fitter for that place than Earth. 115

ANNE
And thou unfit for any place but hell.

RICHARD
Yes, one place else, if you will hear me name it.

ANNE   Some dungeon.

RICHARD   Your bedchamber.

ANNE
Ill rest betide the chamber where thou liest! 120

RICHARD
So will it, madam, till I lie with you.

ANNE
I hope so.

RICHARD   I know so. But, gentle Lady Anne,
To leave this keen encounter of our wits
And fall something into a slower method: 125
Is not the causer of the timeless deaths
Of these Plantagenets, Henry and Edward,
As blameful as the executioner?

ANNE
Thou wast the cause and most accursed effect.

RICHARD
Your beauty was the cause of that effect— 130
Your beauty, that did haunt me in my sleep
To undertake the death of all the world,
So I might live one hour in your sweet bosom.

ANNE
If I thought that, I tell thee, homicide,

137. **wrack:** destruction

143. **would:** wish

146. **quarrel:** cause, reason (Richard, [line 144], used **quarrel** in the sense of "dispute, argument.")

151. **He lives that:** i.e., there is one man alive who; **he:** Edward, Anne's late husband

153. **Plantagenet:** the (French) name of the royal family in England from the twelfth to the fifteenth centuries, including the members of the families of Lancaster and York (**Plantagenet** was the family name of Geoffrey, count of Anjou, ancestor of Edward III, from whom both the Lancasters and Yorks descended. See "The Line of Edward III," pages 2–3, above.)

These nails should rend that beauty from my   135
  cheeks.
RICHARD
These eyes could not endure that beauty's wrack.
You should not blemish it, if I stood by.
As all the world is cheerèd by the sun,
So I by that. It is my day, my life.   140
ANNE
Black night o'ershade thy day, and death thy life.
RICHARD
Curse not thyself, fair creature; thou art both.
ANNE
I would I were, to be revenged on thee.
RICHARD
It is a quarrel most unnatural
To be revenged on him that loveth thee.   145
ANNE
It is a quarrel just and reasonable
To be revenged on him that killed my husband.
RICHARD
He that bereft thee, lady, of thy husband
Did it to help thee to a better husband.
ANNE
His better doth not breathe upon the earth.   150
RICHARD
He lives that loves thee better than he could.
ANNE
Name him.
RICHARD   Plantagenet.
ANNE   Why, that was he.
RICHARD
The selfsame name, but one of better nature.   155
ANNE
Where is he?
RICHARD   Here. (⟨*She*⟩ *spits at him.*) Why dost
  thou spit at me?

159. **mortal:** deadly

161. **poison . . . toad:** In popular belief, toads were poisonous.

164. **basilisks':** i.e., the **eyes** of basilisks, mythical creatures whose glances were deadly, often identified with the cockatrice (See pages 34 and 200.)

169. **aspects:** appearance, looks; **store:** plenty, an abundance

170. **remorseful:** compassionate, pitying

171. **Edward:** Richard's brother, now Edward IV (See picture, page 50.)

172. **Rutland:** Richard's brother, whose murder by the Lancastrian supporter **Clifford** is presented in Shakespeare's *Henry VI, Part 3*

174. **thy . . . father:** the earl of Warwick

177. **That:** i.e., so that

180. **thence exhale:** i.e., draw forth from my eyes

183. **sued to:** petitioned, appealed to

184. **smoothing:** flattering

185. **now:** i.e., now that; **my fee:** i.e., the reward I desire (The image is of a lawyer arguing in return for a **fee,** an image continued with **sues** in line 186.)

186. **sues:** petitions

ANNE
  Would it were mortal poison for thy sake.
RICHARD
  Never came poison from so sweet a place.   160
ANNE
  Never hung poison on a fouler toad.
  Out of my sight! Thou dost infect mine eyes.
RICHARD
  Thine eyes, sweet lady, have infected mine.
ANNE
  Would they were basilisks' to strike thee dead.
RICHARD
  I would they were, that I might die at once,   165
  For now they kill me with a living death.
  Those eyes of thine from mine have drawn salt
      tears,
  Shamed their aspects with store of childish drops.
  These eyes, which never shed remorseful tear—   170
  No, when my father York and Edward wept
  To hear the piteous moan that Rutland made
  When black-faced Clifford shook his sword at him;
  Nor when thy warlike father, like a child,
  Told the sad story of my father's death   175
  And twenty times made pause to sob and weep,
  That all the standers-by had wet their cheeks
  Like trees bedashed with rain—in that sad time,
  My manly eyes did scorn an humble tear;
  And what these sorrows could not thence exhale   180
  Thy beauty hath, and made them blind with
      weeping.
  I never sued to friend nor enemy;
  My tongue could never learn sweet smoothing word.
  But now thy beauty is proposed my fee,   185
  My proud heart sues and prompts my tongue to
      speak.   *She looks scornfully at him.*
  Teach not thy lip such scorn, for it was made

194. **lay it naked:** i.e., bare my breast
195 SD. **open:** i.e., bare; **offers:** makes an attempt
198. **dispatch:** make haste
200 SD. **falls:** i.e., lets fall
212. **figured:** exhibited, displayed
213. **fear me:** i.e., fear
215. **put up:** i.e., sheathe

A basilisk. (1.2.164; 4.1.58)
From Edward Topsell, *The history of four-footed beasts and serpents . . .* (1658).

For kissing, lady, not for such contempt.
If thy revengeful heart cannot forgive,   190
Lo, here I lend thee this sharp-pointed sword,
Which if thou please to hide in this true breast
And let the soul forth that adoreth thee,
I lay it naked to the deadly stroke
And humbly beg the death upon my knee.   195
            He ⌜*kneels and*⌝ *lays his breast open;*
                  she offers at ⌜*it*⌝ *with his sword.*
Nay, do not pause, for I did kill King Henry—
But 'twas thy beauty that provokèd me.
Nay, now dispatch; 'twas I that stabbed young
      Edward—
But 'twas thy heavenly face that set me on.   200
                        She falls the sword.
Take up the sword again, or take up me.

ANNE
Arise, dissembler. Though I wish thy death,
I will not be thy executioner.

RICHARD, ⌜*rising*⌝
Then bid me kill myself, and I will do it.

ANNE
I have already.   205

RICHARD   That was in thy rage.
Speak it again and, even with the word,
This hand, which for thy love did kill thy love,
Shall for thy love kill a far truer love.
To both their deaths shalt thou be accessory.   210

ANNE   I would I knew thy heart.

RICHARD   'Tis figured in my tongue.

ANNE   I fear me both are false.

RICHARD   Then never ⟨was man⟩ true.

ANNE   Well, well, put up your sword.   215

RICHARD   Say then my peace is made.

ANNE   That shalt thou know hereafter.

RICHARD   But shall I live in hope?

219. **All . . . so:** Proverbial: "Hope leaves not a man" (i.e., everyone has hope).

225. **poor . . . servant:** i.e., suitor, who wishes to serve her as lover

226. **But . . . at:** i.e., beg just one favor from

229. **you leave:** i.e., you to leave

231. **presently:** at once; **Crosby House:** a London residence of Richard's, sometimes called "Crosby Place"

235. **expedient:** speedy

237. **boon:** request

242. **'Tis . . . deserve:** Anne takes literally the meaning of the word **farewell**—i.e., "may you go well."

246. **Whitefriars:** a monastery in London; **attend:** await

ANNE   All men I hope live so.
⟨RICHARD⟩   Vouchsafe to wear this ring.   220
⟨ANNE⟩   To take is not to give.
                  ⌜*He places the ring on her hand.*⌝
RICHARD
    Look how my ring encompasseth thy finger;
    Even so thy breast encloseth my poor heart.
    Wear both of them, for both of them are thine.
    And if thy poor devoted servant may   225
    But beg one favor at thy gracious hand,
    Thou dost confirm his happiness forever.
ANNE   What is it?
RICHARD
    That it may please you leave these sad designs
    To him that hath most cause to be a mourner,   230
    And presently repair to Crosby House,
    Where, after I have solemnly interred
    At Chertsey monast'ry this noble king
    And wet his grave with my repentant tears,
    I will with all expedient duty see you.   235
    For divers unknown reasons, I beseech you,
    Grant me this boon.
ANNE
    With all my heart, and much it joys me too
    To see you are become so penitent.—
    Tressel and Berkeley, go along with me.   240
RICHARD
    Bid me farewell.
ANNE   'Tis more than you deserve;
    But since you teach me how to flatter you,
    Imagine I have said "farewell" already.
           Two exit with Anne. ⌜*The bier is taken up.*⌝
GENTLEMAN   Towards Chertsey, noble lord?   245
RICHARD
    No, to Whitefriars. There attend my coming.
         ⌜*Halberds and gentlemen*⌝ *exit* ⌜*with*⌝ *corse.*

247. **humor:** state of mind, mood

253. **by:** i.e., nearby

254. **bars:** barriers, obstacles

256. **back my suit:** support my wooing

258. **all ... nothing:** i.e., against huge odds (proverbial)

262. **Tewkesbury:** site of the battle in which Edward IV decisively defeated Henry VI

264. **Framed ... nature:** i.e., fashioned by nature at her most lavish

265. **right:** very

266. **afford:** provide, yield

270. **moiety:** half

271. **halts:** limps

272. **My dukedom ... denier:** i.e., I would bet my dukedom against a coin worth the twelfth part of a sou

273. **my person:** my physical appearance

275. **marv'lous proper:** marvelously handsome

276. **I'll ... for:** i.e., I'll bear the expense of buying

277. **entertain:** i.e., take into my service

281. **in:** i.e., into

Was ever woman in this humor wooed?
Was ever woman in this humor won?
I'll have her, but I will not keep her long.
What, I that killed her husband and his father,   250
To take her in her heart's extremest hate,
With curses in her mouth, tears in her eyes,
The bleeding witness of my hatred by,
Having God, her conscience, and these bars against
  me,   255
And I no friends to back my suit ⟨at all⟩
But the plain devil and dissembling looks?
And yet to win her, all the world to nothing!
Ha!
Hath she forgot already that brave prince,   260
Edward, her lord, whom I some three months since
Stabbed in my angry mood at Tewkesbury?
A sweeter and a lovelier gentleman,
Framed in the prodigality of nature,
Young, valiant, wise, and, no doubt, right royal,   265
The spacious world cannot again afford.
And will she yet abase her eyes on me,
That cropped the golden prime of this sweet prince
And made her widow to a woeful bed?
On me, whose all not equals Edward's moiety?   270
On me, that halts and am misshapen thus?
My dukedom to a beggarly denier,
I do mistake my person all this while!
Upon my life, she finds, although I cannot,
Myself to be a marv'lous proper man.   275
I'll be at charges for a looking glass
And entertain a score or two of tailors
To study fashions to adorn my body.
Since I am crept in favor with myself,
I will maintain it with some little cost.   280
But first I'll turn yon fellow in his grave

283. **glass:** looking glass, mirror

1.3   Queen Elizabeth bemoans her situation in the face of her husband's serious illness; Richard quarrels with Queen Elizabeth, her brother, and Grey, her son by her first marriage. Queen Margaret, King Henry VI's widow, curses them all. After the others have departed, Richard dispatches his agents to kill Clarence.

---

4. **brook it ill:** i.e., take it badly   **brook:** tolerate
5. **entertain good comfort:** accept consolation
6. **quick:** lively
7. **betide on:** befall
10. **goodly:** fine, splendid
12. **his minority:** the period during which he is too young to govern
16. **determined:** decided; **concluded:** finally arranged
17. **miscarry:** perish

And then return lamenting to my love.
Shine out, fair sun, till I have bought a glass,
That I may see my shadow as I pass.

He exits.

Scene 3

Enter Queen ⌜Elizabeth, the Lord Marquess of Dorset,⌝
Lord Rivers, and Lord Grey.

RIVERS
Have patience, madam. There's no doubt his
    Majesty
Will soon recover his accustomed health.
GREY
In that you brook it ill, it makes him worse.
Therefore, for God's sake, entertain good comfort   5
And cheer his Grace with quick and merry eyes.
QUEEN ELIZABETH
If he were dead, what would betide on me?
GREY
No other harm but loss of such a lord.
QUEEN ELIZABETH
The loss of such a lord includes all harms.
GREY
The heavens have blessed you with a goodly son   10
To be your comforter when he is gone.
QUEEN ELIZABETH
Ah, he is young, and his minority
Is put unto the trust of Richard Gloucester,
A man that loves not me nor none of you.
RIVERS
Is it concluded he shall be Protector?   15
QUEEN ELIZABETH
It is determined, not concluded yet;
But so it must be if the King miscarry.

21. **Countess Richmond:** i.e., Stanley's wife, Margaret Beaufort, whose first marriage was to Edmund Tudor, earl of Richmond

27. **envious:** malicious

30. **wayward sickness:** illness that does not respond to treatment; **grounded:** firmly established

34. **amendment:** recovery from illness

37. **atonement:** harmony

38. **brothers:** Only one of Queen Elizabeth's historical brothers, Lord Rivers, is given a speaking role in the play. In history this brother was known by his proper name, Anthony Woodeville, and by his two titles, the earl of Rivers and Lord Scales. However, in the play, these three titles are transformed into three separate characters, each of whom Richard calls by name in 2.1.68, 70. (Sir Thomas More's biography of Richard mentions "Sir Anthony Woodville, Lord Rivers, and brother to the queen." This list refers to a single person, but it could easily be read as naming three different men.)

40. **warn:** summon

Enter Buckingham and ⌜Lord Stanley, Earl of⌝ Derby.

GREY
Here comes the lord of Buckingham, and Derby.
BUCKINGHAM, ⌜to Queen Elizabeth⌝
Good time of day unto your royal Grace.
STANLEY
God make your Majesty joyful, as you have been.   20
QUEEN ELIZABETH
The Countess Richmond, good my lord of Derby,
To your good prayer will scarcely say amen.
Yet, Derby, notwithstanding she's your wife
And loves not me, be you, good lord, assured
I hate not you for her proud arrogance.   25
STANLEY
I do beseech you either not believe
The envious slanders of her false accusers,
Or if she be accused on true report,
Bear with her weakness, which I think proceeds
From wayward sickness and no grounded malice.   30
QUEEN ELIZABETH
Saw you the King today, my lord of Derby?
STANLEY
But now the Duke of Buckingham and I
Are come from visiting his Majesty.
QUEEN ELIZABETH
What likelihood of his amendment, lords?
BUCKINGHAM
Madam, good hope. His Grace speaks cheerfully.   35
QUEEN ELIZABETH
God grant him health. Did you confer with him?
BUCKINGHAM
Ay, madam. He desires to make atonement
Between the Duke of Gloucester and your brothers,
And between them and my Lord Chamberlain,
And sent to warn them to his royal presence.   40

46. **holy Paul:** i.e., St. Paul; **lightly:** i.e., little

48. **look fair:** appear agreeable or kindly

49. **smooth:** flatter; **cog:** use fraud or deceit

50. **Duck ... nods:** i.e., bow in an affected way

51. **held:** considered, regarded

54. **With:** by; **silken:** ingratiating, flattering; **Jacks:** fellows of low breeding

55. **presence:** company

56. **nor ... nor:** neither ... nor

62. **scarce ... while:** i.e., scarcely for the time it takes to draw a breath

63. **lewd:** ill-mannered

64. **Brother:** i.e., brother-in-law; **matter:** cause, reason (for the King's having summoned you to him)

65. **on ... disposition:** i.e., of his own inclination

66. **suitor else:** other suitor

67. **Aiming belike at:** i.e., probably conjecturing about

70. **Makes:** causes; **ground:** i.e., the grounds "of your ill will," as the quarto goes on to say, perhaps superfluously, in a phrase adopted by many editors

QUEEN ELIZABETH
  Would all were well—but that will never be.
  I fear our happiness is at the height.

  Enter Richard, ⌐Duke of Gloucester, and Hastings.⌐

RICHARD
  They do me wrong, and I will not endure it!
  Who is it that complains unto the King
  That I, forsooth, am stern and love them not?   45
  By holy Paul, they love his Grace but lightly
  That fill his ears with such dissentious rumors.
  Because I cannot flatter and look fair,
  Smile in men's faces, smooth, deceive, and cog,
  Duck with French nods and apish courtesy,   50
  I must be held a rancorous enemy.
  Cannot a plain man live and think no harm,
  But thus his simple truth must be abused
  With silken, sly, insinuating Jacks?

GREY
  To who in all this presence speaks your Grace?   55

RICHARD
  To thee, that hast nor honesty nor grace.
  When have I injured thee? When done thee
      wrong?—
  Or thee?—Or thee? Or any of your faction?
  A plague upon you all! His royal Grace,   60
  Whom God preserve better than you would wish,
  Cannot be quiet scarce a breathing while
  But you must trouble him with lewd complaints.

QUEEN ELIZABETH
  Brother of Gloucester, you mistake the matter.
  The King, on his own royal disposition,   65
  And not provoked by any suitor else,
  Aiming belike at your interior hatred
  That in your outward action shows itself
  Against my children, brothers, and myself,
  Makes him to send, that he may learn the ground.   70

72. **make prey:** i.e., behave like birds of prey

73. **Jack became a gentleman:** Proverbial: "Jack would be a gentleman."

74. **gentle:** noble, honorable

77. **friends':** kinsmen's

79. **we:** i.e., my family and I

85. **scarce:** i.e., scarcely

86. **noble:** a coin worth, according to some contemporary reporters, about a third of a pound

87. **careful height:** i.e., eminent position that is full of cares or worries

88. **hap:** fortune

93. **draw:** ensnare; **suspects:** suspicions

94. **mean:** cause, agent

99. **fair:** desirable

RICHARD
   I cannot tell. The world is grown so bad
   That wrens make prey where eagles dare not perch.
   Since every Jack became a gentleman,
   There's many a gentle person made a Jack.
QUEEN ELIZABETH
   Come, come, we know your meaning, brother   75
     Gloucester.
   You envy my advancement, and my friends'.
   God grant we never may have need of you.
RICHARD
   Meantime God grants that ⟨we⟩ have need of
     you.   80
   Our brother is imprisoned by your means,
   Myself disgraced, and the nobility
   Held in contempt, while great promotions
   Are daily given to ennoble those
   That scarce some two days since were worth a   85
     noble.
QUEEN ELIZABETH
   By Him that raised me to this careful height
   From that contented hap which I enjoyed,
   I never did incense his Majesty
   Against the Duke of Clarence, but have been   90
   An earnest advocate to plead for him.
   My lord, you do me shameful injury
   Falsely to draw me in these vile suspects.
RICHARD
   You may deny that you were not the mean
   Of my Lord Hastings' late imprisonment.   95
RIVERS   She may, my lord, for—
RICHARD
   She may, Lord Rivers. Why, who knows not so?
   She may do more, sir, than denying that.
   She may help you to many fair preferments

101. **lay . . . on:** credit those honors to; **desert:** deserts, merits

102. **marry:** indeed (originally an oath on the name of the Virgin Mary)

106. **Iwis:** certainly; **worser:** i.e., worse

110. **gross:** flagrant

116. **state:** greatness; **seat:** throne; **is:** i.e., are; **due to me:** i.e., properly mine

117. **threat:** i.e., threaten

119. **avouch:** acknowledge

120. **adventure to be:** risk being

121. **pains:** trouble taken (on King Edward's behalf)

122. **Out:** an exclamation of abhorrence

126. **packhorse:** drudge

And then deny her aiding hand therein, 100
And lay those honors on your high desert.
What may she not? She may, ay, marry, may she—
RIVERS What, marry, may she?
RICHARD
What, marry, may she? Marry with a king,
A bachelor, and a handsome stripling too. 105
Iwis, your grandam had a worser match.
QUEEN ELIZABETH
My lord of Gloucester, I have too long borne
Your blunt upbraidings and your bitter scoffs.
By heaven, I will acquaint his Majesty
Of those gross taunts that oft I have endured. 110
I had rather be a country servant-maid
Than a great queen with this condition,
To be so baited, scorned, and stormèd at.

Enter old Queen Margaret, ⌐apart from the others.⌐

Small joy have I in being England's queen.
QUEEN MARGARET, ⌐*aside*⌐
And lessened be that small, God I beseech Him! 115
Thy honor, state, and seat is due to me.
RICHARD, ⌐*to Queen Elizabeth*⌐
What, threat you me with telling of the King?
⟨Tell him and spare not. Look, what I have said,⟩
I will avouch 't in presence of the King;
I dare adventure to be sent to th' Tower. 120
'Tis time to speak. My pains are quite forgot.
QUEEN MARGARET, ⌐*aside*⌐
Out, devil! I do remember them too well:
Thou killed'st my husband Henry in the Tower,
And Edward, my poor son, at Tewkesbury.
RICHARD, ⌐*to Queen Elizabeth*⌐
Ere you were queen, ay, or your husband king, 125
I was a packhorse in his great affairs,
A weeder-out of his proud adversaries,

129. **spent:** i.e., shed

132. **for:** on behalf of

133. **your husband:** i.e., Sir John Grey

134. **battle:** army

137. **Withal:** at the same time

139. **father:** i.e., father-in-law (See longer note, page 305.)

140. **forswore:** perjured.

143. **meed:** reward; **mewed up:** i.e., imprisoned (literally, caged up)

148. **cacodemon:** evil spirit

Edward IV.
From John Taylor, *All the workes of* . . . (1630).

A liberal rewarder of his friends.
To royalize his blood, I spent mine own.

QUEEN MARGARET, ⌜*aside*⌝
Ay, and much better blood than his or thine.   130

RICHARD, ⌜*to Queen Elizabeth*⌝
In all which time, you and your husband Grey
Were factious for the House of Lancaster.—
And, Rivers, so were you.—Was not your husband
In Margaret's battle at Saint Albans slain?
Let me put in your minds, if you forget,   135
What you have been ere this, and what you are;
Withal, what I have been, and what I am.

QUEEN MARGARET, ⌜*aside*⌝
A murd'rous villain, and so still thou art.

RICHARD, ⌜*to Queen Elizabeth*⌝
Poor Clarence did forsake his father Warwick,
Ay, and forswore himself—which Jesu pardon!—   140

QUEEN MARGARET, ⌜*aside*⌝   Which God revenge!

RICHARD
To fight on Edward's party for the crown;
And for his meed, poor lord, he is mewed up.
I would to God my heart were flint, like Edward's,
Or Edward's soft and pitiful, like mine.   145
I am too childish-foolish for this world.

QUEEN MARGARET, ⌜*aside*⌝
Hie thee to hell for shame, and leave this world,
Thou cacodemon! There thy kingdom is.

RIVERS
My lord of Gloucester, in those busy days
Which here you urge to prove us enemies,   150
We followed then our lord, our sovereign king.
So should we you, if you should be our king.

RICHARD
If I should be? I had rather be a peddler.
Far be it from my heart, the thought thereof.

155–58. As . . . thereof: i.e., you may judge how little joy **I** have in being queen by equating it to the little joy you suppose you would have if you were king

162. fall out: quarrel

163. pilled: pillaged, plundered

165–66. If not . . . rebels: i.e., if you do not bow down to me as your queen, you still tremble before me because you are the rebels that deposed me

167. gentle: well-born

168–69. what mak'st thou in my sight: i.e., what are you doing here (Queen Margaret answers as if the question had its literal meaning.)

170. But repetition: merely recital, narration; **marred:** Proverbial: "To make and/or mar."

172. banishèd: The historical Queen Margaret was, at the time of Clarence's death (ordered at the end of this scene), in exile in France.

174. here by my abode: i.e., because of my abiding (staying) here

QUEEN ELIZABETH
As little joy, my lord, as you suppose   155
You should enjoy were you this country's king,
As little joy you may suppose in me
That I enjoy, being the queen thereof.
QUEEN MARGARET, ⌜*aside*⌝
⌜As⌝ little joy enjoys the queen thereof,
For I am she, and altogether joyless.   160
I can no longer hold me patient.
                            ⌜*She steps forward.*⌝
Hear me, you wrangling pirates, that fall out
In sharing that which you have pilled from me!
Which of you trembles not that looks on me?
If not, that I am queen, you bow like subjects,   165
Yet that, by you deposed, you quake like rebels.—
Ah, gentle villain, do not turn away.
RICHARD
Foul, wrinkled witch, what mak'st thou in my
    sight?
QUEEN MARGARET
But repetition of what thou hast marred.   170
That will I make before I let thee go.
RICHARD
Wert thou not banishèd on pain of death?
QUEEN MARGARET
I was, but I do find more pain in banishment
Than death can yield me here by my abode.
A husband and a son thou ow'st to me;   175
⌜*To Queen Elizabeth.*⌝ And thou a kingdom;—all
    of you, allegiance.
This sorrow that I have by right is yours,
And all the pleasures you usurp are mine.
RICHARD
The curse my noble father laid on thee   180
When thou didst crown his warlike brows with
    paper,

184. **clout:** cloth, rag
185. **Rutland:** See note to 1.2.172.
190. **that babe:** i.e., Rutland
193. **No man but:** i.e., everyone
198. **York's dread curse:** the **curse** described by Richard in lines 180–88
202. **but:** only, merely; **peevish:** foolish, silly
204. **quick:** caustic, sharp
206. **surfeit:** sickness caused by overindulgence
207. **As ours by:** i.e., just as our king died through
211. **like:** similar

And with thy scorns drew'st rivers from his eyes,
And then, to dry them, gav'st the Duke a clout
Steeped in the faultless blood of pretty Rutland—　　185
His curses then, from bitterness of soul
Denounced against thee, are all fall'n upon thee,
And God, not we, hath plagued thy bloody deed.

QUEEN ELIZABETH
So just is God to right the innocent.

HASTINGS
O, 'twas the foulest deed to slay that babe,　　190
And the most merciless that e'er was heard of!

RIVERS
Tyrants themselves wept when it was reported.

DORSET
No man but prophesied revenge for it.

BUCKINGHAM
Northumberland, then present, wept to see it.

QUEEN MARGARET
What, were you snarling all before I came,　　195
Ready to catch each other by the throat,
And turn you all your hatred now on me?
Did York's dread curse prevail so much with
　　heaven
That Henry's death, my lovely Edward's death,　　200
Their kingdom's loss, my woeful banishment,
Should all but answer for that peevish brat?
Can curses pierce the clouds and enter heaven?
Why then, give way, dull clouds, to my quick
　　curses!　　205
Though not by war, by surfeit die your king,
As ours by murder to make him a king.
⌈*To Queen Elizabeth.*⌉ Edward thy son, that now is
　　Prince of Wales,
For Edward our son, that was Prince of Wales,　　210
Die in his youth by like untimely violence.
Thyself a queen, for me that was a queen,

216. **stalled:** installed, enthroned

222. **God I pray Him:** i.e., I pray to God

224. **But . . . accident:** i.e., but be by some unforeseen disaster or mishap

225. **charm:** curse

230. **them:** i.e., heaven

233. **still:** always, continually

239. **elvish-marked:** marked at birth by elves, often thought of as malignant, spiteful supernatural creatures; **abortive:** prematurely born; **hog:** Richard's heraldic emblem was the boar.

240. **sealed:** permanently stamped

242. **heavy:** sad, grieved (Or, perhaps, **heavy** is a transferred epithet that modifies **womb.**)

The boar, the heraldic emblem of Richard III.
(1.2.109; 1.3.239; 3.2.11, 29–34; 5.2.7)
From Thomas Willement, *Armorial bearings* . . . (1833).

Outlive thy glory, like my wretched self.
Long mayst thou live to wail thy children's death
And see another, as I see thee now,   215
Decked in thy rights, as thou art stalled in mine.
Long die thy happy days before thy death,
And, after many lengthened hours of grief,
Die neither mother, wife, nor England's queen.—
Rivers and Dorset, you were standers-by,   220
And so wast thou, Lord Hastings, when my son
Was stabbed with bloody daggers. God I pray Him
That none of you may live his natural age,
But by some unlooked accident cut off.

RICHARD
Have done thy charm, thou hateful, withered hag.   225

QUEEN MARGARET
And leave out thee? Stay, dog, for thou shalt hear
    me.
If heaven have any grievous plague in store
Exceeding those that I can wish upon thee,
O, let them keep it till thy sins be ripe   230
And then hurl down their indignation
On thee, the troubler of the poor world's peace.
The worm of conscience still begnaw thy soul.
Thy friends suspect for traitors while thou liv'st,
And take deep traitors for thy dearest friends.   235
No sleep close up that deadly eye of thine,
Unless it be while some tormenting dream
Affrights thee with a hell of ugly devils.
Thou elvish-marked, abortive, rooting hog,
Thou that wast sealed in thy nativity   240
The slave of nature and the son of hell,
Thou slander of thy heavy mother's womb,
Thou loathèd issue of thy father's loins,
Thou rag of honor, thou detested—

RICHARD   Margaret.   245

249. **I cry thee mercy:** i.e., I beg your pardon

252. **make the period to:** i.e., conclude, complete

255. **painted:** imitation; **vain flourish:** worthless or foolish decoration; **my fortune:** i.e., the throne

256. **sugar:** i.e., sweet words; **bottled:** i.e., shaped like a leather bottle, swollen, hunchbacked

258. **thou . . . thyself:** Proverbial: "To cut one's throat with one's own knife."

260. **bunch-backed:** i.e., humpbacked

262. **False-boding:** falsely prophesying

263. **move:** i.e., disturb

265. **well served:** treated as you deserve

266. **do me duty:** show me homage, reverence

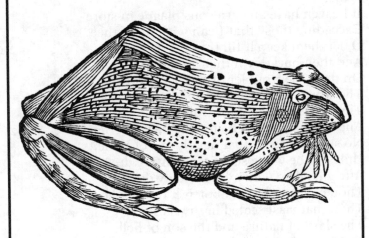

A "bunch-backed toad." (1.3.260–61)
From Edward Topsell, *The historie of serpents* . . . (1608).

QUEEN MARGARET Richard!

RICHARD Ha?

QUEEN MARGARET I call thee not.

RICHARD
I cry thee mercy, then, for I did think
That thou hadst called me all these bitter names.   250

QUEEN MARGARET
Why, so I did, but looked for no reply.
O, let me make the period to my curse!

RICHARD
'Tis done by me and ends in "Margaret."

QUEEN ELIZABETH, ⌈*to Queen Margaret*⌉
Thus have you breathed your curse against yourself.

QUEEN MARGARET
Poor painted queen, vain flourish of my fortune,   255
Why strew'st thou sugar on that bottled spider,
Whose deadly web ensnareth thee about?
Fool, fool, thou whet'st a knife to kill thyself.
The day will come that thou shalt wish for me
To help thee curse this poisonous bunch-backed   260
  toad.

HASTINGS
False-boding woman, end thy frantic curse,
Lest to thy harm thou move our patience.

QUEEN MARGARET
Foul shame upon you, you have all moved mine.

RIVERS
Were you well served, you would be taught your   265
  duty.

QUEEN MARGARET
To serve me well, you all should do me duty:
Teach me to be your queen, and you my subjects.
O, serve me well, and teach yourselves that duty!

DORSET, ⌈*to Rivers*⌉
Dispute not with her; she is lunatic.   270

271. **malapert:** saucy, impudent

272. **Your ... current:** i.e., your noble title has been stamped on you so recently that it can hardly be accepted as genuine currency (The figure of speech is drawn from the minting of coins.)

279. **touches:** applies to

281. **Our ... top:** Compare Ezekial 17.3: "... the great eagle ... came ... and took the highest branch of the cedar." **aerie:** eagle's brood (The word can also mean the nest of the eagle. See page 62.)

282. **dallies ... sun:** Proverbial: "The highest trees abide the sharpest winds" and "Only the eagle can gaze at the sun."

288. **suffer:** allow

289. **is won:** i.e., was won

295. **My charity ... shame:** perhaps, "My only charitable feeling is fury, and to continue living is shame to me"; or, perhaps, "the only charity extended to me is terrible violence, and a life of shame is all that is granted me"

296. **still ... rage:** may my sorrows' rage live on

QUEEN MARGARET
Peace, Master Marquess, you are malapert.
Your fire-new stamp of honor is scarce current.
O, that your young nobility could judge
What 'twere to lose it and be miserable!
They that stand high have many blasts to shake   275
  them,
And if they fall, they dash themselves to pieces.
RICHARD
Good counsel, marry.—Learn it, learn it, marquess.
DORSET
It touches you, my lord, as much as me.
RICHARD
Ay, and much more; but I was born so high.   280
Our aerie buildeth in the cedar's top,
And dallies with the wind and scorns the sun.
QUEEN MARGARET
And turns the sun to shade. Alas, alas,
Witness my son, now in the shade of death,
Whose bright out-shining beams thy cloudy wrath   285
Hath in eternal darkness folded up.
Your aerie buildeth in our aerie's nest.
O God, that seest it, do not suffer it!
As it is won with blood, lost be it so.
BUCKINGHAM
Peace, peace, for shame, if not for charity.   290
QUEEN MARGARET
Urge neither charity nor shame to me.
⌜*Addressing the others.*⌝ Uncharitably with me have
  you dealt,
And shamefully my hopes by you are butchered.
My charity is outrage, life my shame,   295
And in that shame still live my sorrows' rage.
BUCKINGHAM   Have done, have done.
QUEEN MARGARET
O princely Buckingham, I'll kiss thy hand

299. **In sign:** i.e., as a sign; **league:** alliance

300. **fair:** i.e., good fortune; **house:** family

305. **think but:** i.e., think otherwise but that

308. **yonder dog:** i.e., Richard

309. **Look when:** whenever (Proverbial: "These fawning curs will not bark till they bite.")

310. **venom:** venomous; **rankle to the death:** i.e., cause a deadly festering wound

313. **attend on:** wait upon, serve

315. **respect:** heed

316. **gentle:** courteous

317. **soothe:** humor, flatter

323. **an end:** i.e., on end

324. **muse:** wonder, marvel

An aerie. (1.3.281, 287)
From Joachim Camerarius, *Symbolorum et emblematum* . . . (1605).

In sign of league and amity with thee.
Now fair befall thee and thy noble house!   300
Thy garments are not spotted with our blood,
Nor thou within the compass of my curse.

BUCKINGHAM
Nor no one here, for curses never pass
The lips of those that breathe them in the air.

QUEEN MARGARET
I will not think but they ascend the sky,   305
And there awake God's gentle sleeping peace.
⌜*Aside to Buckingham.*⌝ O Buckingham, take heed of
    yonder dog!
Look when he fawns, he bites; and when he bites,
His venom tooth will rankle to the death.   310
Have not to do with him. Beware of him.
Sin, death, and hell have set their marks on him,
And all their ministers attend on him.

RICHARD
What doth she say, my lord of Buckingham?

BUCKINGHAM
Nothing that I respect, my gracious lord.   315

QUEEN MARGARET
What, dost thou scorn me for my gentle counsel,
And soothe the devil that I warn thee from?
O, but remember this another day,
When he shall split thy very heart with sorrow,
And say poor Margaret was a prophetess.—   320
Live each of you the subjects to his hate,
And he to yours, and all of you to God's.   *She exits.*

BUCKINGHAM
My hair doth stand an end to hear her curses.

RIVERS
And so doth mine. I muse why she's at liberty.

RICHARD
I cannot blame her. By God's holy mother,   325

329. **vantage:** benefit; **her wrong:** i.e., the wrong done to her

330. **somebody:** i.e., King Edward IV

333. **franked up to fatting:** penned up like a beast in a sty that is being fatted for slaughter; **pains:** trouble taken (on Edward's behalf)

336. **scathe:** harm

337. **ever:** always; **well advised:** judicious, wary

344. **brawl:** wrangle, squabble

345. **mischiefs:** evils; **set abroach:** set afoot

346. **I . . . others:** i.e., I blame on others

347. **who:** i.e., whom; **cast in darkness:** Compare Matthew 8.12: ". . . the children of the kingdom shall be cast out into utter darkness: there shall be weeping and gnashing of teeth."

348. **beweep:** i.e., weep about; **gulls:** i.e., gullible people

She hath had too much wrong, and I repent
My part thereof that I have done to her.
QUEEN ELIZABETH
I never did her any, to my knowledge.
RICHARD
Yet you have all the vantage of her wrong.
I was too hot to do somebody good   330
That is too cold in thinking of it now.
Marry, as for Clarence, he is well repaid;
He is franked up to fatting for his pains.
God pardon them that are the cause thereof.
RIVERS
A virtuous and a Christian-like conclusion   335
To pray for them that have done scathe to us.
RICHARD
So do I ever—(*speaks to himself*) being well advised,
For had I cursed now, I had cursed myself.

Enter Catesby.

CATESBY
Madam, his Majesty doth call for you,—
And for your Grace,—and yours, my gracious   340
⟨lords.⟩
QUEEN ELIZABETH
Catesby, I come.—Lords, will you go with me?
RIVERS   We wait upon your Grace.
        All but ⌈Richard, Duke of⌉ Gloucester exit.
RICHARD
I do the wrong and first begin to brawl.
The secret mischiefs that I set abroach   345
I lay unto the grievous charge of others.
Clarence, who I indeed have cast in darkness,
I do beweep to many simple gulls,
Namely, to Derby, Hastings, Buckingham,
And tell them 'tis the Queen and her allies   350
That stir the King against the Duke my brother.

352. **withal:** in addition; **whet:** urge

355. **do ... evil:** a biblical commonplace: Matthew 5.44, Luke 6.27, etc.   **for:** in return for

356–58. **And ... devil:** Proverbial: "The devil can cite scripture for his own purpose."   **odd old ends:** (1) random old commonplaces; (2) scraps of old clothes, rags   **forth of:** i.e., from

360. **mates:** fellows

365. **Crosby Place:** See note to 1.2.231.

367. **Withal:** moreover

369. **mark:** listen to, pay attention to

370. **stand to prate:** i.e., stop to chat

371. **Talkers ... doers:** Proverbial: "The greatest talkers are the least doers."

373. **Your ... millstones:** proverbial description of an utter lack of compassion; **fall:** shed

375. **straight:** straightway, immediately

Now they believe it and withal whet me
To be revenged on Rivers, Dorset, Grey;
But then I sigh and, with a piece of scripture,
Tell them that God bids us do good for evil;   355
And thus I clothe my naked villainy
With odd old ends stol'n forth of Holy Writ,
And seem a saint when most I play the devil.

Enter two Murderers.

But soft, here come my executioners.—
How now, my hardy, stout, resolvèd mates?   360
Are you now going to dispatch this thing?
⌜MURDERER⌝
We are, my lord, and come to have the warrant
That we may be admitted where he is.
RICHARD
Well thought upon. I have it here about me.
                                        ⌜*He gives a paper.*⌝
When you have done, repair to Crosby Place.   365
But, sirs, be sudden in the execution,
Withal obdurate; do not hear him plead,
For Clarence is well-spoken and perhaps
May move your hearts to pity if you mark him.
⌜MURDERER⌝
Tut, tut, my lord, we will not stand to prate.   370
Talkers are no good doers. Be assured
We go to use our hands and not our tongues.
RICHARD
Your eyes drop millstones when fools' eyes fall
    tears.
I like you lads. About your business straight.   375
Go, go, dispatch.
⌜MURDERERS⌝   We will, my noble lord.
                                        ⟨*They exit.*⟩

1.4 Richard's agents murder the imprisoned Clarence.

---

0 SD. **Keeper:** jailer
1. **heavily:** sorrowful
9. **Methoughts:** i.e., it seemed to me
11. **Gloucester:** i.e., Richard
12. **tempted:** persuaded, invited
13. **hatches:** i.e., deck
15. **cited up:** recalled; **heavy:** sad
18. **giddy:** dizzying
20. **that . . . stay:** who intended to stop him (from falling)
21. **main:** open ocean
25. **fearful:** dreadful; **wracks:** wrecked ships
28. **Inestimable, unvalued:** i.e., precious beyond one's ability to evaluate

Scene 4
Enter Clarence and Keeper.

KEEPER
  Why looks your Grace so heavily today?
CLARENCE
  O, I have passed a miserable night,
  So full of fearful dreams, of ugly sights,
  That, as I am a Christian faithful man,
  I would not spend another such a night   5
  Though 'twere to buy a world of happy days,
  So full of dismal terror was the time.
KEEPER
  What was your dream, my lord? I pray you tell me.
CLARENCE
  Methoughts that I had broken from the Tower
  And was embarked to cross to Burgundy,   10
  And in my company my brother Gloucester,
  Who from my cabin tempted me to walk
  Upon the hatches. ⟨Thence⟩ we looked toward
      England
  And cited up a thousand heavy times,   15
  During the wars of York and Lancaster,
  That had befall'n us. As we paced along
  Upon the giddy footing of the hatches,
  Methought that Gloucester stumbled, and in falling
  Struck me, that thought to stay him, overboard   20
  Into the tumbling billows of the main.
  O Lord, methought what pain it was to drown,
  What dreadful noise of ⟨waters⟩ in ⟨my⟩ ears,
  What sights of ugly death within ⟨my⟩ eyes.
  Methoughts I saw a thousand fearful wracks,   25
  A thousand men that fishes gnawed upon,
  Wedges of gold, great anchors, heaps of pearl,
  Inestimable stones, unvalued jewels,
  All scattered in the bottom of the sea.

38. **the ghost:** my spirit or soul (Compare Matthew 27.50: "Then Jesus cried again with a loud voice, and yielded up the ghost.") **envious:** malicious; **flood:** ocean, water

39. **Stopped in:** i.e., closed in, as in a stoppered vessel

42. **Who:** i.e., which

43. **sore:** oppressively severe

46. **melancholy flood:** i.e., the river Styx in the underworld of classical mythology (The underworld of Clarence's dream is a blend of the classical Hades, the abode of the shades of the dead visited by Aeneas in Virgil's *Aeneid*—i.e., **this dark monarchy**—and the Hell of Christian theology, visited by Dante in the *Inferno*—i.e., the **legion of foul fiends.**)

47. **sour ferryman:** i.e., Charon, who ferried souls to Hades (See page 78.)

52. **false:** treacherous, faithless (See longer note to 1.3.139, page 305.)

54. **shadow:** shade, ghost (who turns out to be Prince Edward, son to Henry VI)

55. **Dabbled in:** splattered with

56. **fleeting:** unstable, fickle

59. **furies:** avenging, tormenting infernal spirits (See page 74.)

Some lay in dead men's skulls, and in the holes   30
Where eyes did once inhabit, there were crept—
As 'twere in scorn of eyes—reflecting gems,
That wooed the slimy bottom of the deep
And mocked the dead bones that lay scattered by.

KEEPER
Had you such leisure in the time of death   35
To gaze upon these secrets of the deep?

CLARENCE
Methought I had, and often did I strive
To yield the ghost, but still the envious flood
Stopped in my soul and would not let it forth
To find the empty, vast, and wand'ring air,   40
But smothered it within my panting bulk,
Who almost burst to belch it in the sea.

KEEPER
Awaked you not in this sore agony?

CLARENCE
No, no, my dream was lengthened after life.
O, then began the tempest to my soul.   45
I passed, methought, the melancholy flood,
With that sour ferryman which poets write of,
Unto the kingdom of perpetual night.
The first that there did greet my stranger-soul
Was my great father-in-law, renownèd Warwick,   50
Who spake aloud "What scourge for perjury
Can this dark monarchy afford false Clarence?"
And so he vanished. Then came wand'ring by
A shadow like an angel, with bright hair
Dabbled in blood, and he shrieked out aloud   55
"Clarence is come—false, fleeting, perjured
    Clarence,
That stabbed me in the field by Tewkesbury.
Seize on him, furies. Take him unto torment."
With that, ⟨methoughts,⟩ a legion of foul fiends   60

61. **Environed:** surrounded
63. **season:** while
66. **affrighted:** frightened
70. **Edward's:** i.e., King Edward IV's
71. **deep:** solemn; or, profoundly felt
76. **heavy:** (1) sad; (2) sleepy; **fain:** gladly
78–79. **breaks . . . noontide night:** Compare Job 17.11–12: "My days are past, my enterprises are broken, and the thoughts of mine heart have changed the night for the day, and the light that approached, for darkness." **breaks:** interrupts **seasons:** Compare Ecclesiastes 3.1: "To every thing there is a season." **reposing hours:** i.e., proper time for sleep **noontide:** noontime
80. **but:** only
81. **toil:** strife, turmoil
82. **for unfelt imaginations:** i.e., in return for pleasures that are merely imagined
84. **low name:** the status of the commoner

Environed me and howlèd in mine ears
Such hideous cries that with the very noise
I trembling waked, and for a season after
Could not believe but that I was in hell,
Such terrible impression made my dream.   65
KEEPER
No marvel, lord, though it affrighted you.
I am afraid, methinks, to hear you tell it.
CLARENCE
Ah keeper, keeper, I have done these things,
That now give evidence against my soul,
For Edward's sake, and see how he requites me.—   70
O God, if my deep prayers cannot appease thee,
But thou wilt be avenged on my misdeeds,
Yet execute thy wrath in me alone!
O, spare my guiltless wife and my poor children!—
Keeper, I prithee sit by me awhile.   75
My soul is heavy, and I fain would sleep.
KEEPER
I will, my lord. God give your Grace good rest.
                                    ⌜*Clarence sleeps.*⌝

            Enter Brakenbury the Lieutenant.

BRAKENBURY
Sorrow breaks seasons and reposing hours,
Makes the night morning, and the noontide night.
Princes have but their titles for their glories,   80
An outward honor for an inward toil,
And, for unfelt imaginations,
They often feel a world of restless cares,
So that between their titles and low name
There's nothing differs but the outward fame.   85

            Enter two Murderers.

FIRST MURDERER   Ho, who's here?

87. **how:** i.e., on whose authority
97. **will not:** i.e., wish not to
112. **remorse:** pity, compassion

The Furies. (1.4.59)
From Vincenzo Cartari, *Le vere e noue imagini de gli delli antichi . . .* (1615).

BRAKENBURY
What wouldst thou, fellow? And how cam'st thou
    hither?
SECOND MURDERER   I would speak with Clarence, and I
    came hither on my legs.   90
BRAKENBURY   What, so brief?
FIRST MURDERER   'Tis better, sir, than to be tedious.—
    Let him see our commission, and talk no more.
                    ⌜*Brakenbury*⌝ *reads* ⌜*the commission.*⌝
BRAKENBURY
I am in this commanded to deliver
The noble Duke of Clarence to your hands.   95
I will not reason what is meant hereby
Because I will be guiltless from the meaning.
There lies the Duke asleep, and there the keys.
                        ⌜*He hands them keys.*⌝
I'll to the King and signify to him
That thus I have resigned to you my charge.   100
FIRST MURDERER   You may, sir. 'Tis a point of wisdom.
    Fare you well.
                ⌜*Brakenbury and the Keeper*⌝ *exit.*
SECOND MURDERER   What, shall ⟨I⟩ stab him as he
    sleeps?
FIRST MURDERER   No. He'll say 'twas done cowardly,   105
    when he wakes.
SECOND MURDERER   Why, he shall never wake until the
    great Judgment Day.
FIRST MURDERER   Why, then he'll say we stabbed him
    sleeping.   110
SECOND MURDERER   The urging of that word "judg-
    ment" hath bred a kind of remorse in me.
FIRST MURDERER   What, art thou afraid?
SECOND MURDERER   Not to kill him, having a warrant,
    but to be damned for killing him, from the which   115
    no warrant can defend me.
FIRST MURDERER   I thought thou hadst been resolute.

122. **passionate humor:** i.e., inclination toward compassion

123. **wont:** accustomed; **but . . . twenty:** i.e., only for the count of twenty

129. **Zounds:** i.e., God's wounds (a strong oath)

137. **entertain it:** i.e., receive my conscience as a guest, or accept it as a servant

141. **checks:** stops, restrains

147. **turned out of . . . for:** evicted from . . . as

152. **Take . . . mind:** perhaps, seize upon or arrest your conscience (i.e., **the devil**); or perhaps, accept **the devil** (instead of your conscience) into your mind

"A legion of foul fiends." (1.4.60)
From Olaus Magnus, *Historia de gentibus septentrionalibus . . .* (1555).

SECOND MURDERER   So I am—to let him live.

FIRST MURDERER   I'll back to the Duke of Gloucester
and tell him so.   120

SECOND MURDERER   Nay, I prithee stay a little. I hope
this passionate humor of mine will change. It was
wont to hold me but while one tells twenty.

FIRST MURDERER   How dost thou feel thyself now?

SECOND MURDERER   ⟨Faith,⟩ some certain dregs of con-   125
science are yet within me.

FIRST MURDERER   Remember our reward when the
deed's done.

SECOND MURDERER   ⟨Zounds,⟩ he dies! I had forgot the
reward.   130

FIRST MURDERER   Where's thy conscience now?

SECOND MURDERER   O, in the Duke of Gloucester's
purse.

FIRST MURDERER   When he opens his purse to give us
our reward, thy conscience flies out.   135

SECOND MURDERER   'Tis no matter. Let it go. There's
few or none will entertain it.

FIRST MURDERER   What if it come to thee again?

SECOND MURDERER   I'll not meddle with it. It makes a
man a coward: a man cannot steal but it accuseth   140
him; a man cannot swear but it checks him; a man
cannot lie with his neighbor's wife but it detects
him. 'Tis a blushing, shamefaced spirit that muti-
nies in a man's bosom. It fills a man full of
obstacles. It made me once restore a purse of gold   145
that by chance I found. It beggars any man that
keeps it. It is turned out of towns and cities for a
dangerous thing, and every man that means to live
well endeavors to trust to himself and live without it.

FIRST MURDERER   ⟨Zounds,⟩ 'tis even now at my elbow,   150
persuading me not to kill the Duke.

SECOND MURDERER   Take the devil in thy mind, and

151. **him:** i.e., your conscience
153. **insinuate:** ingratiate himself
157. **tall:** brave
159. **Take:** attack; **costard:** head (slang)
160. **hilts:** i.e., hilt
161. **malmsey butt:** barrel of sweet wine
162. **device:** scheme
163. **sop:** cake broken up and soaked in wine
164. **Soft:** i.e., wait a moment
166. **reason:** talk
168. **anon:** soon
173. **thy . . . humble:** i.e., you look like someone of low social status
175. **darkly:** ominously; **deadly:** implacably
177. **Wherefore:** why

Charon, "that sour ferryman." (1.4.47)
From Vincenzo Cartari, *Le vere e noue imagini de gli delli antichi . . .* (1615).

78

believe him not. He would insinuate with thee but
to make thee sigh.

FIRST MURDERER I am strong-framed. He cannot pre-   155
vail with me.

SECOND MURDERER Spoke like a tall man that respects
thy reputation. Come, shall we fall to work?

FIRST MURDERER Take him on the costard with the
hilts of thy sword, and then throw him into the   160
malmsey butt in the next room.

SECOND MURDERER O, excellent device—and make a
sop of him!

FIRST MURDERER Soft, he wakes.

SECOND MURDERER Strike!   165

FIRST MURDERER No, we'll reason with him.
⌜*Clarence wakes.*⌝

CLARENCE
Where art thou, keeper? Give me a cup of wine.

SECOND MURDERER
You shall have wine enough, my lord, anon.

CLARENCE
In God's name, what art thou?

FIRST MURDERER   A man, as you are.   170

CLARENCE But not, as I am, royal.

FIRST MURDERER Nor you, as we are, loyal.

CLARENCE
Thy voice is thunder, but thy looks are humble.

FIRST MURDERER
My voice is now the King's, my looks mine own.

CLARENCE
How darkly and how deadly dost thou speak!   175
Your eyes do menace me. Why look you pale?
Who sent you hither? Wherefore do you come?

SECOND MURDERER To, to, to—

CLARENCE To murder me?

BOTH Ay, ay.   180

187. **drawn forth ... men:** i.e., selected from among the whole of humanity

190. **quest:** inquest, or body of persons appointed to conduct a judicial inquiry

193. **convict:** i.e., pronounced guilty

195. **charge:** command

195–96. **to have redemption ... sins:** We, like other editors, adopt the quarto reading here because we suspect that the Folio reading ("for any goodness") may have been produced by censorship of the explicit reference to Christ.

201. **Erroneous:** misguided

202. **the table of His law:** i.e., the Ten Commandments (For the commandments themselves, see Exodus 20.3–17. For the narrative of Moses writing God's commandments on tables of stone, see Exodus 32.15 and 34.1–29.)

204. **Spurn at:** reject with contempt

CLARENCE
  You scarcely have the hearts to tell me so
  And therefore cannot have the hearts to do it.
  Wherein, my friends, have I offended you?
FIRST MURDERER
  Offended us you have not, but the King.
CLARENCE
  I shall be reconciled to him again.   185
SECOND MURDERER
  Never, my lord. Therefore prepare to die.
CLARENCE
  Are you drawn forth among a world of men
  To slay the innocent? What is my offense?
  Where is the evidence that doth accuse me?
  What lawful quest have given their verdict up   190
  Unto the frowning judge? Or who pronounced
  The bitter sentence of poor Clarence' death
  Before I be convict by course of law?
  To threaten me with death is most unlawful.
  I charge you, as you hope ⟨to have redemption,   195
  By Christ's dear blood shed for our grievous sins,⟩
  That you depart, and lay no hands on me.
  The deed you undertake is damnable.
FIRST MURDERER
  What we will do, we do upon command.
SECOND MURDERER
  And he that hath commanded is our king.   200
CLARENCE
  Erroneous vassals, the great King of kings
  Hath in the table of His law commanded
  That thou shalt do no murder. Will you then
  Spurn at His edict and fulfill a man's?
  Take heed, for He holds vengeance in His hand   205
  To hurl upon their heads that break His law.
SECOND MURDERER
  And that same vengeance doth He hurl on thee

208. **false forswearing:** oath breaking

209–10. **Thou . . . Lancaster:** i.e., you took an oath upon the Eucharist to fight on behalf of Henry VI

214. **Unrippedst:** laid open; **thy sovereign's son:** Prince Edward, son of Henry VI

217. **in . . . degree:** i.e., to such a grievous extent

218. **ill:** evil

221. **deep:** i.e., involved in guilt

227. **minister:** agent

228. **gallant-springing, brave Plantagenet:** i.e., splendid and lively Prince Edward

229. **novice:** i.e., youth (literally, beginner)

235. **meed:** reward

For false forswearing and for murder too.
Thou didst receive the sacrament to fight
In quarrel of the House of Lancaster.   210
FIRST MURDERER
And, like a traitor to the name of God,
Didst break that vow, and with thy treacherous
    blade
⌜Unrippedst⌝ the bowels of thy sovereign's son.
SECOND MURDERER
Whom thou wast sworn to cherish and defend.   215
FIRST MURDERER
How canst thou urge God's dreadful law to us
When thou hast broke it in such dear degree?
CLARENCE
Alas! For whose sake did I that ill deed?
For Edward, for my brother, for his sake.
He sends you not to murder me for this,   220
For in that sin he is as deep as I.
If God will be avengèd for the deed,
O, know you yet He doth it publicly!
Take not the quarrel from His powerful arm;
He needs no indirect or lawless course   225
To cut off those that have offended Him.
FIRST MURDERER
Who made thee then a bloody minister
When gallant-springing, brave Plantagenet,
That princely novice, was struck dead by thee?
CLARENCE
My brother's love, the devil, and my rage.   230
FIRST MURDERER
Thy brother's love, our duty, and thy faults
Provoke us hither now to slaughter thee.
CLARENCE
If you do love my brother, hate not me.
I am his brother, and I love him well.
If you are hired for meed, go back again,   235

245. **arm:** Here the quarto provides the line "And charged us from his soul to love each other."

248. **millstones:** See note to 1.3.373. **lessoned:** instructed

249. **kind:** i.e., good-hearted (The First Murderer's reply plays on the meaning of **kind** as natural.)

253. **bewept:** wept for; **fortune:** i.e., misfortune (of imprisonment)

255. **labor:** exert his influence in urging

257. **Earth's thralldom:** i.e., enslavement of life on Earth

And I will send you to my brother Gloucester,
Who shall reward you better for my life
Than Edward will for tidings of my death.
SECOND MURDERER
  You are deceived. Your brother Gloucester hates
    you.   240
CLARENCE
  O no, he loves me, and he holds me dear.
  Go you to him from me.
FIRST MURDERER   Ay, so we will.
CLARENCE
  Tell him, when that our princely father York
  Blessed his three sons with his victorious arm,   245
  He little thought of this divided friendship.
  Bid Gloucester think ⟨of⟩ this, and he will weep.
FIRST MURDERER
  Ay, millstones, as he lessoned us to weep.
CLARENCE
  O, do not slander him, for he is kind.
FIRST MURDERER
  Right, as snow in harvest. Come, you deceive   250
    yourself.
  'Tis he that sends us to destroy you here.
CLARENCE
  It cannot be, for he bewept my fortune,
  And hugged me in his arms, and swore with sobs
  That he would labor my delivery.   255
FIRST MURDERER
  Why, so he doth, when he delivers you
  From this Earth's thralldom to the joys of heaven.
SECOND MURDERER
  Make peace with God, for you must die, my lord.
CLARENCE
  Have you that holy feeling in your souls
  To counsel me to make my peace with God,   260
  And are you yet to your own souls so blind

268. **pent from liberty:** i.e., imprisoned, closely confined

284. **fain:** gladly; **like Pilate:** See Matthew 27.24.

That you will war with God by murd'ring me?
O sirs, consider: they that set you on
To do this deed will hate you for the deed.

SECOND MURDERER, ⌜*to First Murderer*⌝
What shall we do?   265

CLARENCE   Relent, and save your souls.
Which of you—if you were a prince's son
Being pent from liberty, as I am now—
If two such murderers as yourselves came to you,
Would not entreat for life? ⌜Ay,⌝ you would beg,   270
Were you in my distress.

FIRST MURDERER
Relent? No. 'Tis cowardly and womanish.

CLARENCE
Not to relent is beastly, savage, devilish.
⌜*To Second Murderer.*⌝ My friend, I spy some pity
in thy looks.   275
O, if thine eye be not a flatterer,
Come thou on my side and entreat for me.
A begging prince what beggar pities not?

SECOND MURDERER   Look behind you, my lord.

FIRST MURDERER
Take that, and that. (*Stabs him.*) If all this will not   280
do,
I'll drown you in the malmsey butt within.
                           He exits ⌜*with the body.*⌝

SECOND MURDERER
A bloody deed, and desperately dispatched.
How fain, like Pilate, would I wash my hands
Of this most grievous murder.   285

                  Enter First Murderer.

FIRST MURDERER
How now? What mean'st thou that thou help'st me
not?

290. **would:** wish
292. **repent me:** i.e., repent
297. **this will out:** Proverbial: "Murder will out" (i.e., cannot be hidden).

By ⟨heavens,⟩ the Duke shall know how slack you
   have been.
SECOND MURDERER
   I would he knew that I had saved his brother.   290
   Take thou the fee, and tell him what I say,
   For I repent me that the Duke is slain.   *He exits.*
FIRST MURDERER
   So do not I. Go, coward as thou art.
   Well, I'll go hide the body in some hole
   Till that the Duke give order for his burial.   295
   And when I have my meed, I will away,
   For this will out, and then I must not stay.
                                        He exits.

The Tragedy of

RICHARD III

ACT 2

2.1 The dying King Edward IV attempts to reconcile the quarreling factions in his royal court. Queen Elizabeth and her kindred, on the one side, and Hastings, Buckingham, and Richard, on the other, vow to make and keep peace among themselves. Rejoicing about this "united league" is interrupted by news of Clarence's murder, which King Edward blames on himself and Richard blames on the Queen's kindred.

---

0 SD. **Flourish:** trumpets to announce the approach of a dignitary, here the monarch himself

3. **embassage:** ambassador; message

4. **redeem:** deliver; **hence:** from this world

8. **Dissemble not:** i.e., do not merely cover up or conceal

10. **seal:** ratify

14–15. **award . . . end:** appoint or sentence you to be each other's downfall

ACT 2

Scene 1

Flourish. Enter King ⌐Edward,¬ sick, Queen ⌐Elizabeth,¬
Lord Marquess Dorset, Rivers, Hastings, Buckingham,
Woodeville, ⌐Grey, and Scales.¬

KING EDWARD
  Why, so. Now have I done a good day's work.
  You peers, continue this united league.
  I every day expect an embassage
  From my Redeemer to redeem me hence,
  And more ⟨in⟩ peace my soul shall part to heaven   5
  Since I have made my friends at peace on earth.
  ⟨Rivers and Hastings,⟩ take each other's hand.
  Dissemble not your hatred. Swear your love.
RIVERS, ⌐*taking Hastings' hand*¬
  By heaven, my soul is purged from grudging hate,
  And with my hand I seal my true heart's love.   10
HASTINGS
  So thrive I as I truly swear the like.
KING EDWARD
  Take heed you dally not before your king,
  Lest He that is the supreme King of kings
  Confound your hidden falsehood and award
  Either of you to be the other's end.   15
HASTINGS
  So prosper I as I swear perfect love.

93

19. **son:** i.e., stepson
20. **been factious:** i.e., formed factions
25–26. **Lord Marquess:** i.e., Dorset
31. **embracements to:** i.e., embraces of
34–35. **but . . . Doth:** i.e., and . . . does not
38. **And most:** i.e., and am most
39. **Deep:** very cunning or crafty
42. **cordial:** medicine, food, or drink that invigorates the heart

RIVERS
    And I as I love Hastings with my heart.
KING EDWARD, ⌈*to Queen Elizabeth*⌉
    Madam, yourself is not exempt from this,—
    Nor you, son Dorset,—Buckingham, nor you.
    You have been factious one against the other.—   20
    Wife, love Lord Hastings. Let him kiss your hand,
    And what you do, do it unfeignedly.
QUEEN ELIZABETH
    There, Hastings, I will never more remember
    Our former hatred, so thrive I and mine.
                            ⌈*Hastings kisses her hand.*⌉
KING EDWARD
    Dorset, embrace him.—Hastings, love Lord   25
        Marquess.
DORSET
    This interchange of love, I here protest,
    Upon my part shall be inviolable.
HASTINGS   And so swear I.   ⌈*They embrace.*⌉
KING EDWARD
    Now, princely Buckingham, seal thou this league   30
    With thy embracements to my wife's allies
    And make me happy in your unity.
BUCKINGHAM, ⌈*to Queen Elizabeth*⌉
    Whenever Buckingham doth turn his hate
    Upon your Grace, but with all duteous love
    Doth cherish you and yours, God punish me   35
    With hate in those where I expect most love.
    When I have most need to employ a friend,
    And most assurèd that he is a friend,
    Deep, hollow, treacherous, and full of guile
    Be he unto me: this do I beg of ⟨God,⟩   40
    When I am cold in love to you or yours.
            ⌈*Queen Elizabeth and Buckingham*⌉ embrace.
KING EDWARD
    A pleasing cordial, princely Buckingham,

44. **wanteth:** lacks
45. **period:** conclusion
48. **morrow:** morning
51. **charity:** Christian love of one's fellow man
53. **swelling:** indignant; **wrong-incensèd:** i.e., mistakenly angry
55. **heap:** multitude
59. **hardly borne:** resented
60. **presence:** company
61. **me:** i.e., myself
69. **all without desert:** entirely without my deserving it
70. **Lord Woodeville and Lord Scales:** See note to 1.3.38.
73. **any jot:** i.e., the least bit

Is this thy vow unto my sickly heart.
There wanteth now our brother Gloucester here
To make the blessèd period of this peace. 45
BUCKINGHAM   And in good time
Here comes Sir Richard Ratcliffe and the Duke.

Enter Ratcliffe, and ⌐Richard, Duke of⌐ Gloucester.

RICHARD
Good morrow to my sovereign king and queen,
And, princely peers, a happy time of day.
KING EDWARD
Happy indeed, as we have spent the day. 50
Gloucester, we have done deeds of charity,
Made peace of enmity, fair love of hate,
Between these swelling, wrong-incensèd peers.
RICHARD
A blessèd labor, my most sovereign lord.
Among this princely heap, if any here 55
By false intelligence or wrong surmise
Hold me a foe,
If I ⟨unwittingly,⟩ or in my rage,
Have aught committed that is hardly borne
⟨By⟩ any in this presence, I desire 60
To reconcile me to his friendly peace.
'Tis death to me to be at enmity;
I hate it, and desire all good men's love.
First, madam, I entreat true peace of you,
Which I will purchase with my duteous service;— 65
Of you, my noble cousin Buckingham,
If ever any grudge were lodged between us;—
Of you and you, Lord Rivers and of Dorset,
That all without desert have frowned on me;—
Of you, Lord Woodeville and Lord Scales;—of you, 70
Dukes, earls, lords, gentlemen; indeed, of all.
I do not know that Englishman alive
With whom my soul is any jot at odds

77. **compounded:** settled

79. **to your grace:** i.e., into your favor

83. **corse:** corpse

85. **what a world is this:** proverbial

87. **in the presence:** i.e., in attendance here upon the king

88. **forsook:** i.e., forsaken, left

91. **wingèd Mercury:** the messenger of the gods, often depicted with wings at his heels (See below.)

93. **lag:** late

94–97. **some . . . suspicion:** a veiled reference to the Queen and her relatives **blood:** i.e., blood relation **go current:** are taken to be genuine (as if legal currency) **from:** i.e., free from

"Wingèd Mercury." (2.1.91; 4.3.59)
From Innocenzio Ringhieri, *Cento giuochi liberali . . .* (1580).

More than the infant that is born tonight.
I thank my God for my humility.   75
QUEEN ELIZABETH
A holy day shall this be kept hereafter.
I would to God all strifes were well compounded.
My sovereign lord, I do beseech your Highness
To take our brother Clarence to your grace.
RICHARD
Why, madam, have I offered love for this,   80
To be so flouted in this royal presence?
Who knows not that the gentle duke is dead?
                                        They all start.
You do him injury to scorn his corse.
KING EDWARD
Who knows not he is dead! Who knows he is?
QUEEN ELIZABETH
All-seeing heaven, what a world is this!   85
BUCKINGHAM
Look I so pale, Lord Dorset, as the rest?
DORSET
Ay, my good lord, and no man in the presence
But his red color hath forsook his cheeks.
KING EDWARD
Is Clarence dead? The order was reversed.
RICHARD
But he, poor man, by your first order died,   90
And that a wingèd Mercury did bear.
Some tardy cripple bare the countermand,
That came too lag to see him burièd.
God grant that some, less noble and less loyal,
Nearer in bloody thoughts, and not in blood,   95
Deserve not worse than wretched Clarence did,
And yet go current from suspicion.

     Enter ⌐Lord Stanley,⌐ Earl of Derby.

98. **boon:** favor

102. **forfeit . . . life:** i.e., release of my servant from the death penalty

103. **riotous:** belligerent

104. **Lately attendant on:** i.e., who was recently in the service of

105. **doom . . . death:** condemn my brother to death

106. **slave:** wretch

107. **his . . . thought:** Proverbial: "Thought is free"—i.e., one cannot be punished for only thinking something.

109. **sued to me for him:** i.e., begged my favor toward him

110. **advised:** judicious, prudent

112. **poor soul:** i.e., Clarence

117. **lay:** i.e., were resting

120. **thin:** i.e., thinly clothed; **numb-cold:** i.e., numbingly cold

123. **grace:** i.e., graciousness

124. **waiting vassals:** servants

125–26. **defaced . . . Redeemer:** i.e., destroyed another human being

STANLEY, ⌜*kneeling*⌝
  A boon, my sovereign, for my service done.
KING EDWARD
  I prithee, peace. My soul is full of sorrow.
STANLEY
  I will not rise unless your Highness hear me.   100
KING EDWARD
  Then say at once what is it thou requests.
STANLEY
  The forfeit, sovereign, of my servant's life,
  Who slew today a riotous gentleman
  Lately attendant on the Duke of Norfolk.
KING EDWARD
  Have I a tongue to doom my brother's death,   105
  And shall that tongue give pardon to a slave?
  My brother killed no man; his fault was thought,
  And yet his punishment was bitter death.
  Who sued to me for him? Who, in my wrath,
  Kneeled ⟨at⟩ my feet, and ⟨bade⟩ me be advised?   110
  Who spoke of brotherhood? Who spoke of love?
  Who told me how the poor soul did forsake
  The mighty Warwick and did fight for me?
  Who told me, in the field at Tewkesbury,
  When Oxford had me down, he rescued me,   115
  And said "Dear brother, live, and be a king"?
  Who told me, when we both lay in the field
  Frozen almost to death, how he did lap me
  Even in his garments and did give himself,
  All thin and naked, to the numb-cold night?   120
  All this from my remembrance brutish wrath
  Sinfully plucked, and not a man of you
  Had so much grace to put it in my mind.
  But when your carters or your waiting vassals
  Have done a drunken slaughter and defaced   125
  The precious image of our dear Redeemer,

127. **straight:** straightway, immediately
130. **Nor I:** i.e., nor did I
132. **beholding:** beholden, indebted
136. **closet:** private chamber
138. **Marked:** noticed
141. **they . . . King:** i.e., they were always trying to persuade the King to do it

2.2 As the Duchess of York mourns Clarence's death, Queen Elizabeth enters grieving for the death of King Edward IV. Richard and Buckingham make plans to escort King Edward's heir, Prince Edward, to London.

———————

4. **unhappy:** unfortunate

You straight are on your knees for pardon, pardon,
And I, unjustly too, must grant it you.
                              ⌜*Stanley rises.*⌝
But for my brother, not a man would speak,
Nor I, ungracious, speak unto myself   130
For him, poor soul. The proudest of you all
Have been beholding to him in his life,
Yet none of you would once beg for his life.
O God, I fear Thy justice will take hold
On me and you, and mine and yours for this!—   135
Come, Hastings, help me to my closet.—
Ah, poor Clarence.
                    Some exit with King and Queen.
RICHARD
This is the fruits of rashness. Marked you not
How that the guilty kindred of the Queen
Looked pale when they did hear of Clarence' death?   140
O, they did urge it still unto the King.
God will revenge it. Come, lords, will you go
To comfort Edward with our company?
BUCKINGHAM   We wait upon your Grace.
                                        They exit.

Scene 2
Enter the old Duchess of York with the two
children of Clarence.

BOY
Good grandam, tell us, is our father dead?
DUCHESS   No, boy.
DAUGHTER
Why do ⟨you⟩ weep so oft, and beat your breast,
And cry "O Clarence, my unhappy son"?
BOY
Why do you look on us and shake your head,   5

8. **cousins:** kin (a term for any relatives)

11. **It were . . . lost:** Proverbial: "For a lost thing care not."

15. **all:** entirely

19. **Incapable:** i.e., not capable of understanding

23. **impeachments:** charges

27. **And he:** i.e., and said he

28. **shape:** appearance (also, theatrical role)

29. **visor:** mask, disguise (See below.)

Men and women in visors. (2.2.29)
From Giacomo Franco, *Habiti d'huomeni . . .* (1609).

And call us orphans, wretches, castaways,
If that our noble father were alive?

DUCHESS
My pretty cousins, you mistake me both.
I do lament the sickness of the King,
As loath to lose him, not your father's death.   10
It were lost sorrow to wail one that's lost.

BOY
Then, you conclude, my grandam, he is dead.
The King mine uncle is to blame for it.
God will revenge it, whom I will importune
With earnest prayers, all to that effect.   15

DAUGHTER   And so will I.

DUCHESS
Peace, children, peace. The King doth love you
    well.
Incapable and shallow innocents,
You cannot guess who caused your father's death.   20

BOY
Grandam, we can, for my good uncle Gloucester
Told me the King, provoked to it by the Queen,
Devised impeachments to imprison him;
And when my uncle told me so, he wept,
And pitied me, and kindly kissed my cheek,   25
Bade me rely on him as on my father,
And he would love me dearly as a child.

DUCHESS
Ah, that deceit should steal such gentle shape,
And with a virtuous visor hide deep vice.
He is my son, ay, and therein my shame,   30
Yet from my dugs he drew not this deceit.

BOY
Think you my uncle did dissemble, grandam?

DUCHESS   Ay, boy.

BOY
I cannot think it. Hark, what noise is this?

34 SD. her hair about her ears: a stage signal to show grief and lamentation

39. rude: violent; **impatience:** failure to endure suffering with equanimity

40. make . . . violence: perform the violent emotion that is appropriate to tragedy

43. want: lack

44. brief: hasty

48. interest: legal right or share

49. title: ownership (as his mother)

50. bewept: wept for

51. lived with: i.e., preserved my life by; **images:** i.e., sons

52. semblance: appearance

53. malignant: malicious

54. glass: mirror

62. moiety: portion

63. overgo . . . woes: surpass you in grieving

Enter Queen ⌐Elizabeth⌐ with her hair about her ears,
Rivers and Dorset after her.

QUEEN ELIZABETH
Ah, who shall hinder me to wail and weep,   35
To chide my fortune and torment myself?
I'll join with black despair against my soul
And to myself become an enemy.
DUCHESS
What means this scene of rude impatience?
QUEEN ELIZABETH
To make an act of tragic violence.   40
Edward, my lord, thy son, our king, is dead.
Why grow the branches when the root is gone?
Why wither not the leaves that want their sap?
If you will live, lament. If die, be brief,
That our swift-wingèd souls may catch the King's,   45
Or, like obedient subjects, follow him
To his new kingdom of ne'er-changing night.
DUCHESS
Ah, so much interest have ⟨I⟩ in thy sorrow
As I had title in thy noble husband.
I have bewept a worthy husband's death   50
And lived with looking on his images;
But now two mirrors of his princely semblance
Are cracked in pieces by malignant death,
And I, for comfort, have but one false glass
That grieves me when I see my shame in him.   55
Thou art a widow, yet thou art a mother,
And hast the comfort of thy children left,
But death hath snatched my husband from mine
    arms
And plucked two crutches from my feeble hands,   60
Clarence and Edward. O, what cause have I,
Thine being but a moiety of my moan,
To overgo thy woes and drown thy cries!

65. **kindred tears:** (1) tears of relatives; (2) similar tears

67. **widow-dolor:** i.e., sorrow as a widow

69. **barren . . . forth:** unable to give birth to

70. **All springs reduce:** i.e., let all springs bring or lead

71. **watery moon:** Because the moon controls the oceans' tides, it is called "watery" or "moist."

76. **stay:** support

79. **Was never widow:** i.e., there was never before a widow who; **dear:** severe, grievous

83. **Their . . . general:** i.e., they each suffer a particular loss, while I suffer the loss of all   **parceled:** divided into smaller portions

BOY, ⌈*to Queen Elizabeth*⌉
  Ah, aunt, you wept not for our father's death.
  How can we aid you with our kindred tears?   65
DAUGHTER, ⌈*to Queen Elizabeth*⌉
  Our fatherless distress was left unmoaned.
  Your widow-dolor likewise be unwept!
QUEEN ELIZABETH
  Give me no help in lamentation.
  I am not barren to bring forth complaints.
  All springs reduce their currents to mine eyes,   70
  That I, being governed by the watery moon,
  May send forth plenteous tears to drown the world.
  Ah, for my husband, for my dear lord Edward!
CHILDREN
  Ah, for our father, for our dear lord Clarence!
DUCHESS
  Alas for both, both mine, Edward and Clarence!   75
QUEEN ELIZABETH
  What stay had I but Edward? And he's gone.
CHILDREN
  What stay had we but Clarence? And he's gone.
DUCHESS
  What stays had I but they? And they are gone.
QUEEN ELIZABETH
  Was never widow had so dear a loss.
CHILDREN
  Were never orphans had so dear a loss.   80
DUCHESS
  Was never mother had so dear a loss.
  Alas, I am the mother of these griefs.
  Their woes are parceled; mine is general.
  She for an Edward weeps, and so do I;
  I for a Clarence ⟨weep;⟩ so doth not she.   85
  These babes for Clarence weep, ⟨and so do I;
  I for an Edward weep;⟩ so do not they.
  Alas, you three, on me, threefold distressed,

89. **nurse:** i.e., wet nurse

96. **opposite with:** opposed to

97. **For:** because

98. **bethink you:** i.e., think

106. **none . . . them:** Proverbial: "Sorrow helps not."

107. **I . . . mercy:** i.e., I beg your pardon

113. **butt end:** last part

115. **cloudy:** darkened by grief (Buckingham's speeches in this scene are sometimes obscure; their obscurity has been read as signaling his political skill.)

Pour all your tears. I am your sorrow's nurse,
And I will pamper it with lamentation.   90
DORSET, ⌈*to Queen Elizabeth*⌉
Comfort, dear mother. God is much displeased
That you take with unthankfulness His doing.
In common worldly things, 'tis called ungrateful
With dull unwillingness to repay a debt
Which with a bounteous hand was kindly lent;   95
Much more to be thus opposite with heaven,
For it requires the royal debt it lent you.
RIVERS
Madam, bethink you, like a careful mother,
Of the young prince your son. Send straight for
    him.   100
Let him be crowned. In him your comfort lives.
Drown desperate sorrow in dead Edward's grave
And plant your joys in living Edward's throne.

Enter Richard, ⌈Duke of Gloucester,⌉ Buckingham, ⌈Lord
    Stanley, Earl of⌉ Derby, Hastings, and Ratcliffe.

RICHARD, ⌈*to Queen Elizabeth*⌉
Sister, have comfort. All of us have cause
To wail the dimming of our shining star,   105
But none can help our harms by wailing them.—
Madam my mother, I do cry you mercy;
I did not see your Grace. Humbly on my knee
I crave your blessing.   ⌈*He kneels.*⌉
DUCHESS
God bless thee, and put meekness in thy breast,   110
Love, charity, obedience, and true duty.
RICHARD, ⌈*standing*⌉
Amen. ⌈*Aside.*⌉ And make me die a good old man!
That is the butt end of a mother's blessing;
I marvel that her Grace did leave it out.
BUCKINGHAM
You cloudy princes and heart-sorrowing peers   115

116. **moan:** grief

120–22. **broken ... kept:** Buckingham seems to compare the hatred between court factions to fractures of bones that have festered (**high-swoll'n**) and have only recently been treated; although they have begun to heal, the bones are fragile. **splintered:** splinted

123. **Meseemeth:** it seems to me; **some little train:** a small entourage

124. **Ludlow:** in Shropshire, near Wales; **fet:** fetched

128. **Marry:** indeed

131. **By how much:** i.e., to the extent that; **the estate:** i.e., the state, England under Edward V; **green:** not fully developed or matured

133. **his commanding rein:** i.e., the rein by which it should be commanded

134. **as please himself:** i.e., as the horse pleases

137. **with:** i.e., among

140. **green:** young, i.e., recent

140–42. **it should ... urged:** The fear shared by Buckingham and Rivers, which is expressed for the first time with some directness in these lines, is that one faction may amass so large a company of armed men to fetch the Prince that this faction will not be able to resist taking control of England before the Prince can establish himself. **haply:** perhaps

That bear this heavy mutual load of moan,
Now cheer each other in each other's love.
Though we have spent our harvest of this king,
We are to reap the harvest of his son.
The broken rancor of your high-swoll'n hates,   120
But lately splintered, knit, and joined together,
Must gently be preserved, cherished, and kept.
Meseemeth good that with some little train
Forthwith from Ludlow the young prince be fet
Hither to London, to be crowned our king.   125
RIVERS
Why "with some little train," my lord of
  Buckingham?
BUCKINGHAM
Marry, my lord, lest by a multitude
The new-healed wound of malice should break out,
Which would be so much the more dangerous   130
By how much the estate is green and yet
  ungoverned.
Where every horse bears his commanding rein
And may direct his course as please himself,
As well the fear of harm as harm apparent,   135
In my opinion, ought to be prevented.
RICHARD
I hope the King made peace with all of us;
And the compact is firm and true in me.
RIVERS
And so in me, and so, I think, in all.
Yet since it is but green, it should be put   140
To no apparent likelihood of breach,
Which haply by much company might be urged.
Therefore I say with noble Buckingham
That it is meet so few should fetch the Prince.
HASTINGS   And so say I.   145
RICHARD
Then be it so, and go we to determine

147. **straight:** straightway, immediately; **post:** travel with great speed (as if on post-horses)

149. **Madam ... sister:** addressed to the duchess of York and Queen Elizabeth

150. **censures:** judgments, opinions

153. **by:** i.e., along; **sort occasion:** choose an opportunity

154. **index:** preface; **late:** recently

156. **My other self:** Proverbial: "A friend is one's second self." **council's consistory:** council's meeting place

157. **cousin:** Like the Yorks and the Lancastrians, Buckingham was a descendant of Edward III. (He was the great-great-grandson of Thomas of Woodstock, one of the sons of Edward III.)

158. **by thy direction:** according to your instructions

2.3 Three citizens discuss the possibly tumultuous succession of Prince Edward.

---

5. **Ill:** unfavorable, disastrous; **by 'r Lady:** i.e., by Our Lady (an oath on a title of the Virgin Mary); **Seldom ... better:** proverbial

6. **giddy:** mad, insane

7. **speed:** i.e., make you prosper

Who they shall be that straight shall post to
⟨Ludlow.⟩—
Madam, and you, my sister, will you go
To give your censures in this business? 150
All but Buckingham and Richard exit.

BUCKINGHAM
My lord, whoever journeys to the Prince,
For ⟨God's⟩ sake let not us two stay at home.
For by the way I'll sort occasion,
As index to the story we late talked of,
To part the Queen's proud kindred from the Prince. 155

RICHARD
My other self, my council's consistory,
My oracle, my prophet, my dear cousin,
I, as a child, will go by thy direction.
Toward ⟨Ludlow⟩ then, for we'll not stay behind.
They exit.

Scene 3
Enter one Citizen at one door, and another at the other.

FIRST CITIZEN
Good morrow, neighbor, whither away so fast?

SECOND CITIZEN
I promise you I scarcely know myself.
Hear you the news abroad?

FIRST CITIZEN   Yes, that the King is dead.

SECOND CITIZEN
Ill news, by 'r Lady. Seldom comes the better. 5
I fear, I fear, 'twill prove a giddy world.

Enter another Citizen.

THIRD CITIZEN
Neighbors, God speed.

FIRST CITIZEN   Give you good morrow, sir.

9. **Doth . . . hold:** i.e., is the news confirmed

10. **God help the while:** May God help us in this time.

11. **troublous:** unsettled, disturbed

13. **Woe . . . child:** See Ecclesiastes 10.16: "Woe to thee, O land, when thy king is a child."

14–17. **there is a hope . . . well:** i.e., the state will be governed well while he is a minor by his councillors and then, when he grows up, by himself (as king) **nonage:** minority

20. **wot:** knows

22. **politic:** wise, prudent

24. **by . . . mother:** i.e., from his father's family and his mother's

27. **emulation:** rivalry; **nearest:** i.e., to the Prince

28. **touch . . . near:** i.e., concern us all too closely

30. **haught:** i.e., haughty

33. **solace:** take comfort

THIRD CITIZEN
  Doth the news hold of good King Edward's death?
SECOND CITIZEN
  Ay, sir, it is too true, God help the while.   10
THIRD CITIZEN
  Then, masters, look to see a troublous world.
FIRST CITIZEN
  No, no, by God's good grace, his son shall reign.
THIRD CITIZEN
  Woe to that land that's governed by a child.
SECOND CITIZEN
  In him there is a hope of government,
  Which, in his nonage, council under him,   15
  And, in his full and ripened years, himself,
  No doubt shall then, and till then, govern well.
FIRST CITIZEN
  So stood the state when Henry the Sixth
  Was crowned in Paris but at nine months old.
THIRD CITIZEN
  Stood the state so? No, no, good friends, God wot,   20
  For then this land was famously enriched
  With politic grave counsel; then the King
  Had virtuous uncles to protect his Grace.
FIRST CITIZEN
  Why, so hath this, both by his father and mother.
THIRD CITIZEN
  Better it were they all came by his father,   25
  Or by his father there were none at all,
  For emulation who shall now be nearest
  Will touch us all too near if God prevent not.
  O, full of danger is the Duke of Gloucester,
  And the Queen's sons and brothers haught and   30
     proud,
  And were they to be ruled, and not to rule,
  This sickly land might solace as before.

39. **Untimely:** unseasonable
40. **sort:** ordain, order
43. **You . . . man:** i.e., there is hardly a man to talk to
44. **heavily:** sad
45. **still:** always
46–48. **By . . . storm:** These lines argue a parallel between men's instinctive fear of coming danger and the phenomenon of the ocean's pre-storm swelling. Siemon notes the same parallel in More's biography of Richard III.   **proof:** experience

2.4 As Queen Elizabeth awaits the coming of Prince Edward, news arrives that Richard has imprisoned her brother Rivers, her son Grey, and Sir Thomas Vaughan. She rushes to sanctuary with her son the Duke of York.

———————

1, 2. **Stony Stratford, Northampton:** See longer note, page 306.

FIRST CITIZEN
  Come, come, we fear the worst. All will be well.
THIRD CITIZEN
  When clouds are seen, wise men put on their   35
    cloaks;
  When great leaves fall, then winter is at hand;
  When the sun sets, who doth not look for night?
  Untimely storms makes men expect a dearth.
  All may be well; but if God sort it so,   40
  'Tis more than we deserve or I expect.
SECOND CITIZEN
  Truly, the hearts of men are full of fear.
  You cannot reason almost with a man
  That looks not heavily and full of dread.
THIRD CITIZEN
  Before the days of change, still is it so.   45
  By a divine instinct, men's minds mistrust
  Ensuing danger, as by proof we see
  The water swell before a boist'rous storm.
  But leave it all to God. Whither away?
SECOND CITIZEN
  Marry, we were sent for to the Justices.   50
THIRD CITIZEN
  And so was I. I'll bear you company.
                              They exit.

                              Scene 4
Enter Archbishop, ⌜the⌝ young ⌜Duke of⌝ York,
Queen ⌜Elizabeth,⌝ and the Duchess ⌜of York.⌝

ARCHBISHOP
  Last night, I ⟨hear,⟩ they lay at Stony Stratford,
  And at Northampton they do rest tonight.
  Tomorrow or next day they will be here.

9. **cousin:** kinsman

14. **grace:** virtue

14–15. **great . . . apace:** Proverbial: "An ill weed grows apace."

16. **since:** ever since; **methinks I would not grow:** i.e., I would prefer not to grow

17. **slow:** i.e., in growing

19. **hold:** remain true

20. **object . . . thee:** bring the same saying forward against you

23. **rule:** maxim, adage; **gracious:** filled with the grace promised to "small herbs" (See line 14.)

26. **by my troth:** a mild oath; **had been remembered:** i.e., had remembered

27. **my uncle's Grace:** his Grace, my uncle

28. **To . . . mine:** i.e., more directly related to his growth than his saying was to my growth

DUCHESS

    I long with all my heart to see the Prince.

    I hope he is much grown since last I saw him. 5

QUEEN ELIZABETH

    But I hear no; they say my son of York

    Has almost overta'en him in his growth.

YORK

    Ay, mother, but I would not have it so.

DUCHESS

    Why, my good cousin? It is good to grow.

YORK

    Grandam, one night as we did sit at supper, 10

    My uncle Rivers talked how I did grow

    More than my brother. "Ay," quoth my uncle

      Gloucester,

    "Small herbs have grace; great weeds do grow

      apace." 15

    And since, methinks I would not grow so fast

    Because sweet flowers are slow and weeds make

      haste.

DUCHESS

    Good faith, good faith, the saying did not hold

    In him that did object the same to thee! 20

    He was the wretched'st thing when he was young,

    So long a-growing and so leisurely,

    That if his rule were true, he should be gracious.

YORK

    And so no doubt he is, my gracious madam.

DUCHESS

    I hope he is, but yet let mothers doubt. 25

YORK

    Now, by my troth, if I had been remembered,

    I could have given my uncle's Grace a flout

    To touch his growth nearer than he touched mine.

DUCHESS

    How, my young York? I prithee let me hear it.

38. **parlous:** perilously cunning, mischievous; **Go to:** an expression of impatience; **shrewd:** naughty; abusive; artfully cunning

40. **Pitchers have ears:** Proverbial: "Little pitchers have wide ears."

46. **Pomfret:** Pontefract, a castle in the north of England

48. **committed them:** i.e., sent them to prison

51. **can:** know

53. **all:** entirely

YORK
  Marry, they say my uncle grew so fast   30
  That he could gnaw a crust at two hours old.
  'Twas full two years ere I could get a tooth.
  Grandam, this would have been a biting jest.
DUCHESS
  I prithee, pretty York, who told thee this?
YORK   Grandam, his nurse.   35
DUCHESS
  His nurse? Why, she was dead ere thou wast born.
YORK
  If 'twere not she, I cannot tell who told me.
QUEEN ELIZABETH
  A parlous boy! Go to, you are too shrewd.
DUCHESS
  Good madam, be not angry with the child.
QUEEN ELIZABETH   Pitchers have ears.   40

            Enter a Messenger.

ARCHBISHOP   Here comes a messenger.—What news?
MESSENGER
  Such news, my lord, as grieves me to report.
QUEEN ELIZABETH   How doth the Prince?
MESSENGER   Well, madam, and in health.
DUCHESS   What is thy news?   45
MESSENGER
  Lord Rivers and Lord Grey are sent to Pomfret,
  And, with them, Sir Thomas Vaughan, prisoners.
DUCHESS   Who hath committed them?
MESSENGER
  The mighty dukes, Gloucester and Buckingham.
ARCHBISHOP   For what offense?   50
MESSENGER
  The sum of all I can, I have disclosed.
  Why, or for what, the nobles were committed
  Is all unknown to me, my gracious lord.

55. **hind:** female deer
56. **Insulting:** triumphant; **jut:** strike
57. **aweless:** weak, inspiring no awe
59. **map:** image or picture; **end:** destruction
62. **to get:** attempting to get
65. **seated:** i.e., on the English throne
66. **Clean overblown:** i.e., completely blown over or away
67–68. **Make . . . self:** See longer note to 1.3.139, page 305.   **to:** i.e., against
68. **preposterous:** monstrous
69. **spleen:** violent ill-nature
71. **to sanctuary:** i.e., go or flee to sanctuary, a place (often a church or other sacred place) where a fugitive could find protection from capture or punishment
78. **seal:** the Great Seal of England
78–79. **so betide . . . yours:** i.e., may my fate be determined by how well I care for you and yours **tender:** care for

QUEEN ELIZABETH
Ay me! I see the ruin of my house.
The tiger now hath seized the gentle hind.   55
Insulting tyranny begins to jut
Upon the innocent and aweless throne.
Welcome, destruction, blood, and massacre.
I see, as in a map, the end of all.
DUCHESS
Accursèd and unquiet wrangling days,   60
How many of you have mine eyes beheld?
My husband lost his life to get the crown,
And often up and down my sons were tossed
For me to joy, and weep, their gain and loss.
And being seated, and domestic broils   65
Clean overblown, themselves the conquerors
Make war upon themselves, brother to brother,
Blood to blood, self against self. O, preposterous
And frantic outrage, end thy damnèd spleen,
Or let me die, to look on Earth no more.   70
QUEEN ELIZABETH, ⌜*to York*⌝
Come, come, my boy. We will to sanctuary.—
Madam, farewell.
DUCHESS   Stay, I will go with you.
QUEEN ELIZABETH
You have no cause.
ARCHBISHOP, ⌜*to Queen Elizabeth*⌝
              My gracious lady, go,   75
And thither bear your treasure and your goods.
For my part, I'll resign unto your Grace
The seal I keep; and so betide to me
As well I tender you and all of yours.
Go. I'll conduct you to the sanctuary.   80
                       They exit.

The Tragedy of

RICHARD III

ACT 3

3.1 Richard and Buckingham arrive in London with Prince Edward and order that Edward's brother, the Duke of York, be taken from sanctuary. Richard and Buckingham put both boys in the Tower and send Catesby to sound out Hastings about supporting Richard's intention to take the throne for himself.

---

1. **chamber:** capital (According to More's biography as it appears in Holinshed's *Chronicles*, the primary source of this play, "London [is] the King's especial chamber.")

4. **crosses:** vexations

5. **heavy:** oppressive, distressful

9–11. **Nor . . . heart:** Compare 1 Samuel 16.7: "[M]an beholdeth the outward appearance, but the Lord looketh on the heart." **God He knows:** i.e., God knows **jumpeth:** accords

12. **want:** (1) lack; (2) desire

"Young Prince Edward." (3.1.0 SD)
From John Speed, *The theatre of the empire of Great Britaine . . .* (1627 [i.e., 1631]).

[ACT 3]

[Scene 1]
The trumpets sound. Enter young Prince ⌐*Edward,*¬
⌐*Richard Duke of*¬ *Gloucester, Buckingham,*
⌐*the*¬ *Cardinal,* ⌐*Catesby,*¬ *and others.*

BUCKINGHAM
Welcome, sweet prince, to London, to your chamber.
RICHARD, ⌐*to Prince*¬
Welcome, dear cousin, my thoughts' sovereign.
The weary way hath made you melancholy.
PRINCE
No, uncle, but our crosses on the way
Have made it tedious, wearisome, and heavy.   5
I want more uncles here to welcome me.
RICHARD
Sweet prince, the untainted virtue of your years
Hath not yet dived into the world's deceit;
Nor more can you distinguish of a man
Than of his outward show, which, God He knows,   10
Seldom or never jumpeth with the heart.
Those uncles which you want were dangerous.
Your Grace attended to their sugared words
But looked not on the poison of their hearts.
God keep you from them, and from such false   15
    friends.

129

23. **slug:** sluggard, lazy fellow
26. **What:** an interjection introducing a question or exclamation
29. **tender:** young
31. **perforce:** i.e., against his will
32. **indirect:** devious; **peevish:** spiteful, perverse; **course:** proceeding, way of behaving
37. **jealous:** suspicious, fearful; **perforce:** forcibly

The Tower of London. (1.1.47; 3.1.66)
From John Seller, *A book of the prospects of . . . London . . .* (c. 1700?).

PRINCE
God keep me from false friends, but they were none.
RICHARD
My lord, the Mayor of London comes to greet you.

Enter Lord Mayor ⌐with others.⌐

MAYOR
God bless your Grace with health and happy days.
PRINCE
I thank you, good my lord, and thank you all.—   20
I thought my mother and my brother York
Would long ere this have met us on the way.
Fie, what a slug is Hastings that he comes not
To tell us whether they will come or no!

Enter Lord Hastings.

BUCKINGHAM
And in good time here comes the sweating lord.   25
PRINCE
Welcome, my lord. What, will our mother come?
HASTINGS
On what occasion God He knows, not I,
The Queen your mother and your brother York
Have taken sanctuary. The tender prince
Would fain have come with me to meet your Grace,   30
But by his mother was perforce withheld.
BUCKINGHAM
Fie, what an indirect and peevish course
Is this of hers!—Lord Cardinal, will your Grace
Persuade the Queen to send the Duke of York
Unto his princely brother presently?—   35
If she deny, Lord Hastings, go with him,
And from her jealous arms pluck him perforce.
CARDINAL
My lord of Buckingham, if my weak oratory

40. **Anon:** soon

44. **deep:** serious, heinous

45. **senseless:** unreasonably

46. **ceremonious:** scrupulous about observing formalities

47. **grossness:** i.e., lack of refinement

51. **wit:** intelligence

55. **charter:** immunity

62. **our:** i.e., my (the royal "we")

66. **the Tower:** Primarily a fortress and prison, the Tower of London was also sometimes used as a royal residence. (See page 130.)

Can from his mother win the Duke of York,
Anon expect him here; but if she be obdurate   40
To mild entreaties, God in heaven forbid
We should infringe the holy privilege
Of blessèd sanctuary! Not for all this land
Would I be guilty of so deep a sin.

BUCKINGHAM
You are too senseless obstinate, my lord,   45
Too ceremonious and traditional.
Weigh it but with the grossness of this age,
You break not sanctuary in seizing him.
The benefit thereof is always granted
To those whose dealings have deserved the place   50
And those who have the wit to claim the place.
This prince hath neither claimed it nor deserved it
And therefore, in mine opinion, cannot have it.
Then taking him from thence that is not there,
You break no privilege nor charter there.   55
Oft have I heard of sanctuary men,
But sanctuary children, never till now.

CARDINAL
My lord, you shall o'errule my mind for once.—
Come on, Lord Hastings, will you go with me?

HASTINGS   I go, my lord.   60

PRINCE
Good lords, make all the speedy haste you may.
                    [*The Cardinal and Hastings exit.*]
Say, uncle Gloucester, if our brother come,
Where shall we sojourn till our coronation?

RICHARD
Where it seems best unto your royal self.
If I may counsel you, some day or two   65
Your Highness shall repose you at the Tower;
Then where you please and shall be thought most fit
For your best health and recreation.

69. **of any place:** i.e., of all places

70. **Julius Caesar:** Roman conqueror of Britain (See page 136.)

72. **re-edified:** rebuilt

73, 75. **record:** pronounced **recòrd**

76. **registered:** recorded

77. **Methinks:** i.e., it seems to me that

78. **retailed:** recounted, told

79. **the . . . day:** doomsday

80. **So . . . long:** Proverbial: "Too soon wise to live long."

82. **characters:** i.e., written records (literally, graphic symbols)

83. **formal Vice, Iniquity:** i.e., conventional stage figure of the Vice named Iniquity in a morality play (The Vice often equivocated. **Iniquity** is the name of the Vice in two plays that survive from this period, *Darius* and *Nice Wanton.*)

84. **moralize:** interpret; **two . . . word:** i.e., perhaps, of the word *live*, which Richard uses first literally (line 80) and then figuratively in line 82

86. **what:** i.e., that with which

92. **An if:** i.e., if

93. **ancient . . . France:** Between 1337 and 1453, during the Hundred Years War, the English (led most notably by King Edward III and King Henry V) had invaded France in efforts to enforce hereditary claims to the French throne. By 1453, thirty years before the setting of this scene, King Henry VI had lost what his father, Henry V, had won in France. **in:** i.e., to

95. **lightly:** commonly; **a forward:** an early (with wordplay on **forward** as presumptuous, bold)

PRINCE
  I do not like the Tower, of any place.—
  Did Julius Caesar build that place, my lord?   70
BUCKINGHAM
  He did, my gracious lord, begin that place,
  Which, since, succeeding ages have re-edified.
PRINCE
  Is it upon record, or else reported
  Successively from age to age, he built it?
BUCKINGHAM   Upon record, my gracious lord.   75
PRINCE
  But say, my lord, it were not registered,
  Methinks the truth should live from age to age,
  As 'twere retailed to all posterity,
  Even to the general all-ending day.
RICHARD, ⌜*aside*⌝
  So wise so young, they say, do never live long.   80
PRINCE   What say you, uncle?
RICHARD
  I say, without characters fame lives long.
  ⌜*Aside.*⌝ Thus, like the formal Vice, Iniquity,
  I moralize two meanings in one word.
PRINCE
  That Julius Caesar was a famous man.   85
  With what his valor did enrich his wit,
  His wit set down to make his [valor] live.
  Death makes no conquest of this conqueror,
  For now he lives in fame, though not in life.
  I'll tell you what, my cousin Buckingham—   90
BUCKINGHAM   What, my gracious lord?
PRINCE
  An if I live until I be a man,
  I'll win our ancient right in France again
  Or die a soldier, as I lived a king.
RICHARD, ⌜*aside*⌝
  Short summers lightly have a forward spring.   95

100. **late:** recently; **he:** a reference to their father, Edward IV

102. **cousin:** kinsman

103. **gentle:** noble

104. **idle:** worthless

109. **beholding:** beholden, obligated

115. **that:** i.e., who

116. **toy:** trifle; **is no grief:** i.e., it is no hardship

Julius Caesar. (3.1.70)
From Thomas Treterus, *Romanorum imperatorum effigies . . .* (1590).

Enter young ⌐Duke of ⌐ York, Hastings, ⌐and the⌐
Cardinal.

BUCKINGHAM
  Now in good time here comes the Duke of York.
PRINCE
  Richard of York, how fares our loving brother?
YORK
  Well, my dread lord—so must I call you now.
PRINCE
  Ay, brother, to our grief, as it is yours.
  Too late he died that might have kept that title,   100
  Which by his death hath lost much majesty.
RICHARD
  How fares our cousin, noble lord of York?
YORK
  I thank you, gentle uncle. O my lord,
  You said that idle weeds are fast in growth.
  The Prince my brother hath outgrown me far.   105
RICHARD
  He hath, my lord.
YORK   And therefore is he idle?
RICHARD
  O my fair cousin, I must not say so.
YORK
  Then he is more beholding to you than I.
RICHARD
  He may command me as my sovereign,   110
  But you have power in me as in a kinsman.
YORK
  I pray you, uncle, give me this dagger.
RICHARD
  My dagger, little cousin? With all my heart.
PRINCE   A beggar, brother?
YORK
  Of my kind uncle, that I know will give,   115
  And being but a toy, which is no grief to give.

120. **light:** inconsequential (wordplay on "light" in line 119)

121. **say . . . nay:** i.e., refuse one who begs

123. **I . . . heavier:** i.e., I would not think much of it even if it were heavier

128. **cross:** contrary, perverse

132. **ape:** At fairs, an ape was set on the shoulders of a bear; some professional jesters, or Fools, also carried apes on their shoulders. (The word **scorn** [lines 136 and 156] suggests that the duke of York here mocks Richard as a hunchback, the hump on whose back would provide an excellent place for an ape to ride.)

135. **sharp-provided:** clever and ready

139. **pass along:** i.e., continue on your way

RICHARD
  A greater gift than that I'll give my cousin.
YORK
  A greater gift? O, that's the sword to it.
RICHARD
  Ay, gentle cousin, were it light enough.
YORK
  O, then I see you will part but with light gifts.   120
  In weightier things you'll say a beggar nay.
RICHARD
  It is too heavy for your Grace to wear.
YORK
  I weigh it lightly, were it heavier.
RICHARD
  What, would you have my weapon, little lord?
YORK
  I would, that I might thank you as you call me.   125
RICHARD   How?
YORK   Little.
PRINCE
  My lord of York will still be cross in talk.
  Uncle, your Grace knows how to bear with him.
YORK
  You mean, to bear me, not to bear with me.—   130
  Uncle, my brother mocks both you and me.
  Because that I am little, like an ape,
  He thinks that you should bear me on your
      shoulders.
BUCKINGHAM, ⌈*aside*⌉
  With what a sharp-provided wit he reasons!   135
  To mitigate the scorn he gives his uncle,
  He prettily and aptly taunts himself.
  So cunning and so young is wonderful.
RICHARD, ⌈*to Prince*⌉
  My lord, will 't please you pass along?

141. **Will to:** will go to, will visit; **of her:** i.e., her

144. **needs will:** is determined to

151. **they:** The words "With a heavy heart, / Thinking on them" (lines 152–53) suggest that **they** refers to the uncle and stepbrother arrested by Richard. It may also refer to Woodeville and Scales, also his maternal uncles. (See note to 1.3.38.)

153 SD. **sennet:** trumpet sound to signal the arrival or departure of royalty

154. **prating:** chattering

155. **incensèd:** incited, instigated

157. **parlous:** perilously cunning

158. **quick:** lively; **forward:** presumptuous, pert; **capable:** intelligent

160. **let them rest:** i.e., let them be

161. **deeply:** thoroughly

163. **urged . . . way:** i.e., advanced in the course of our journey

Myself and my good cousin Buckingham   140
Will to your mother, to entreat of her
To meet you at the Tower and welcome you.
YORK, ⌈*to Prince*⌉
What, will you go unto the Tower, my lord?
PRINCE
My Lord Protector needs will have it so.
YORK
I shall not sleep in quiet at the Tower.   145
RICHARD   Why, what should you fear?
YORK
Marry, my uncle Clarence' angry ghost.
My grandam told me he was murdered there.
PRINCE   I fear no uncles dead.
RICHARD   Nor none that live, I hope.   150
PRINCE
An if they live, I hope I need not fear.
⌈*To York.*⌉ But come, my lord. With a heavy heart,
Thinking on them, go I unto the Tower.
        [*A sennet. Prince* ⌈*Edward, the Duke of*⌉ *York,*
            ⌈*and*⌉ *Hastings exit. Richard, Buckingham,*
                            and Catesby remain.]
BUCKINGHAM, ⌈*to Richard*⌉
Think you, my lord, this little prating York
Was not incensèd by his subtle mother   155
To taunt and scorn you thus opprobriously?
RICHARD
No doubt, no doubt. O, 'tis a parlous boy,
Bold, quick, ingenious, forward, capable.
He is all the mother's, from the top to toe.
BUCKINGHAM
Well, let them rest.—Come hither, Catesby.   160
Thou art sworn as deeply to effect what we intend
As closely to conceal what we impart.
Thou knowest our reasons, urged upon the way.

166–67. **installment . . . isle:** i.e., installation of Richard as king of England   **seat royal:** throne

168. **his father's:** i.e., the father of the prince, namely, the former king, Edward IV

173. **as . . . off:** i.e., most tactfully; **sound:** sound out, question

174. **doth . . . affected:** i.e., is disposed

176. **sit:** i.e., meet in council

182. **divided councils:** i.e., two separate councils

183. **highly:** extensively

184. **Lord William:** i.e., Hastings

185. **ancient . . . adversaries:** i.e., old enemies

186. **let blood:** i.e., executed (literally, are bled by a barber-surgeon as a medical treatment)

189. **soundly:** properly, thoroughly

What thinkest thou? Is it not an easy matter
To make William Lord Hastings of our mind   165
For the installment of this noble duke
In the seat royal of this famous isle?
CATESBY
He, for his father's sake, so loves the Prince
That he will not be won to aught against him.
BUCKINGHAM
What think'st thou then of Stanley? Will not he?   170
CATESBY
He will do all in all as Hastings doth.
BUCKINGHAM
Well then, no more but this: go, gentle Catesby,
And, as it were far off, sound thou Lord Hastings
How he doth stand affected to our purpose
And summon him tomorrow to the Tower   175
To sit about the coronation.
If thou dost find him tractable to us,
Encourage him and tell him all our reasons.
If he be leaden, icy, cold, unwilling,
Be thou so too, and so break off the talk,   180
And give us notice of his inclination;
For we tomorrow hold divided councils,
Wherein thyself shalt highly be employed.
RICHARD
Commend me to Lord William. Tell him, Catesby,
His ancient knot of dangerous adversaries   185
Tomorrow are let blood at Pomfret Castle,
And bid my lord, for joy of this good news,
Give Mistress Shore one gentle kiss the more.
BUCKINGHAM
Good Catesby, go effect this business soundly.
CATESBY
My good lords both, with all the heed I can.   190
RICHARD
Shall we hear from you, Catesby, ere we sleep?

195. **yield . . . complots:** i.e., consent to our con-
spiracies

197. **look when:** i.e., as soon as

198. **movables:** portable possessions (attached to
the earldom of Hereford and in the possession of
the monarch)

202. **betimes:** early

203. **digest:** arrange; **some form:** good order

3.2 Responding to Catesby, Hastings flatly refuses
to support Richard's bid for the throne, and takes
great satisfaction in the news that the Queen's son
and brother are to be beheaded that very day.

---

2 SP. **within:** offstage

4. **What is 't o'clock?:** i.e., what time is it?

7. **that:** what

CATESBY   You shall, my lord.
RICHARD
   At Crosby House, there shall you find us both.

                           Catesby exits.
BUCKINGHAM
   Now, my lord, what shall we do if we perceive
   Lord Hastings will not yield to our complots?   195
RICHARD
   Chop off his head. Something we will determine.
   And look when I am king, claim thou of me
   The earldom of Hereford, and all the movables
   Whereof the King my brother was possessed.
BUCKINGHAM
   I'll claim that promise at your Grace's hand.   200
RICHARD
   And look to have it yielded with all kindness.
   Come, let us sup betimes, that afterwards
   We may digest our complots in some form.

                               They exit.

Scene 2
Enter a Messenger to the door of Hastings.

MESSENGER, ⌜*knocking*⌝   My lord, my lord.
HASTINGS, ⌜*within*⌝   Who knocks?
MESSENGER   One from the Lord Stanley.
HASTINGS, ⌜*within*⌝ What is 't o'clock?
MESSENGER   Upon the stroke of four.   5

              Enter Lord Hastings.

HASTINGS
   Cannot my Lord Stanley sleep these tedious nights?
MESSENGER
   So it appears by that I have to say.
   First, he commends him to your noble self.

10. **certifies:** informs
11. **boar:** Richard's heraldic emblem (See page 56.); **razèd . . . helm:** (1) cut off his helmet (and, by implication, head); (2) obliterated the heraldic crest on his helmet (symbolic of destroying his family line)
13. **that:** i.e., something
16. **pleasure:** choice, preference
17. **presently:** at once
18. **post:** ride with haste
24. **toucheth:** concerns, affects
25. **intelligence:** information
26. **instance:** cause
27. **for:** i.e., as for; **simple:** foolish
28. **mock'ry:** unreal appearances, dream images (with wordplay on *mockery* as derision)
29. **fly:** flee
31. **mean:** intend
34. **kindly:** i.e., with courtesy (A second, ironic meaning of this word, "according to his nature," would be heard by the audience.)
36. **morrows:** mornings

HASTINGS   What then?

MESSENGER
Then certifies your Lordship that this night   10
He dreamt the boar had razèd off his helm.
Besides, he says there are two councils kept,
And that may be determined at the one
Which may make you and him to rue at th' other.
Therefore he sends to know your Lordship's   15
   pleasure,
If you will presently take horse with him
And with all speed post with him toward the north
To shun the danger that his soul divines.

HASTINGS
Go, fellow, go. Return unto thy lord.   20
Bid him not fear the separated council.
His Honor and myself are at the one,
And at the other is my good friend Catesby,
Where nothing can proceed that toucheth us
Whereof I shall not have intelligence.   25
Tell him his fears are shallow, without instance.
And for his dreams, I wonder he's so simple
To trust the mock'ry of unquiet slumbers.
To fly the boar before the boar pursues
Were to incense the boar to follow us   30
And make pursuit where he did mean no chase.
Go, bid thy master rise and come to me,
And we will both together to the Tower,
Where he shall see the boar will use us kindly.

MESSENGER
I'll go, my lord, and tell him what you say.   *He exits.*   35

Enter Catesby.

CATESBY
Many good morrows to my noble lord.

45. **crown:** i.e., crown of the head
46. **foul:** i.e., foully
47. **canst thou guess:** i.e., do you think
48. **forward:** zealous
49. **Upon his party:** i.e., on his side
54. **still:** always
56. **To . . . descent:** i.e., to bar from the crown the heirs truly descended from Edward IV
60–61. **That . . . tragedy:** i.e., that I have lived to see the tragedy (downfall and death) of those who incited King Edward IV to hate me (See 1.1.67–73.)

HASTINGS
  Good morrow, Catesby. You are early stirring.
  What news, what news in this our tott'ring state?
CATESBY
  It is a reeling world indeed, my lord,
  And I believe will never stand upright   40
  Till Richard wear the garland of the realm.
HASTINGS
  How "wear the garland"? Dost thou mean the
    crown?
CATESBY Ay, my good lord.
HASTINGS
  I'll have this crown of mine cut from my shoulders   45
  Before I'll see the crown so foul misplaced.
  But canst thou guess that he doth aim at it?
CATESBY
  Ay, on my life, and hopes to find you forward
  Upon his party for the gain thereof;
  And thereupon he sends you this good news,   50
  That this same very day your enemies,
  The kindred of the Queen, must die at Pomfret.
HASTINGS
  Indeed, I am no mourner for that news,
  Because they have been still my adversaries.
  But that I'll give my voice on Richard's side   55
  To bar my master's heirs in true descent,
  God knows I will not do it, to the death.
CATESBY
  God keep your Lordship in that gracious mind.
HASTINGS
  But I shall laugh at this a twelve-month hence,
  That they which brought me in my master's hate,   60
  I live to look upon their tragedy.
  Well, Catesby, ere a fortnight make me older
  I'll send some packing that yet think not on 't.

71. **make . . . of:** i.e., have high regard for

72. **account:** consider; reckon on; **head . . . Bridge:** The heads of those executed for treason were displayed on poles on London Bridge. (See page 156.)

77. **Holy Rood:** the cross of Christ

78. **several:** separate

82. **but that I know:** i.e., if I did not know; **state:** condition

83. **triumphant:** exultant

87. **o'ercast:** became overcast

88. **stab of rancor:** probably, Richard's recent hateful thrust against the Queen's faction

89. **a needless coward:** i.e., needlessly afraid

90. **spent:** well under way

CATESBY
'Tis a vile thing to die, my gracious lord,
When men are unprepared and look not for it.   65

HASTINGS
O monstrous, monstrous! And so falls it out
With Rivers, Vaughan, Grey; and so 'twill do
With some men else that think themselves as safe
As thou and I, who, as thou know'st, are dear
To princely Richard and to Buckingham.   70

CATESBY
The Princes both make high account of you—
⌜*Aside.*⌝ For they account his head upon the Bridge.

HASTINGS
I know they do, and I have well deserved it.

Enter Lord Stanley.

Come on, come on. Where is your boar-spear, man?
Fear you the boar and go so unprovided?   75

STANLEY
My lord, good morrow.—Good morrow, Catesby.—
You may jest on, but, by the Holy Rood,
I do not like these several councils, I.

HASTINGS
My lord, I hold my life as dear as ⟨you do⟩ yours,
And never in my days, I do protest,   80
Was it so precious to me as 'tis now.
Think you but that I know our state secure,
I would be so triumphant as I am?

STANLEY
The lords at Pomfret, when they rode from London,
Were jocund and supposed their states were sure,   85
And they indeed had no cause to mistrust;
But yet you see how soon the day o'ercast.
This sudden stab of rancor I misdoubt.
Pray God, I say, I prove a needless coward!
What, shall we toward the Tower? The day is spent.   90

91. **Have with you:** i.e., let's go; **Wot:** know

93. **truth:** loyalty

94. **wear their hats:** i.e., keep their offices

95 SD. **Pursuivant:** a royal or state messenger or warrant officer; or, a junior officer serving under a herald (In the quarto, this character is also called Hastings, and many editors include this proper name.)

97. **sirrah:** a form of address to a man of lesser status

98. **that . . . ask:** i.e., that it pleases you to ask (Proverbial: "The better for your asking.")

102. **By the suggestion:** because of the false charges; **allies:** relatives

105. **state:** condition

106. **hold:** preserve

107. **Gramercy:** many thanks

110. **Sir:** a title of courtesy for a priest

HASTINGS
Come, come. Have with you. Wot you what, my lord?
Today the lords you ⟨talked⟩ of are beheaded.
STANLEY
They, for their truth, might better wear their heads
Than some that have accused them wear their hats.
But come, my lord, let's away.   95

Enter a Pursuivant.

HASTINGS
Go on before. I'll talk with this good fellow.
                    Lord Stanley and Catesby exit.
How now, sirrah? How goes the world with thee?
PURSUIVANT
The better that your Lordship please to ask.
HASTINGS
I tell thee, man, 'tis better with me now
Than when thou met'st me last where now we meet.   100
Then was I going prisoner to the Tower
By the suggestion of the Queen's allies.
But now, I tell thee—keep it to thyself—
This day those enemies are put to death,
And I in better state than e'er I was.   105
PURSUIVANT
God hold it, to your Honor's good content!
HASTINGS
Gramercy, fellow. There, drink that for me.
                    Throws him his purse.
PURSUIVANT   I thank your Honor.   *Pursuivant exits.*

Enter a Priest.

PRIEST
Well met, my lord. I am glad to see your Honor.
HASTINGS
I thank thee, good Sir John, with all my heart.   110

111. **exercise:** sermon
112. **content:** compensate
113. **wait upon:** attend upon
116. **shriving work:** making a confession and receiving absolution
121. **thence:** from there
122. **like:** i.e., likely; **stay:** i.e., stay for

3.3 The Queen's brother Rivers, her son Grey, and Sir Thomas Vaughan are led to execution. They recall Margaret's curse, and pray that it will fall as well on Hastings, Buckingham, and Richard, whom she also cursed.

———————

0 SD. **Halberds:** halberdiers; **carrying:** i.e., leading

I am in your debt for your last exercise.
Come the next sabbath, and I will content you.
PRIEST   I'll wait upon your Lordship.   ⌐*Priest exits.*¬

                    Enter Buckingham.

BUCKINGHAM
   What, talking with a priest, Lord Chamberlain?
   Your friends at Pomfret, they do need the priest;   115
   Your Honor hath no shriving work in hand.
HASTINGS
   Good faith, and when I met this holy man,
   The men you talk of came into my mind.
   What, go you toward the Tower?
BUCKINGHAM
   I do, my lord, but long I cannot stay there.   120
   I shall return before your Lordship thence.
HASTINGS
   Nay, like enough, for I stay dinner there.
BUCKINGHAM, ⌐*aside*¬
   And supper too, although thou know'st it not.—
   Come, will you go?
HASTINGS   I'll wait upon your Lordship.   125
                                        They exit.

                    Scene 3
Enter Sir Richard Ratcliffe, with Halberds, carrying the
nobles ⟨Rivers, Grey, and Vaughan⟩ to death at Pomfret.

RIVERS
   Sir Richard Ratcliffe, let me tell thee this:
   Today shalt thou behold a subject die
   For truth, for duty, and for loyalty.
GREY, ⌐*to Ratcliffe*¬
   God bless the Prince from all the pack of you!
   A knot you are of damnèd bloodsuckers.   5

7. **Dispatch:** make haste; **limit . . . out:** duration
. . . is over

10. **closure:** bounds

12. **slander:** discredit, disgrace; **dismal:** sinister,
boding disaster; **seat:** site

15. **exclaimed on:** accused, blamed

21. **my sister:** i.e., Queen Elizabeth

24. **expiate:** fully come

Heads "upon the Bridge." (3.2.72)
From Claes Jansz Visscher, *Londinum florentissima
Britanniae urbs* . . . [c. 1625].

VAUGHAN, ⌜*to Ratcliffe*⌝
  You live that shall cry woe for this hereafter.
RATCLIFFE
  Dispatch. The limit of your lives is out.
RIVERS
  O Pomfret, Pomfret! O thou bloody prison,
  Fatal and ominous to noble peers!
  Within the guilty closure of thy walls,   10
  Richard the Second here was hacked to death,
  And, for more slander to thy dismal seat,
  We give to thee our guiltless blood to drink.
GREY
  Now Margaret's curse is fall'n upon our heads,
  When she exclaimed on Hastings, you, and I,   15
  For standing by when Richard stabbed her son.
RIVERS
  Then cursed she Richard. Then cursed she
    Buckingham.
  Then cursed she Hastings. O, remember, God,
  To hear her prayer for them as now for us!   20
  And for my sister and her princely sons,
  Be satisfied, dear God, with our true blood,
  Which, as thou know'st, unjustly must be spilt.
RATCLIFFE
  Make haste. The hour of death is expiate.
RIVERS
  Come, Grey. Come, Vaughan. Let us here embrace. 25
                     ⌜*They embrace.*⌝
  Farewell until we meet again in heaven.
                           They exit.

3.4   A council of lords meets to plan the coronation of Edward V. Richard, learning from Buckingham of Hastings' refusal to support them, accuses Hastings' mistress of witchcraft and orders Hastings' execution. Hastings, led off to his death, remembers Stanley's warning dream and Margaret's curse.

---

  2. **determine of:** make a decision about
  4. **Is:** i.e., are
  5. **It . . . nomination:** i.e., all things are ready; all that is lacking is the naming of the day (for the coronation of Prince Edward as Edward V)
  6. **happy:** favorable
  8. **inward:** intimate
  11. **for:** i.e., as for
  16. **purpose in:** intention concerning
  17. **sounded:** questioned; **delivered:** pronounced
  18. **pleasure:** choice, preference
  20. **in:** i.e., on; **voice:** vote
  21. **in gentle part:** in good part, without offense

Scene 4

Enter Buckingham, ⌐Lord Stanley, Earl of ¬ Derby,
Hastings, Bishop of Ely, Norfolk, Ratcliffe, Lovell, with
others, at a table.

HASTINGS
Now, noble peers, the cause why we are met
Is to determine of the coronation.
In God's name, speak. When is the royal day?
BUCKINGHAM
Is all things ready for the royal time?
STANLEY
It is, and wants but nomination.   5
ELY
Tomorrow, then, I judge a happy day.
BUCKINGHAM
Who knows the Lord Protector's mind herein?
Who is most inward with the noble duke?
ELY
Your Grace, we think, should soonest know his
    mind.   10
BUCKINGHAM
We know each other's faces; for our hearts,
He knows no more of mine than I of yours,
Or I of his, my lord, than you of mine.—
Lord Hastings, you and he are near in love.
HASTINGS
I thank his Grace, I know he loves me well.   15
But for his purpose in the coronation,
I have not sounded him, nor he delivered
His gracious pleasure any way therein.
But you, my honorable lords, may name the time,
And in the Duke's behalf I'll give my voice,   20
Which I presume he'll take in gentle part.

    Enter ⌐Richard, Duke of ¬ Gloucester.

22. **happy:** fortunate

23. **cousins:** The term *cousin* was used by a sovereign in addressing his noblemen. Richard may be speaking as if he were already the sovereign. Or he may be addressing both his kinsman Buckingham and possibly other kinsmen.

25. **neglect:** cause to be neglected

32. **Holborn:** site of the Bishop of Ely's palace

33. **strawberries:** This fruit was associated in contemporary emblems with adders and other snakes, which in turn are identified with hypocrisy and treachery. (Paradin's *Heroicall Devises* [1591] reads: "In gathering of flowers, and strawberries that grow low upon the ground, we must be verie carefull for the adder and snake that lieth lurking in the grass." See page 162.)

35. **Marry and:** i.e., indeed I

40. **worshipfully . . . it:** i.e., respectfully he puts it

43. **triumph:** public festivity

44. **too sudden:** i.e., too early a date

45. **provided:** prepared

46. **else:** otherwise; **prolonged:** postponed

ELY
    In happy time here comes the Duke himself.
RICHARD
    My noble lords and cousins all, good morrow.
    I have been long a sleeper; but I trust
    My absence doth neglect no great design   25
    Which by my presence might have been concluded.
BUCKINGHAM
    Had you not come upon your cue, my lord,
    William Lord Hastings had pronounced your part—
    I mean your voice for crowning of the King.
RICHARD
    Than my Lord Hastings no man might be bolder.   30
    His Lordship knows me well and loves me well.—
    My lord of Ely, when I was last in Holborn
    I saw good strawberries in your garden there;
    I do beseech you, send for some of them.
ELY
    Marry and will, my lord, with all my heart.   35
                                    Exit Bishop ⌐*of Ely.*⌐
RICHARD
    Cousin of Buckingham, a word with you.
                                    ⌐*They move aside.*⌐
    Catesby hath sounded Hastings in our business
    And finds the testy gentleman so hot
    That he will lose his head ere give consent
    His master's child, as worshipfully he terms it,   40
    Shall lose the royalty of England's throne.
BUCKINGHAM
    Withdraw yourself awhile. I'll go with you.
                            ⌐*Richard and Buckingham*⌐ *exit.*
STANLEY
    We have not yet set down this day of triumph.
    Tomorrow, in my judgment, is too sudden,
    For I myself am not so well provided   45
    As else I would be, were the day prolonged.

49. **cheerfully and smooth:** i.e., cheerful and affable

51. **conceit:** conception, idea; **likes:** pleases

55. **straight:** straightway, immediately

57. **livelihood:** liveliness

59. **looks:** Here the quarto gives a metrically deficient line to Stanley, "I pray God he be not, I say," which is included by many modern editors.

61. **conspire:** i.e., conspire to bring about

63. **charms:** spells

65. **forward:** ready, prompt; **presence:** company

66. **doom:** condemn

Strawberries with a lurking adder. (3.4.33)
Claude Paradin, *The heroicall deuises of . . .* (1591).

Enter the Bishop of Ely.

ELY
  Where is my lord the Duke of Gloucester?
  I have sent for these strawberries.
HASTINGS
  His Grace looks cheerfully and smooth this
      morning.   50
  There's some conceit or other likes him well
  When that he bids good morrow with such spirit.
  I think there's never a man in Christendom
  Can lesser hide his love or hate than he,
  For by his face straight shall you know his heart.   55
STANLEY
  What of his heart perceive you in his face
  By any livelihood he showed today?
HASTINGS
  Marry, that with no man here he is offended,
  For were he, he had shown it in his looks.

Enter Richard and Buckingham.

RICHARD
  I pray you all, tell me what they deserve   60
  That do conspire my death with devilish plots
  Of damnèd witchcraft, and that have prevailed
  Upon my body with their hellish charms?
HASTINGS
  The tender love I bear your Grace, my lord,
  Makes me most forward in this princely presence   65
  To doom th' offenders, whosoe'er they be.
  I say, my lord, they have deservèd death.
RICHARD
  Then be your eyes the witness of their evil.
                         ⌈*He shows his arm.*⌉
  Look how I am bewitched! Behold mine arm
  Is like a blasted sapling withered up;   70

72. **Consorted with:** in league with

82. **fond:** foolish

84. **fly:** flee

85. **foot-cloth horse:** a horse adorned with a large ornamental cloth as a sign of the rider's dignity

86. **started:** i.e., moved as if startled or frightened

90. **too triumphing:** i.e., exulting too much

95. **dispatch:** make haste; **would:** wishes to

97. **short shrift:** brief confession

98–99. **O . . . God:** Compare Jeremiah 17.5: "Cursed be the man that trusteth in man . . . and whose heart departeth from the Lord." **grace of mortal men:** human favor

A council meeting. (3.4)
From Raphael Holinshed, *Chronicles of England . . .* (1577).

And this is Edward's wife, that monstrous witch,
Consorted with that harlot, strumpet Shore,
That by their witchcraft thus have markèd me.
HASTINGS
If they have done this deed, my noble lord—
RICHARD
If? Thou protector of this damnèd strumpet,   75
Talk'st thou to me of "ifs"? Thou art a traitor.—
Off with his head. Now by Saint Paul I swear
I will not dine until I see the same.—
Lovell and Ratcliffe, look that it be done.—
The rest that love me, rise and follow me.   80
          They exit. Lovell and Ratcliffe remain,
                    with the Lord Hastings.
HASTINGS
Woe, woe for England! Not a whit for me,
For I, too fond, might have prevented this.
Stanley did dream the boar did ⟨raze his helm,⟩
And I did scorn it and disdain to fly.
Three times today my foot-cloth horse did stumble,   85
And started when he looked upon the Tower,
As loath to bear me to the slaughterhouse.
O, now I need the priest that spake to me!
I now repent I told the pursuivant,
As too triumphing, how mine enemies   90
Today at Pomfret bloodily were butchered,
And I myself secure in grace and favor.
O Margaret, Margaret, now thy heavy curse
Is lighted on poor Hastings' wretched head.
RATCLIFFE
Come, come, dispatch. The Duke would be at   95
    dinner.
Make a short shrift. He longs to see your head.
HASTINGS
O momentary grace of mortal men,
Which we more hunt for than the grace of God!

100. **Who:** i.e., he who; **in air of your good looks:** i.e., on the airy foundation of your apparent favor

101–3. **Lives . . . deep:** Compare Proverbs 23.31–34: "Look not thou upon the wine when it is red. . . . And thou shalt be as one that sleepeth in the middle of the sea, and as he that sleepeth in the top of the mast."

105. **bloody:** bloodthirsty

108. **him:** i.e., Richard

3.5 Richard and Buckingham excuse the summary execution of Hastings to the Mayor of London by staging an "uprising" that they blame on Hastings' treachery. Richard then sends Buckingham to persuade Londoners that the crown should be taken from the heirs of Edward IV and given to Richard. Buckingham is to claim that Edward IV himself was illegitimate, and that therefore Richard is the legitimate heir.

---

0 SD. **rotten:** rusted; or, crumbling to pieces; **marvelous ill-favored:** i.e., marvelously ugly

1–2. **change thy color:** grow pale or flushed

6. **counterfeit:** imitate; **deep:** profoundly crafty; **tragedian:** tragic actor

7. **pry . . . side:** peer all over the place

8. **wagging of a straw:** the movement of only a piece of straw

9. **Intending:** signifying

11. **offices:** functions

Who builds his hope in air of your good looks   100
Lives like a drunken sailor on a mast,
Ready with every nod to tumble down
Into the fatal bowels of the deep.

LOVELL
Come, come, dispatch. 'Tis bootless to exclaim.

HASTINGS
O bloody Richard! Miserable England,   105
I prophesy the fearfull'st time to thee
That ever wretched age hath looked upon.—
Come, lead me to the block. Bear him my head.
They smile at me who shortly shall be dead.
                              They exit.

                    ⌜Scene 5⌝
    Enter Richard and Buckingham, in rotten armor,
                marvelous ill-favored.

RICHARD
Come, cousin, canst thou quake and change thy
    color,
Murder thy breath in middle of a word,
And then again begin, and stop again,
As if thou were distraught and mad with terror?   5

BUCKINGHAM
Tut, I can counterfeit the deep tragedian,
Speak, and look back, and pry on every side,
Tremble and start at wagging of a straw,
Intending deep suspicion. Ghastly looks
Are at my service, like enforcèd smiles,   10
And both are ready, in their offices,
At any time to grace my stratagems.
But what, is Catesby gone?

RICHARD
He is; and see he brings the Mayor along.

16. **Look . . . there:** Here Richard and Buckingham begin to pretend that they are under attack.

18. **o'erlook:** look over the top of

20. **back:** i.e., behind you

22. **patient:** calm

26. **harmless:** i.e., most harmless

28. **book:** i.e., commonplace book

31. **apparent:** evident, obvious

32. **conversation:** sexual intimacy

33. **from . . . suspects:** i.e., free from the dishonor of any suspicion

34. **covert'st:** most secretive and deceitful; **sheltered:** protected

37. **by great preservation:** through being protected (by God or providence)

Enter the Mayor and Catesby.

BUCKINGHAM   Lord Mayor—   15
RICHARD   Look to the drawbridge there!
BUCKINGHAM   Hark, a drum!
RICHARD   Catesby, o'erlook the walls.
                              ⌐*Catesby exits.*⌐
BUCKINGHAM   Lord Mayor, the reason we have sent—
RICHARD
   Look back! Defend thee! Here are enemies.   20
BUCKINGHAM
   God and our ⟨innocence⟩ defend and guard us!

   Enter Lovell and Ratcliffe, with Hastings' head.

RICHARD
   Be patient. They are friends, Ratcliffe and Lovell.
LOVELL
   Here is the head of that ignoble traitor,
   The dangerous and unsuspected Hastings.
RICHARD
   So dear I loved the man that I must weep.   25
   I took him for the plainest harmless creature
   That breathed upon the Earth a Christian;
   Made him my book, wherein my soul recorded
   The history of all her secret thoughts.
   So smooth he daubed his vice with show of virtue   30
   That, his apparent open guilt omitted—
   I mean his conversation with Shore's wife—
   He lived from all attainder of suspects.
BUCKINGHAM
   Well, well, he was the covert'st sheltered traitor
   That ever lived.—   35
   Would you imagine, or almost believe,
   Were 't not that by great preservation
   We live to tell it, that the subtle traitor

45. **But:** except

48. **fair befall you:** i.e., may good fortune be yours

49. **well proceeded:** acted properly

50. **the like:** similar

51. **at his hands:** i.e., from him

55. **these our friends:** Lovell and Ratcliffe

56. **Something:** somewhat; **meanings:** intentions; **prevented:** forestalled

60. **signified:** indicated

61. **haply:** perhaps

62. **Misconster . . . him:** i.e., misunderstand our treatment of him

64. **as I:** i.e., as if I

65. **right:** truly; **noble princes both:** See note to line 2.2.157.

66. **But:** i.e., but that

69. **T' avoid:** i.e., so that we can avoid

This day had plotted, in the council house,
To murder me and my good lord of Gloucester?   40
MAYOR   Had he done so?
RICHARD
What, think you we are Turks or infidels?
Or that we would, against the form of law,
Proceed thus rashly in the villain's death,
But that the extreme peril of the case,   45
The peace of England, and our persons' safety
Enforced us to this execution?
MAYOR
Now fair befall you! He deserved his death,
And your good Graces both have well proceeded
To warn false traitors from the like attempts.   50
BUCKINGHAM
I never looked for better at his hands
After he once fell in with Mistress Shore.
Yet had we not determined he should die
Until your Lordship came to see his end
(Which now the loving haste of these our friends,   55
Something against our meanings, have prevented),
Because, my lord, I would have had you heard
The traitor speak and timorously confess
The manner and the purpose of his treasons,
That you might well have signified the same   60
Unto the citizens, who haply may
Misconster us in him, and wail his death.
MAYOR
But, my good lord, your Graces' words shall serve
As well as I had seen and heard him speak;
And do not doubt, right noble princes both,   65
But I'll acquaint our duteous citizens
With all your just proceedings in this case.
RICHARD
And to that end we wished your Lordship here,
T' avoid the censures of the carping world.

70. **Which . . . intent:** i.e., although you have come too late to fulfill our original intention for you

71. **witness:** i.e., bear witness to

73. **Go after:** i.e., follow (the Mayor)

74. **Guildhall:** the hall of the Corporation of the City of London, used for meetings, etc. (See page 190.) **in all post:** i.e., with all speed

75. **at . . . time:** i.e., at the most appropriate moment for you to do so

76. **Infer:** imply

77. **them:** i.e., the citizens of London

79. **house:** perhaps, alehouse

80. **Which . . . so:** i.e., which was called the Crown because of the sign it bore

81. **luxury:** lechery

82. **change of lust:** i.e., always changing the object of his desire

85. **raging:** roving, wanton

87. **for a need:** i.e., if need be

88–89. **went . . . Edward:** i.e., was carrying in her womb the child who became this insatiable Edward

92. **the issue . . . begot:** i.e., the child (Edward) could not have been fathered by him

95. **touch:** i.e., touch on, mention; **as . . . off:** i.e., most tactfully

97. **Doubt:** fear

98. **golden fee:** i.e., the crown (which Buckingham will secure for Richard if he is successful in pleading, or persuading citizens of the illegitimacy of Edward IV and his heirs)

100. **Baynard's Castle:** Richard's residence on the north bank of the Thames River in London between Blackfriars and London Bridge (See page 180.)

BUCKINGHAM

Which since you come too late of our intent, 70
Yet witness what you hear we did intend.
And so, my good Lord Mayor, we bid farewell.

Mayor exits.

RICHARD

Go after, after, cousin Buckingham.
The Mayor towards Guildhall hies him in all post.
There, at your meetest vantage of the time, 75
Infer the bastardy of Edward's children.
Tell them how Edward put to death a citizen
Only for saying he would make his son
Heir to the Crown—meaning indeed his house,
Which, by the sign thereof, was termèd so. 80
Moreover, urge his hateful luxury
And bestial appetite in change of lust,
Which stretched unto their servants, daughters,
  wives,
Even where his raging eye or savage heart, 85
Without control, lusted to make a prey.
Nay, for a need, thus far come near my person:
Tell them when that my mother went with child
Of that insatiate Edward, noble York
My princely father then had wars in France, 90
And, by true computation of the time,
Found that the issue was not his begot,
Which well appearèd in his lineaments,
Being nothing like the noble duke my father.
Yet touch this sparingly, as 'twere far off, 95
Because, my lord, you know my mother lives.

BUCKINGHAM

Doubt not, my lord. I'll play the orator
As if the golden fee for which I plead
Were for myself. And so, my lord, adieu.

RICHARD

If you thrive well, bring them to Baynard's Castle, 100

105. **Doctor:** i.e., doctor of divinity
109. **take . . . order:** i.e., give a secret order
111. **no manner person:** i.e., no one whatsoever
112. **recourse:** access, admission

3.6 The professional scribe who has just finished transcribing Hastings' indictment shows how the charge against Hastings had been prepared and the transcribing begun long before Hastings had even been accused or arrested.

---

0 SD. **Scrivener:** professional copyist; notary (See page 182.)
2. **in . . . engrossed:** i.e., is now properly transcribed   **set hand:** a style of handwriting used for copying legal documents   **fairly:** clearly, legibly
3. **read . . . Paul's:** proclaimed at Paul's Cross, outside of St. Paul's Cathedral (See page 192.)
4. **mark:** notice; **sequel:** sequence (of events)
7. **precedent . . . a-doing:** i.e., the original from which my copy was made took just as long to write
8. **within . . . hours:** i.e., five hours ago
9. **Untainted:** free of allegations
10. **Here's . . . while:** i.e., what a world we live in; **gross:** stupid

Where you shall find me well accompanied
With reverend fathers and well-learnèd bishops.

BUCKINGHAM
I go; and towards three or four o'clock
Look for the news that the Guildhall affords.

Buckingham exits.

RICHARD
Go, Lovell, with all speed to Doctor Shaa.   105
⌈*To Ratcliffe.*⌉ Go thou to Friar Penker. Bid them
    both
Meet me within this hour at Baynard's Castle.

⌈*Ratcliffe and Lovell*⌉ *exit.*

Now will I go to take some privy order
To draw the brats of Clarence out of sight,   110
And to give order that no manner person
Have any time recourse unto the Princes.

⟨*He exits.*⟩

⌈Scene 6⌉
Enter a Scrivener.

SCRIVENER
Here is the indictment of the good Lord Hastings,
Which in a set hand fairly is engrossed,
That it may be today read o'er in Paul's.
And mark how well the sequel hangs together:
Eleven hours I have spent to write it over,   5
For yesternight by Catesby was it sent me;
The precedent was full as long a-doing,
And yet within these five hours Hastings lived,
Untainted, unexamined, free, at liberty.
Here's a good world the while! Who is so gross   10
That cannot see this palpable device?
Yet who so bold but says he sees it not?

13. **naught:** evil
14. **ill:** evil; **must . . . thought:** i.e., cannot be uttered

3.7 Richard and Buckingham, having failed to persuade London's officials and citizens that Richard should be king, stage a scene of Richard's great piety. Richard "yields" to the Mayor's plea that Richard accept the kingship.

———————————

0 SD. **several:** separate
4. **Touched you:** i.e., did you mention
5. **contract with:** i.e., engagement to; **Lady Lucy:** Elizabeth Lucy, one of Edward's mistresses
6. **by . . . France:** Edward sent the earl of Warwick as his **deputy** to France to secure a marriage to the Lady Bona, sister-in-law to the French king, but then changed his mind. (See Shakespeare's *Henry VI, Part 3* [2.6.90–103, 3.2, and 3.3].)
7. **unsatiate:** insatiable
8. **enforcement:** (sexual) forcing, compelling
9. **tyranny for trifles:** i.e., cruel sentences for small offenses
10. **got:** conceived
11. **Duke:** the duke of York, Richard's father
12. **Withal:** in addition; **infer:** mention
13. **right idea:** proper image
19. **slightly handled:** i.e., treated carelessly or slightingly

Bad is the world, and all will come to naught
When such ill dealing must be seen in thought.
                                        He exits.

⌜Scene 7⌝
Enter Richard and Buckingham at several doors.

RICHARD
  How now, how now? What say the citizens?
BUCKINGHAM
  Now, by the holy mother of our Lord,
  The citizens are mum, say not a word.
RICHARD
  Touched you the bastardy of Edward's children?
BUCKINGHAM
  I did; with his contract with Lady Lucy   5
  And his contract by deputy in France;
  Th' unsatiate greediness of his desire
  And his enforcement of the city wives;
  His tyranny for trifles; his own bastardy,
  As being got, your father then in France,   10
  And his resemblance being not like the Duke.
  Withal, I did infer your lineaments,
  Being the right idea of your father,
  Both in your form and nobleness of mind;
  Laid open all your victories in Scotland,   15
  Your discipline in war, wisdom in peace,
  Your bounty, virtue, fair humility;
  Indeed, left nothing fitting for your purpose
  Untouched or slightly handled in discourse.
  And when ⟨mine⟩ oratory drew toward end,   20
  I bid them that did love their country's good
  Cry "God save Richard, England's royal king!"
RICHARD   And did they so?

26. **each on other:** i.e., at each other

30. **Recorder:** municipal legal official

33. **inferred:** reported

34. **in warrant from himself:** on his own authority

38. **vantage of:** i.e., opportunity provided by

42. **brake:** broke

45. **brethren:** i.e., fellow civic officials

46. **Intend:** i.e., pretend

47. **but . . . suit:** i.e., until you are most insistently petitioned

50. **on . . . descant:** (1) on that plainsong or melody I'll raise a harmonious song; (2) on that basis I'll comment on your holiness

52. **Play . . . it:** Proverbial: "Maids say nay and take it." **still answer:** keep answering

53. **An if:** i.e., if; **for them:** i.e., on their behalf

55. **happy issue:** fortunate outcome

BUCKINGHAM
  No. So God help me, they spake not a word
  But, like dumb statues or breathing stones,   25
  Stared each on other and looked deadly pale;
  Which when I saw, I reprehended them
  And asked the Mayor what meant this willful silence.
  His answer was, the people were not used
  To be spoke to but by the Recorder.   30
  Then he was urged to tell my tale again:
  "Thus saith the Duke. Thus hath the Duke
    inferred"—
  But nothing spoke in warrant from himself.
  When he had done, some followers of mine own,   35
  At lower end of the hall, hurled up their caps,
  And some ten voices cried "God save King Richard!"
  And thus I took the vantage of those few.
  "Thanks, gentle citizens and friends," quoth I.
  "This general applause and cheerful shout   40
  Argues your ⟨wisdoms⟩ and your love to Richard"—
  And even here brake off and came away.
RICHARD
  What tongueless blocks were they! Would they not
    speak?
  Will not the Mayor then and his brethren come?   45
BUCKINGHAM
  The Mayor is here at hand. Intend some fear;
  Be not you spoke with but by mighty suit.
  And look you get a prayer book in your hand
  And stand between two churchmen, good my lord,
  For on that ground I'll make a holy descant.   50
  And be not easily won to our requests.
  Play the maid's part: still answer "nay," and take it.
RICHARD
  I go. An if you plead as well for them
  As I can say "nay" to thee for myself,
  No doubt we bring it to a happy issue.   55
                    ⌜*Knocking within.*⌝

56. **leads:** lead-covered roof (here perhaps represented by the gallery above the stage)

57. **dance attendance:** i.e., am left to kick my heels waiting (for Richard)

58. **withal:** with

64. **in:** i.e., by; **worldly suits:** secular petitions; **moved:** persuaded

65. **holy exercise:** spiritual devotions

70. **conference:** conversation

71. **straight:** straightway, immediately

76. **deep:** learned

77. **engross:** fatten

78. **watchful:** unsleeping

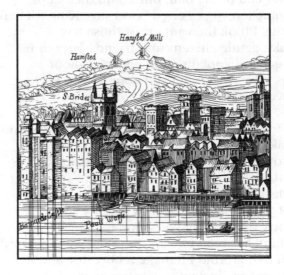

Baynard's Castle. (3.5.100)
From Claes Jansz Visscher, *Londinum florentissima Britanniae urbs . . .* [c. 1625].

BUCKINGHAM
Go, go, up to the leads. The Lord Mayor knocks.
⟨⌜*Richard*⌝ *exits.*⟩

Enter the Mayor and Citizens.

Welcome, my lord. I dance attendance here.
I think the Duke will not be spoke withal.

Enter Catesby.

Now, Catesby, what says your lord to my request?
CATESBY
He doth entreat your Grace, my noble lord,   60
To visit him tomorrow or next day.
He is within, with two right reverend fathers,
Divinely bent to meditation,
And in no worldly suits would he be moved
To draw him from his holy exercise.   65
BUCKINGHAM
Return, good Catesby, to the gracious duke.
Tell him myself, the Mayor, and aldermen,
In deep designs, in matter of great moment
No less importing than our general good,
Are come to have some conference with his Grace.   70
CATESBY
I'll signify so much unto him straight.   *He exits.*
BUCKINGHAM
Ah ha, my lord, this prince is not an Edward!
He is not lolling on a lewd love-bed,
But on his knees at meditation;
Not dallying with a brace of courtesans,   75
But meditating with two deep divines;
Not sleeping, to engross his idle body,
But praying, to enrich his watchful soul.
Happy were England would this virtuous prince

82. **defend:** forbid

85. **to what end:** for what purpose

94. **at their beads:** i.e., praying (literally, saying the rosary)

95 SD. **aloft:** See page xlvi, above, for possible early staging practices.

98. **stay:** prevent; **the ... vanity:** i.e., sinning through vanity

100. **to know:** i.e., by which to identify

Scriveners at work. (3.6.0 SD)
From Raphael Holinshed, *Chronicles of England . . .* (1577).

Take on his Grace the sovereignty thereof.   80
But sure I fear we shall not win him to it.
MAYOR
Marry, God defend his Grace should say us nay.
BUCKINGHAM
I fear he will. Here Catesby comes again.

Enter Catesby.

Now, Catesby, what says his Grace?
CATESBY
He wonders to what end you have assembled   85
Such troops of citizens to come to him,
His Grace not being warned thereof before.
He fears, my lord, you mean no good to him.
BUCKINGHAM
Sorry I am my noble cousin should
Suspect me that I mean no good to him.   90
By heaven, we come to him in perfect love,
And so once more return and tell his Grace.
                              ⟨*Catesby*⟩ *exits.*
When holy and devout religious men
Are at their beads, 'tis much to draw them thence,
So sweet is zealous contemplation.   95

Enter Richard aloft, between two Bishops.
⌜*Catesby reenters.*⌝

MAYOR
See where his Grace stands, 'tween two clergymen.
BUCKINGHAM
Two props of virtue for a Christian prince,
To stay him from the fall of vanity;
And, see, a book of prayer in his hand,
True ornaments to know a holy man.—   100
Famous Plantagenet, most gracious prince,
Lend favorable ear to our requests,

104. **right:** true, proper
113. **disgracious:** displeasing
118. **Else wherefore:** otherwise why
121. **office:** position of authority
122. **Your state of fortune:** i.e., power and great-ness awarded you by fortune
123. **house:** family
127. **want . . . limbs:** lack her own limbs
129. **graft:** grafted (See below.)
130. **in:** i.e., into
132. **recure:** restore

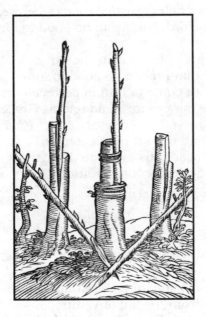

"Stock graft with . . . plants." (3.7.129)
From Marco Bussato, *Giardino di agricoltura . . .* (1599).

And pardon us the interruption
Of thy devotion and right Christian zeal.
RICHARD
My lord, there needs no such apology.   105
I do beseech your Grace to pardon me,
Who, earnest in the service of my God,
Deferred the visitation of my friends.
But, leaving this, what is your Grace's pleasure?
BUCKINGHAM
Even that, I hope, which pleaseth God above   110
And all good men of this ungoverned isle.
RICHARD
I do suspect I have done some offense
That seems disgracious in the city's eye,
And that you come to reprehend my ignorance.
BUCKINGHAM
You have, my lord. Would it might please your   115
    Grace,
On our entreaties, to amend your fault.
RICHARD
Else wherefore breathe I in a Christian land?
BUCKINGHAM
Know, then, it is your fault that you resign
The supreme seat, the throne majestical,   120
The sceptered office of your ancestors,
Your state of fortune, and your due of birth,
The lineal glory of your royal house,
To the corruption of a blemished stock,
Whiles in the mildness of your sleepy thoughts,   125
Which here we waken to our country's good,
The noble isle doth want ⟨her⟩ proper limbs—
⟨Her⟩ face defaced with scars of infamy,
⌈Her⌉ royal stock graft with ignoble plants,
And almost shouldered in the swallowing gulf   130
Of dark forgetfulness and deep oblivion;
Which to recure, we heartily solicit

136. **factor:** agent

137. **successively . . . to blood:** i.e., succeeding by right of immediate descent

138. **empery:** absolute dominion

139. **consorted with:** in the company of

140. **worshipful:** honorable

142. **move:** persuade

143. **if:** whether

145. **fitteth:** becomes; **degree:** rank; **condition:** social status

146. **not to:** i.e., I do not; **haply:** perhaps

149. **fondly:** foolishly

150. **If to:** i.e., if I were to; **suit:** petition

152. **on the other side:** i.e., going to the other extreme; **checked:** reprimanded

156–57. **desert / Unmeritable:** unworthiness (literally, "meritless merit")

159. **that:** if; **even:** straightforward, direct; smooth

160. **As . . . birth:** i.e., as my possession to claim by right of birth

161. **poverty of spirit:** See Matthew 5.3: "Blessed are the poor in spirit: for theirs is the kingdom of heaven." (The parallel passage at Luke 6.20 is glossed marginally in the Geneva Bible with this explanation: "They that are humble and submit themselves willingly to obey God.")

163. **my greatness:** i.e., my title to the throne

164. **bark:** boat; **brook:** endure

Your gracious self to take on you the charge
And kingly government of this your land,
Not as Protector, steward, substitute,   135
Or lowly factor for another's gain,
But as successively, from blood to blood,
Your right of birth, your empery, your own.
For this, consorted with the citizens,
Your very worshipful and loving friends,   140
And by their vehement instigation,
In this just cause come I to move your Grace.

RICHARD
I cannot tell if to depart in silence
Or bitterly to speak in your reproof
Best fitteth my degree or your condition.   145
If not to answer, you might haply think
Tongue-tied ambition, not replying, yielded
To bear the golden yoke of sovereignty,
Which fondly you would here impose on me.
If to reprove you for this suit of yours,   150
So seasoned with your faithful love to me,
Then on the other side I checked my friends.
Therefore, to speak, and to avoid the first,
And then, in speaking, not to incur the last,
Definitively thus I answer you: 155
Your love deserves my thanks, but my desert
Unmeritable shuns your high request.
First, if all obstacles were cut away
And that my path were even to the crown
As the ripe revenue and due of birth,   160
Yet so much is my poverty of spirit,
So mighty and so many my defects,
That I would rather hide me from my greatness,
Being a bark to brook no mighty sea,
Than in my greatness covet to be hid   165
And in the vapor of my glory smothered.
But, God be thanked, there is no need of me,

168. **I need:** I lack

169. **The . . . fruit:** See Matthew 12.33: "Either make the tree good, and his fruit good; or else make the tree evil, and his fruit evil: for the tree is known by his fruit."

170. **stealing:** i.e., imperceptively passing

171. **become:** grace, adorn

173. **that:** what, that which

174. **happy stars:** i.e., fortunate destiny

176. **this . . . conscience:** i.e., this speech proves that there is conscientiousness

177. **the respects thereof:** the considerations supporting your argument; **nice:** slight

178. **well:** i.e., being well

179. **Edward:** i.e., Prince Edward

180. **Edward's:** i.e., **your brother's** (line 179), King Edward IV's

181. **contract:** contracted, engaged

184. **sister:** See note to 3.7.6.

185. **poor petitioner:** Elizabeth Grey, the Queen Elizabeth of this play (whom Edward met when she came to petition him for help). See *Henry VI, Part 3*, 3.2.

189. **prize, purchase:** plunder, booty

190. **Seduced:** enticed; **pitch:** i.e., pinnacle (literally, the highest point reached by a falcon in its flight); **degree:** rank

191. **declension:** falling away

192. **got:** i.e., begot, conceived

195. **some alive:** perhaps a reference to the duchess of York, King Edward IV's and Richard's mother

196. **I . . . tongue:** i.e., I speak with restraint

199. **withal:** as well

And much I need to help you, were there need.
The royal tree hath left us royal fruit,
Which, mellowed by the stealing hours of time,   170
Will well become the seat of majesty,
And make, no doubt, us happy by his reign.
On him I lay that you would lay on me,
The right and fortune of his happy stars,
Which God defend that I should wring from him.   175

BUCKINGHAM
My lord, this argues conscience in your Grace,
But the respects thereof are nice and trivial,
All circumstances well consberèd.
You say that Edward is your brother's son;
So say we too, but not by Edward's wife.   180
For first was he contract to Lady Lucy—
Your mother lives a witness to his vow—
And afterward by substitute betrothed
To Bona, sister to the King of France.
These both put off, a poor petitioner,   185
A care-crazed mother to a many sons,
A beauty-waning and distressèd widow,
Even in the afternoon of her best days,
Made prize and purchase of his wanton eye,
Seduced the pitch and height of his degree   190
To base declension and loathed bigamy.
By her in his unlawful bed he got
This Edward, whom our manners call "the Prince."
More bitterly could I expostulate,
Save that, for reverence to some alive,   195
I give a sparing limit to my tongue.
Then, good my lord, take to your royal self
This proffered benefit of dignity,
If not to bless us and the land withal,
Yet to draw forth your noble ancestry   200
From the corruption of abusing times
Unto a lineal, true-derivèd course.

207. **state:** pomp

210. **as:** being

213. **kind, effeminate remorse:** i.e., natural compassion

214. **noted:** observed; **to:** i.e., toward

215. **all estates:** all kinds of people

216. **whe'er:** i.e., whether

219. **house:** family

221. **Zounds:** i.e., God's or Christ's wounds (a strong oath)

Guildhall. (3.5.74)
From John Seller, *A book of the prospects of . . .
London . . .* (c. 1700?).

MAYOR
 Do, good my lord. Your citizens entreat you.
BUCKINGHAM
 Refuse not, mighty lord, this proffered love.
CATESBY
 O, make them joyful. Grant their lawful suit.   205
RICHARD
 Alas, why would you heap this care on me?
 I am unfit for state and majesty.
 I do beseech you, take it not amiss;
 I cannot, nor I will not, yield to you.
BUCKINGHAM
 If you refuse it, as in love and zeal   210
 Loath to depose the child, your brother's son—
 As well we know your tenderness of heart
 And gentle, kind, effeminate remorse,
 Which we have noted in you to your kindred
 And equally indeed to all estates—   215
 Yet know, whe'er you accept our suit or no,
 Your brother's son shall never reign our king,
 But we will plant some other in the throne,
 To the disgrace and downfall of your house.
 And in this resolution here we leave you.— 220
 Come, citizens. ⟨Zounds, I'll⟩ entreat no more.
⟨RICHARD
 O, do not swear, my lord of Buckingham!⟩
      ⌜*Buckingham and some others*⌝ *exit.*
CATESBY
 Call him again, sweet prince. Accept their suit.
 If you deny them, all the land will rue it.
RICHARD
 Will you enforce me to a world of cares?   225
 Call them again. I am not made of stones,
 But penetrable to your kind entreaties,
 Albeit against my conscience and my soul.

    Enter Buckingham and the rest.

230. **Fortune:** the goddess Fortuna
235. **mere:** utter, absolute; **acquittance:** acquit

Paul's Cross. (3.6.3)
From Robert Wilkinson, *Londina illustrata* ... (1819–25).

Cousin of Buckingham and sage, grave men,
Since you will buckle Fortune on my back, 230
To bear her burden, whe'er I will or no,
I must have patience to endure the load;
But if black scandal or foul-faced reproach
Attend the sequel of your imposition,
Your mere enforcement shall acquittance me 235
From all the impure blots and stains thereof,
For God doth know, and you may partly see,
How far I am from the desire of this.

MAYOR
God bless your Grace! We see it and will say it.

RICHARD
In saying so, you shall but say the truth. 240

BUCKINGHAM
Then I salute you with this royal title:
Long live Richard, England's worthy king!

ALL Amen.

BUCKINGHAM
Tomorrow may it please you to be crowned?

RICHARD
Even when you please, for you will have it so. 245

BUCKINGHAM
Tomorrow, then, we will attend your Grace,
And so most joyfully we take our leave.

RICHARD, ⌜*to the Bishops*⌝
Come, let us to our holy work again.—
Farewell, my ⟨cousin.⟩ Farewell, gentle friends.
                                        They exit.

The Tragedy of

RICHARD III

ACT 4

4.1 Queen Elizabeth, her son Dorset, and the Duchess of York meet Lady Anne and Clarence's daughter as all approach the Tower to visit Prince Edward and the Duke of York. They are denied entry. Then Stanley comes to take Lady Anne to be crowned Richard's queen. At Elizabeth's urging, Dorset leaves for France to join Stanley's stepson, Henry Tudor, Earl of Richmond.

---

1. **My niece Plantagenet:** The Duchess of York is referring to Clarence's daughter. Here, as often at the time, *niece* means granddaughter.
3. **for my life:** a mild oath
4. **On:** i.e., motivated by; **tender:** young
5. **Daughter:** daughter-in-law
8. **sister:** sister-in-law
10. **Upon . . . devotion:** i.e., to perform the same devout act
11. **gratulate:** greet, salute

ACT 4

Scene 1
⟨*Enter Queen* ⌈*Elizabeth, with the*⌉ *Duchess of York,* ⌈*and
the Lord*⌉ *Marquess* ⌈*of*⌉ *Dorset, at one door;* ⌈*Anne,*⌉
Duchess of Gloucester ⌈*with Clarence's daughter,*⌉ *at
another door.*⟩

DUCHESS
Who meets us here? My niece Plantagenet
Led in the hand of her kind aunt of Gloucester?
Now, for my life, she's wandering to the Tower,
On pure heart's love, to greet the tender prince.—
Daughter, well met.   5
ANNE   God give your Graces both
A happy and a joyful time of day.
QUEEN ELIZABETH
As much to you, good sister. Whither away?
ANNE
No farther than the Tower, and, as I guess,
Upon the like devotion as yourselves,   10
To gratulate the gentle princes there.
QUEEN ELIZABETH
Kind sister, thanks. We'll enter all together.

            Enter ⌈*Brakenbury,*⌉ *the Lieutenant.*

And in good time here the Lieutenant comes.—
Master Lieutenant, pray you, by your leave,
How doth the Prince and my young son of York?   15

16. **Right:** very; **By your patience:** a polite phrase requesting one's indulgence or acquiescence

17. **suffer:** allow

18. **charged:** commanded

22. **bounds:** boundaries

25. **in law:** by marriage

27. **office:** obligation, duty

28. **leave it so:** i.e., abdicate my responsibility

31. **mother:** mother-in-law

32. **reverend looker-on:** honored beholder; **two fair queens:** Queen Elizabeth and Anne (soon to be crowned)

34. **Westminster:** i.e., Westminster Abbey

36. **lace:** cord that closes the bodice of her dress

39. **Despiteful:** cruel, malicious

BRAKENBURY
Right well, dear madam. By your patience,
I may not suffer you to visit them.
The King hath strictly charged the contrary.

QUEEN ELIZABETH
The King? Who's that?

BRAKENBURY   I mean, the Lord Protector.   20

QUEEN ELIZABETH
The Lord protect him from that kingly title!
Hath he set bounds between their love and me?
I am their mother. Who shall bar me from them?

DUCHESS
I am their father's mother. I will see them.

ANNE
Their aunt I am in law, in love their mother.   25
Then bring me to their sights. I'll bear thy blame
And take thy office from thee, on my peril.

BRAKENBURY
No, madam, no. I may not leave it so.
I am bound by oath, and therefore pardon me.
                    ⌈*Brakenbury the*⌉ *Lieutenant exits.*

                    Enter Stanley.

STANLEY
Let me but meet you ladies one hour hence,   30
And I'll salute your Grace of York as mother
And reverend looker-on of two fair queens.
⌈*To Anne.*⌉ Come, madam, you must straight to
    Westminster,
There to be crownèd Richard's royal queen.   35

QUEEN ELIZABETH   Ah, cut my lace asunder
That my pent heart may have some scope to beat,
Or else I swoon with this dead-killing news!

ANNE
Despiteful tidings! O, unpleasing news!

45. **from:** beyond

46. **hie thee:** make haste

48. **the thrall of:** in bondage to

49. **Nor . . . nor:** i.e., neither . . . nor; **counted:** accounted, recognized, esteemed

53. **son:** stepson (i.e., Richmond)

55. **ta'en:** taken

56. **ill:** evil

58. **cockatrice:** a mythical creature whose glance was deadly, often identified with the basilisk (See below and page 34.)

62–63. **the inclusive . . . metal:** i.e., the crown

63. **round:** i.e., go around

68. **humor:** mood, state of feeling

A cockatrice. (1.2.164; 4.1.58)
From Joachim Camerarius, *Symbolorum et emblematum . . .* (1605).

DORSET, ⌜*to Queen Elizabeth*⌝
  Be of good cheer, mother. How fares your Grace?   40
QUEEN ELIZABETH
  O Dorset, speak not to me. Get thee gone.
  Death and destruction dogs thee at thy heels.
  Thy mother's name is ominous to children.
  If thou wilt outstrip death, go, cross the seas,
  And live with Richmond, from the reach of hell.   45
  Go, hie thee, hie thee from this slaughterhouse,
  Lest thou increase the number of the dead
  And make me die the thrall of Margaret's curse,
  Nor mother, wife, nor England's counted queen.
STANLEY
  Full of wise care is this your counsel, madam.   50
  ⌜*To Dorset.*⌝ Take all the swift advantage of the
    hours.
  You shall have letters from me to my son
  In your behalf, to meet you on the way.
  Be not ta'en tardy by unwise delay.   55
DUCHESS
  O ill-dispersing wind of misery!
  O my accursèd womb, the bed of death!
  A cockatrice hast thou hatched to the world,
  Whose unavoided eye is murderous.
STANLEY, ⌜*to Anne*⌝
  Come, madam, come. I in all haste was sent.   60
ANNE
  And I with all unwillingness will go.
  O, would to God that the inclusive verge
  Of golden metal that must round my brow
  Were red-hot steel to sear me to the brains!
  Anointed let me be with deadly venom,   65
  And die ere men can say "God save the Queen."
QUEEN ELIZABETH
  Go, go, poor soul, I envy not thy glory.
  To feed my humor, wish thyself no harm.

70. **corse:** corpse
71. **scarce:** scarcely; **his:** i.e., Richard's
73. **angel husband:** i.e., Prince Edward, son of Henry VI
74. **dear saint:** i.e., Henry VI
84. **Grossly:** stupidly
86. **hitherto:** as yet
89. **with:** by; **still:** continually
90. **for:** because of
92. **complaining:** complaint

ANNE

No? Why? When he that is my husband now
Came to me as I followed Henry's corse,   70
When scarce the blood was well washed from his
    hands
Which issued from my other angel husband
And that dear saint which then I weeping followed—
O, when, I say, I looked on Richard's face,   75
This was my wish: be thou, quoth I, accursed
For making me, so young, so old a widow;
And, when thou wedd'st, let sorrow haunt thy bed;
And be thy wife, if any be so mad,
More miserable by the life of thee   80
Than thou hast made me by my dear lord's death.
Lo, ere I can repeat this curse again,
Within so small a time my woman's heart
Grossly grew captive to his honey words
And proved the subject of mine own soul's curse,   85
Which hitherto hath held ⟨my⟩ eyes from rest,
For never yet one hour in his bed
Did I enjoy the golden dew of sleep,
But with his timorous dreams was still awaked.
Besides, he hates me for my father Warwick,   90
And will, no doubt, shortly be rid of me.

QUEEN ELIZABETH

Poor heart, adieu. I pity thy complaining.

ANNE

No more than with my soul I mourn for yours.

DORSET

Farewell, thou woeful welcomer of glory.

ANNE

Adieu, poor soul that tak'st thy leave of it.   95

DUCHESS, ⌜*to Dorset*⌝

Go thou to Richmond, and good fortune guide thee.
⌜*To Anne.*⌝ Go thou to Richard, and good angels
    tend thee.

103. **wracked:** destroyed; **teen:** grief, woe
106. **envy:** malice
108. **Rude:** harsh; **playfellow:** playmate

4.2 The newly crowned Richard asks Buckingham to arrange the deaths of Prince Edward and the Duke of York. When Buckingham resists the request, Richard procures "a discontented gentleman," James Tyrrel, to kill the boys. Richard decides to have Lady Anne killed and to marry Elizabeth, daughter of Edward IV and Queen Elizabeth. He then refuses a promised earldom to Buckingham, and Buckingham flees.

---

1. **apart:** aside
8. **Still live they:** i.e., may they always continue
9–10. **play . . . gold:** test you to determine if you are real gold **touch:** touchstone **current gold:** genuine gold coin, used as currency (See page 210.)

⌜*To Queen Elizabeth.*⌝ Go thou to sanctuary, and
  good thoughts possess thee. 100
I to my grave, where peace and rest lie with me.
Eighty-odd years of sorrow have I seen,
And each hour's joy wracked with a week of teen.

QUEEN ELIZABETH
  Stay, yet look back with me unto the Tower.—
  Pity, you ancient stones, those tender babes 105
  Whom envy hath immured within your walls—
  Rough cradle for such little pretty ones.
  Rude ragged nurse, old sullen playfellow
  For tender princes, use my babies well.
  So foolish sorrows bids your stones farewell. 110

They exit.

Scene 2

Sound a sennet. Enter Richard in pomp; Buckingham,
Catesby, Ratcliffe, Lovell, ⌜and others, including a Page.⌝

RICHARD
  Stand all apart.—Cousin of Buckingham.
             ⌜*The others move aside.*⌝

BUCKINGHAM My gracious sovereign.

RICHARD
  Give me thy hand.
    ⟨*Here he ascendeth the throne.*⟩ *Sound* ⌜*trumpets.*⌝
             Thus high, by thy advice
  And thy assistance is King Richard seated. 5
  But shall we wear these glories for a day,
  Or shall they last and we rejoice in them?

BUCKINGHAM
  Still live they, and forever let them last.

RICHARD
  Ah, Buckingham, now do I play the touch,
  To try if thou be current gold indeed: 10
  Young Edward lives; think now what I would speak.

17. **consequence:** sequel
19. **wont:** accustomed
21. **suddenly:** immediately
26. **breath:** i.e., breathing space (in which to make a decision)
28. **resolve you:** make known to you my decision; **presently:** soon
30. **I . . . with:** i.e., I have no one to talk with but
31. **unrespective:** heedless; **are for me:** i.e., will be taken into my confidence
32. **considerate:** thoughtful, deliberate, prudent
37. **close:** secret

"Thus high . . . is King Richard seated." (4.2.4–5)
From Raphael Holinshed, *Chronicles of England . . .* (1577).

BUCKINGHAM   Say on, my loving lord.
RICHARD
Why, Buckingham, I say I would be king.
BUCKINGHAM
Why so you are, my thrice-renownèd lord.
RICHARD
Ha! Am I king? 'Tis so—but Edward lives.   15
BUCKINGHAM
True, noble prince.
RICHARD   O bitter consequence
That Edward still should live "true noble prince"!
Cousin, thou wast not wont to be so dull.
Shall I be plain? I wish the bastards dead,   20
And I would have it suddenly performed.
What sayst thou now? Speak suddenly. Be brief.
BUCKINGHAM   Your Grace may do your pleasure.
RICHARD
Tut, tut, thou art all ice; thy kindness freezes.
Say, have I thy consent that they shall die?   25
BUCKINGHAM
Give me some little breath, some pause, dear lord,
Before I positively speak in this.
I will resolve you herein presently.
                                    Buckingham exits.
CATESBY, ⌜*aside to the other Attendants*⌝
The King is angry. See, he gnaws his lip.
RICHARD, ⌜*aside*⌝
I will converse with iron-witted fools   30
And unrespective boys. None are for me
That look into me with considerate eyes.
High-reaching Buckingham grows circumspect.—
Boy!
PAGE, ⌜*coming forward*⌝   My lord?   35
RICHARD
Know'st thou not any whom corrupting gold
Will tempt unto a close exploit of death?

40. **Gold . . . orators:** Proverbial: "Gold speaks."

45. **deep-revolving:** profoundly thoughtful; **witty:** wise, clever, cunning

47. **held out:** continued, endured

52. **abides:** resides

54. **grievous:** i.e., grievously

55. **will . . . close:** i.e., command that she be kept hidden or secluded

56. **Inquire me out:** i.e., find for me; **mean:** low-born; **poor:** poverty-stricken

57. **straight:** straightway, immediately

59. **dream'st:** i.e., stand daydreaming; **give out:** announce

60. **like:** i.e., likely

61. **About:** i.e., set about; **stands me much upon:** i.e., is imperative for me

62. **all hopes:** i.e., (1) all who might hope to reign; or, (2) all hopes that are resting on potential rivals

63. **brother's daughter:** i.e., Elizabeth, daughter of King Edward IV (See page 234.)

PAGE
I know a discontented gentleman
Whose humble means match not his haughty spirit.
Gold were as good as twenty orators,   40
And will, no doubt, tempt him to anything.
RICHARD
What is his name?
PAGE   His name, my lord, is Tyrrel.
RICHARD
I partly know the man. Go, call him hither, boy.
⌜*Page*⌝ *exits.*

⌜*Aside.*⌝ The deep-revolving witty Buckingham   45
No more shall be the neighbor to my counsels.
Hath he so long held out with me, untired,
And stops he now for breath? Well, be it so.

Enter Stanley.

How now, Lord Stanley, what's the news?
STANLEY   Know, my loving lord,   50
The Marquess Dorset, as I hear, is fled
To Richmond, in the parts where he abides.
⌜*He walks aside.*⌝
RICHARD
Come hither, Catesby. Rumor it abroad
That Anne my wife is very grievous sick.
I will take order for her keeping close.   55
Inquire me out some mean poor gentleman,
Whom I will marry straight to Clarence' daughter.
The boy is foolish, and I fear not him.
Look how thou dream'st! I say again, give out
That Anne my queen is sick and like to die.   60
About it, for it stands me much upon
To stop all hopes whose growth may damage me.
⌜*Catesby exits.*⌝
⌜*Aside.*⌝ I must be married to my brother's daughter,
Or else my kingdom stands on brittle glass.

66. **of gain:** i.e., to prosper

67. **pluck on sin:** i.e., draw more sin after it (In *Macbeth* a similar idea is expressed as "I am in blood / Stepped in so far that . . . / Returning were as tedious as go o'er" [3.4.168–70].)

72. **Prove:** test

74. **Please you:** i.e., if it please you

75. **deep:** great

77. **upon:** i.e., with

79. **open means to come:** i.e., unobstructed access

82. **by this token:** Richard here hands Tyrrel an object that will show that he has Richard's authority to enter the prison.

84. **prefer thee:** i.e., promote you in rank or fortune

Testing gold on a touchstone. (4.2.9)
From George Wither, *A collection of emblemes* . . . (1635).

Murder her brothers, and then marry her—   65
Uncertain way of gain. But I am in
So far in blood that sin will pluck on sin.
Tear-falling pity dwells not in this eye.

Enter Tyrrel.

Is thy name Tyrrel?
TYRREL
James Tyrrel, and your most obedient subject.   70
RICHARD
Art thou indeed?
TYRREL   Prove me, my gracious lord.
RICHARD
Dar'st thou resolve to kill a friend of mine?
TYRREL
Please you. But I had rather kill two enemies.
RICHARD
Why then, thou hast it. Two deep enemies,   75
Foes to my rest, and my sweet sleep's disturbers,
Are they that I would have thee deal upon.
Tyrrel, I mean those bastards in the Tower.
TYRREL
Let me have open means to come to them,
And soon I'll rid you from the fear of them.   80
RICHARD
Thou sing'st sweet music. Hark, come hither, Tyrrel.
              ⌈*Tyrrel approaches Richard and kneels.*⌉
Go, by this token. Rise, and lend thine ear.
              ⌈*Tyrrel rises, and Richard*⌉ *whispers*
                    ⌈*to him. Then Tyrrel steps back.*⌉
There is no more but so. Say it is done,
And I will love thee and prefer thee for it.
TYRREL   I will dispatch it straight.   *He exits.*   85

Enter Buckingham.

87. **late ... in:** i.e., the request about which you recently sounded me out

90. **he:** i.e., Richmond

91. **due:** right

92. **pawned:** pledged

93–94. **Th' earldom ... possess:** See 3.1.197–99.

96. **answer:** i.e., answer for, be accountable for

98. **remember me:** i.e., remember

100. **peevish:** foolish

104. **by:** nearby

108. **Rougemont:** pronounced like "Richmond," and, like "Richmond," meaning "red hill"

Henry VI. (4.2.98)
From John Speed, *The theatre of the empire of Great Britaine* . . . (1627 [i.e., 1631]).

BUCKINGHAM
My lord, I have considered in my mind
The late request that you did sound me in.
RICHARD
Well, let that rest. Dorset is fled to Richmond.
BUCKINGHAM   I hear the news, my lord.
RICHARD
Stanley, he is your wife's son. Well, look unto it.   90
BUCKINGHAM
My lord, I claim the gift, my due by promise,
For which your honor and your faith is pawned—
Th' earldom of ⟨Hereford⟩ and the movables
Which you have promisèd I shall possess.
RICHARD
Stanley, look to your wife. If she convey   95
Letters to Richmond, you shall answer it.
BUCKINGHAM
What says your Highness to my just request?
RICHARD
I do remember me, Henry the Sixth
Did prophesy that Richmond should be king,
When Richmond was a little peevish boy.   100
A king perhaps—
⟨BUCKINGHAM   My lord—
RICHARD
How chance the prophet could not at that time
Have told me, I being by, that I should kill him?
BUCKINGHAM
My lord, your promise for the earldom—   105
RICHARD
Richmond! When last I was at Exeter,
The Mayor in courtesy showed me the castle
And called it Rougemont, at which name I started,
Because a bard of Ireland told me once
I should not live long after I saw Richmond.   110
BUCKINGHAM   My lord—

112. **what's o'clock:** i.e., what time is it?

119. **jack:** i.e., a figure that strikes the bell on the outside of a clock; also, a lowborn fellow; **keep'st the stroke:** (1) continue to strike; (2) keep time (See page 230.)

120. **Betwixt:** between

124. **deep:** great, important

127. **Brecknock:** Buckingham's family estate in southeast Wales (See page 216.)

4.3 Tyrrel reports the deaths of Edward IV's sons. Richard then reveals that Anne is dead and that he will now woo his niece Elizabeth, whom Richmond also seeks in marriage. Ratcliffe informs Richard that Morton, Bishop of Ely, has fled to Richmond, and that Buckingham is "in the field." Richard musters his army.

---

1. **tyrannous:** cruel
2. **most arch:** preeminent
4. **who:** i.e., whom
6. **fleshed villains:** criminals initiated into killing

RICHARD   Ay, what's o'clock?

BUCKINGHAM
I am thus bold to put your Grace in mind
Of what you promised me.

RICHARD   Well, but what's o'clock?   115

BUCKINGHAM   Upon the stroke of ten.

RICHARD   Well, let it strike.

BUCKINGHAM   Why let it strike?

RICHARD
Because that, like a jack, thou keep'st the stroke
Betwixt thy begging and my meditation.   120
I am not in the giving vein today.

BUCKINGHAM
Why then, resolve me whether you will or no.⟩

RICHARD
Thou troublest me; I am not in the vein.
      He exits, ⌜*and is followed by all but Buckingham.*⌝

BUCKINGHAM
And is it thus? Repays he my deep service
With such contempt? Made I him king for this?   125
O, let me think on Hastings and be gone
To Brecknock, while my fearful head is on!
                              He exits.

⌜Scene 3⌝
Enter Tyrrel.

TYRREL
The tyrannous and bloody act is done,
The most arch deed of piteous massacre
That ever yet this land was guilty of.
Dighton and Forrest, who I did suborn
To do this piece of ⌜ruthless⌝ butchery,   5
Albeit they were fleshed villains, bloody dogs,
Melted with tenderness and mild compassion,

8. **their deaths' sad story:** i.e., the sad story of the princes' deaths
   10. **girdling:** i.e., embracing
   11. **alabaster:** i.e., white and smooth
   19. **replenishèd:** full, perfect
   20. **prime:** first; **she framed:** i.e., nature created
   21. **gone:** destroyed, undone
   23. **this:** i.e., these; **bloody:** bloodthirsty
   26. **gave in charge:** i.e., ordered
   34. **after-supper:** dessert
   35. **process:** tale

The town and castle of Brecknock. (4.2.127)
From John Speed, *The theatre of the empire of Great Britaine* . . . (1627 [i.e., 1631]).

Wept like two children in their deaths' sad story.
"O thus," quoth Dighton, "lay the gentle babes."
"Thus, thus," quoth Forrest, "girdling one another   10
Within their alabaster innocent arms.
Their lips were four red roses on a stalk,
And in their summer beauty kissed each other.
A book of prayers on their pillow lay,
Which ⟨once,⟩" quoth Forrest, "almost changed my   15
    mind,
But, O, the devil—" There the villain stopped;
When Dighton thus told on: "We smotherèd
The most replenishèd sweet work of nature
That from the prime creation e'er she framed."   20
Hence both are gone with conscience and remorse;
They could not speak; and so I left them both
To bear this tidings to the bloody king.

Enter Richard.

And here he comes.—All health, my sovereign lord.
RICHARD
Kind Tyrrel, am I happy in thy news?   25
TYRREL
If to have done the thing you gave in charge
Beget your happiness, be happy then,
For it is done.
RICHARD   But did'st thou see them dead?
TYRREL
I did, my lord.   30
RICHARD   And buried, gentle Tyrrel?
TYRREL
The chaplain of the Tower hath buried them,
But where, to say the truth, I do not know.
RICHARD
Come to me, Tyrrel, soon ⟨at⟩ after-supper,
When thou shalt tell the process of their death.   35
Meantime, but think how I may do thee good,

37. **inheritor:** possessor

40. **pent up close:** i.e., securely imprisoned

41. **meanly:** ignobly, basely

42. **in Abraham's bosom:** See Luke 16.22: ". . . the beggar died, and was carried by the angels into Abraham's bosom. . . ."

46. **by that knot:** by virtue of marrying her; **looks . . . crown:** casts an arrogant look at the crown

49. **bluntly:** abruptly, without ceremony

50. **Morton:** i.e., the bishop of Ely

52. **in the field:** i.e., on the march; **power:** army

53. **near:** closely, directly

55. **fearful commenting:** frightened or timorous talk

56. **leaden servitor:** indolent servant

58. **expedition:** speed

59. **Jove's Mercury:** Mercury was the god-messenger (often depicted with wings at his heels) used by Jove, king of the gods in Roman mythology. (See page 98.)

60. **My . . . shield:** i.e., instead of deliberating (taking counsel), I will arm (and fight)

61. **be brief:** act quickly; **brave the field:** challenge us to fight

And be inheritor of thy desire.
Farewell till then.
TYRREL   I humbly take my leave.
                              ⟨*Tyrrel exits.*⟩
RICHARD
The son of Clarence have I pent up close,   40
His daughter meanly have I matched in marriage,
The sons of Edward sleep in Abraham's bosom,
And Anne my wife hath bid this world goodnight.
Now, for I know the Breton Richmond aims
At young Elizabeth, my brother's daughter,   45
And by that knot looks proudly on the crown,
To her go I, a jolly thriving wooer.

                    Enter Ratcliffe.

RATCLIFFE   My lord.
RICHARD
Good or bad news, that thou com'st in so bluntly?
RATCLIFFE
Bad news, my lord. Morton is fled to Richmond,   50
And Buckingham, backed with the hardy Welshmen,
Is in the field, and still his power increaseth.
RICHARD
Ely with Richmond troubles me more near
Than Buckingham and his rash-levied strength.
Come, I have learned that fearful commenting   55
Is leaden servitor to dull delay;
Delay ⟨leads⟩ impotent and snail-paced beggary;
Then fiery expedition be my wing,
Jove's Mercury, and herald for a king.
Go, muster men. My counsel is my shield.   60
We must be brief when traitors brave the field.
                                        They exit.

4.4 Queen Margaret, Queen Elizabeth, and the Duchess of York grieve for their dead. Richard enters on his way to confront Buckingham's army, and he tries to persuade Queen Elizabeth to give him her daughter Elizabeth in marriage. Then a series of messengers bring Richard news of his enemies' maneuvers against him, and of Buckingham's capture.

----

5. **induction:** first part (of a play)
6. **will:** i.e., will go; **consequence:** i.e., what follows the **induction**
10. **tender:** young
11. **unblown:** unopened, still in the bud; **sweets:** flowers; darlings
13. **doom:** judgment
18. **crazed:** cracked, broken
20. **Edward Plantagenet:** probably Edward V (**Plantagenet** was the name of the whole English royal family, whether they were descendants of York or of Lancaster. See note on 1.2.153.)
21. **quit:** requite, pay for; balance
22. **dying debt:** i.e., debt that can be paid only by a death
23. **fly:** flee
25. **When:** i.e., whenever

⌜Scene 4⌝
Enter old Queen Margaret.

QUEEN MARGARET
So now prosperity begins to mellow
And drop into the rotten mouth of death.
Here in these confines slyly have I lurked
To watch the waning of mine enemies.
A dire induction am I witness to,   5
And will to France, hoping the consequence
Will prove as bitter, black, and tragical.
Withdraw thee, wretched Margaret. Who comes
    here?   ⌜*She steps aside.*⌝

Enter Duchess ⟨of York⟩ and Queen ⌜*Elizabeth.*⌝

QUEEN ELIZABETH
Ah, my poor princes! Ah, my tender babes,   10
My ⟨unblown⟩ flowers, new-appearing sweets,
If yet your gentle souls fly in the air
And be not fixed in doom perpetual,
Hover about me with your airy wings
And hear your mother's lamentation.   15
QUEEN MARGARET, ⌜*aside*⌝
Hover about her; say that right for right
Hath dimmed your infant morn to agèd night.
DUCHESS
So many miseries have crazed my voice
That my woe-wearied tongue is still and mute.
Edward Plantagenet, why art thou dead?   20
QUEEN MARGARET, ⌜*aside*⌝
Plantagenet doth quit Plantagenet;
Edward for Edward pays a dying debt.
QUEEN ELIZABETH
Wilt thou, O God, fly from such gentle lambs
And throw them in the entrails of the wolf?
When didst thou sleep when such a deed was done?   25

26. **Harry:** i.e., Henry VI

30. **abstract:** epitome; **record:** pronounced recòrd

33. **that thou:** i.e., if only **England's lawful earth** (line 31); **afford:** provide

35. **hide my bones:** be buried

38. **seigniory:** sovereignty (perhaps with a pun on *seniority*)

39. **on . . . hand:** from a position of superiority or precedence

41. **Tell:** count

44–45. **Edward, Richard:** Queen Elizabeth's young sons

46. **Richard:** i.e., her husband, the late duke of York

47. **holp'st:** helped

51. **dog . . . eyes:** In *Henry VI, Part 3*, Richard describes the cry of women at his birth: "O Jesus bless us, he is born with teeth," adding "And so I was, which plainly signified / That I should snarl, and bite, and play the dog" (5.6.76–78). Queen Margaret refers to the fact that puppies are born blind.

53. **excellent:** preeminent, supreme

54. **That reigns:** who reigns

QUEEN MARGARET, ⌐*aside*¬
  When holy Harry died, and my sweet son.
DUCHESS, ⌐*to Queen Elizabeth*¬
  Dead life, blind sight, poor mortal living ghost,
  Woe's scene, world's shame, grave's due by life
    usurped,
  Brief abstract and record of tedious days,   30
  Rest thy unrest on England's lawful earth,
  Unlawfully made drunk with innocent blood.
QUEEN ELIZABETH, ⌐*as they both sit down*¬
  Ah, that thou wouldst as soon afford a grave
  As thou canst yield a melancholy seat,
  Then would I hide my bones, not rest them here.   35
  Ah, who hath any cause to mourn but we?
QUEEN MARGARET, ⌐*coming forward*¬
  If ancient sorrow be most reverend,
  Give mine the benefit of seigniory,
  And let my griefs frown on the upper hand.
  If sorrow can admit society,   40
  ⟨Tell over your woes again by viewing mine.⟩
  I had an Edward till a Richard killed him;
  I had a husband till a Richard killed him.
  Thou hadst an Edward till a Richard killed him;
  Thou hadst a Richard till a Richard killed him.   45
DUCHESS
  I had a Richard too, and thou did'st kill him;
  I had a Rutland too; thou ⌐holp'st¬ to kill him.
QUEEN MARGARET
  Thou hadst a Clarence too, and Richard killed him.
  From forth the kennel of thy womb hath crept
  A hellhound that doth hunt us all to death—   50
  That dog, that had his teeth before his eyes,
  To worry lambs and lap their gentle blood;
  That excellent grand tyrant of the Earth,
  That reigns in gallèd eyes of weeping souls;
  That foul defacer of God's handiwork   55

58. **carnal:** carnivorous, murderous

60. **pew-fellow:** i.e., fellow sufferer (literally, one sitting in the same church pew)

61. **triumph:** exult

64. **cloy me:** sate myself

65. **Thy Edward:** King Edward IV

66. **other Edward:** Edward V; **quit:** requite, pay for; balance

67. **but boot:** only thrown into the bargain to make up the difference between the **high perfection** (line 68) of Margaret's son Edward and the two Yorkist Edwards

70. **frantic:** insane

71. **adulterate:** adulterous (because of his relations with Mistress Shore)

72. **smothered:** hidden, concealed

73. **intelligencer:** spy

74. **Only ... factor:** i.e., only held back from death so that he can be hell's agent

75. **at hand:** soon

79. **bond:** deed, lease

81–85. **O, thou ... painted queen:** See 1.3.255–61 and notes.   **shadow:** reflected image; actor

86. **presentation:** (1) representation; (2) theatrical presentation; **what I was:** i.e., what I was in actuality

87. **index:** prologue, preface; **direful:** terrible, calamitous

Thy womb let loose to chase us to our graves.
O upright, just, and true-disposing God,
How do I thank thee that this carnal cur
Preys on the issue of his mother's body
And makes her pew-fellow with others' moan!   60
DUCHESS, ⌐*standing*¬
O Harry's wife, triumph not in my woes!
God witness with me, I have wept for thine.
QUEEN MARGARET
Bear with me. I am hungry for revenge,
And now I cloy me with beholding it.
Thy Edward he is dead, that killed my Edward,   65
⟨Thy⟩ other Edward dead, to quit my Edward;
Young York, he is but boot, because both they
Matched not the high perfection of my loss.
Thy Clarence he is dead that stabbed my Edward,
And the beholders of this frantic play,   70
Th' adulterate Hastings, Rivers, Vaughan, Grey,
Untimely smothered in their dusky graves.
Richard yet lives, hell's black intelligencer,
Only reserved their factor to buy souls
And send them thither. But at hand, at hand   75
Ensues his piteous and unpitied end.
Earth gapes, hell burns, fiends roar, saints pray,
To have him suddenly conveyed from hence.
Cancel his bond of life, dear God I pray,
That I may live and say "The dog is dead."   80
QUEEN ELIZABETH, ⌐*standing*¬
O, thou didst prophesy the time would come
That I should wish for thee to help me curse
That bottled spider, that foul bunch-backed toad!
QUEEN MARGARET
I called thee then "vain flourish of my fortune."
I called thee then poor shadow, "painted queen,"   85
The presentation of but what I was,
The flattering index of a direful pageant,

88. **One heaved:** someone who was heaved; **a-high:** on high

91. **shot:** armed soldier

92. **sign:** i.e., empty symbol; **breath, bubble:** Proverbial: "Man is but a breath (or a bubble)."

93. **scene:** stage

96. **sues:** petitions

98. **bending:** bowing; **peers:** i.e., nobles

100. **Decline:** go through and recite (To **decline** a noun in a language that uses inflections is to recite its forms in the different cases: nominative, accusative, etc. Here, perhaps, **decline** also puns on the downward movement from happiness to unhappiness.)

101–7. **For:** i.e., instead of

104. **very caitiff:** true wretch

105. **scorned at:** mocked; **scorned of:** i.e., scorned by

106, 107. **of:** by

110. **no more but thought:** only thoughts

113. **just:** proper

114. **Now . . . yoke:** The image is of the two queens yoked together like oxen drawing a plow. The yoke, while coupling them, also burdens their necks.

One heaved a-high to be hurled down below,
A mother only mocked with two fair babes,
A dream of what thou wast, a garish flag   90
To be the aim of every dangerous shot,
A sign of dignity, a breath, a bubble,
A queen in jest, only to fill the scene.
Where is thy husband now? Where be thy brothers?
Where ⟨are⟩ thy two sons? Wherein dost thou joy?   95
Who sues and kneels and says "God save the
     Queen?"
Where be the bending peers that flattered thee?
Where be the thronging troops that followed thee?
Decline all this, and see what now thou art: 100
For happy wife, a most distressèd widow;
For joyful mother, one that wails the name;
For one being sued to, one that humbly sues;
For queen, a very caitiff crowned with care;
For she that scorned at me, now scorned of me;   105
For she being feared of all, now fearing one;
For she commanding all, obeyed of none.
Thus hath the course of justice whirled about
And left thee but a very prey to time,
Having no more but thought of what thou wast   110
To torture thee the more, being what thou art.
Thou didst usurp my place, and dost thou not
Usurp the just proportion of my sorrow?
Now thy proud neck bears half my burdened yoke,
From which even here I slip my ⟨weary⟩ head   115
And leave the burden of it all on thee.
Farewell, York's wife, and queen of sad mischance.
These English woes shall make me smile in France.
                              ⌜*She begins to exit.*⌝
QUEEN ELIZABETH
O, thou well-skilled in curses, stay awhile,
And teach me how to curse mine enemies.   120

126. **Revolving:** meditating on

127. **quicken:** enliven

132. **succeeders . . . joys:** heirs to joys not passed on by the dead

139. **copious:** profuse; **exclaims:** exclamations, outcries

139 SD. As the textual note on page 331 shows, the quarto stage direction reads *"Enter K. Richard marching with Drummes and Trumpets,"* making clear that Richard is off to war.

140. **expedition:** haste; military enterprise

141. **intercepted:** prevented, hindered

QUEEN MARGARET
  Forbear to sleep the ⟨nights,⟩ and fast the ⟨days;⟩
  Compare dead happiness with living woe;
  Think that thy babes were sweeter than they were,
  And he that slew them fouler than he is.
  Bettering thy loss makes the bad causer worse.   125
  Revolving this will teach thee how to curse.
QUEEN ELIZABETH
  My words are dull. O, quicken them with thine!
QUEEN MARGARET
  Thy woes will make them sharp and pierce like
      mine.   *Margaret exits.*
DUCHESS
  Why should calamity be full of words?   130
QUEEN ELIZABETH
  Windy attorneys to their clients' woes,
  Airy succeeders of ⟨intestate⟩ joys,
  Poor breathing orators of miseries,
  Let them have scope; though what they will impart
  Help nothing else, yet do they ease the heart.   135
DUCHESS
  If so, then be not tongue-tied. Go with me,
  And in the breath of bitter words let's smother
  My damnèd son that thy two sweet sons smothered.
                          ⌜*A trumpet sounds.*⌝
  The trumpet sounds. Be copious in exclaims.

Enter King Richard and his train, ⌜including Catesby.⌝

RICHARD
  Who intercepts me in my expedition?   140
DUCHESS
  O, she that might have intercepted thee,
  By strangling thee in her accursèd womb,
  From all the slaughters, wretch, that thou hast done.

146. **owed:** owned
153. **flourish:** trumpet call or fanfare; **alarum:** call to arms
156. **patient:** calm; **fair:** politely
157. **report:** resounding noise
163. **brook:** endure; **accent:** tone

"Like a jack, thou keep'st the stroke." (4.2.119)
From Angelo Rocca, *De campanis commentarius . . .* (1612).

QUEEN ELIZABETH, ⌜*to Richard*⌝
  Hid'st thou that forehead with a golden crown
  Where should be branded, if that right were right, 145
  The slaughter of the prince that owed that crown
  And the dire death of my poor sons and brothers?
  Tell me, thou villain-slave, where are my children?
DUCHESS, ⌜*to Richard*⌝
  Thou toad, thou toad, where is thy brother Clarence,
  And little Ned Plantagenet his son? 150
QUEEN ELIZABETH, ⌜*to Richard*⌝
  Where is the gentle Rivers, Vaughan, Grey?
DUCHESS, ⌜*to Richard*⌝ Where is kind Hastings?
RICHARD
  A flourish, trumpets! Strike alarum, drums!
  Let not the heavens hear these telltale women
  Rail on the Lord's anointed. Strike, I say! 155
                       Flourish. Alarums.
  Either be patient and entreat me fair,
  Or with the clamorous report of war
  Thus will I drown your exclamations.
DUCHESS Art thou my son?
RICHARD
  Ay, I thank God, my father, and yourself. 160
DUCHESS
  Then patiently hear my impatience.
RICHARD
  Madam, I have a touch of your condition,
  That cannot brook the accent of reproof.
DUCHESS
  O, let me speak!
RICHARD   Do then, but I'll not hear. 165
DUCHESS
  I will be mild and gentle in my words.
RICHARD
  And brief, good mother, for I am in haste.

168. **stayed:** waited (in the labor of childbirth)
171. **Holy Rood:** cross on which Christ died
174. **wayward:** disobedient
175. **frightful:** frightening
177. **prime of:** i.e., early
178. **age confirmed:** maturity
179. **kind in hatred:** Richard says of himself in *Henry VI, Part 3,* "I can smile, and murder whiles I smile, . . . / And wet my cheeks with artificial tears" (3.2.184–86).
180. **comfortable:** pleasant, cheering
182. **Humfrey Hower:** This name has eluded editorial explanation—beyond the obvious pun on **Hower/hour** (line 180).
184. **forth of:** from
185. **disgracious:** displeasing
194. **turn:** i.e., return

DUCHESS
  Art thou so hasty? I have stayed for thee,
  God knows, in torment and in agony.
RICHARD
  And came I not at last to comfort you?   170
DUCHESS
  No, by the Holy Rood, thou know'st it well.
  Thou cam'st on Earth to make the Earth my hell.
  A grievous burden was thy birth to me;
  Tetchy and wayward was thy infancy;
  Thy school days frightful, desp'rate, wild, and   175
    furious;
  Thy prime of manhood daring, bold, and venturous;
  Thy age confirmed, proud, subtle, sly, and bloody,
  More mild, but yet more harmful, kind in hatred.
  What comfortable hour canst thou name,   180
  That ever graced me with thy company?
RICHARD
  Faith, none but Humfrey Hower, that called your
    Grace
  To breakfast once, forth of my company.
  If I be so disgracious in your eye,   185
  Let me march on and not offend you, madam.—
  Strike up the drum.
DUCHESS   I prithee, hear me speak.
RICHARD
  You speak too bitterly.
DUCHESS   Hear me a word,   190
  For I shall never speak to thee again.
RICHARD So.
DUCHESS
  Either thou wilt die by God's just ordinance
  Ere from this war thou turn a conqueror,
  Or I with grief and extreme age shall perish   195
  And nevermore behold thy face again.
  Therefore take with thee my most grievous curse,

199. **complete:** pronounced **còmplete**
202. **Whisper:** i.e., whisper to
204. **Bloody:** bloodthirsty; **bloody:** blood-covered
211. **For my daughters:** i.e., as for my daughters
213. **level:** aim
217. **manners:** morals
220. **So:** i.e., in order that; **of:** i.e., by
224. **safest . . . birth:** i.e., most secure only because she is Edward's child

Elizabeth of York.
From John Speed, *The theatre of the empire of Great
Britaine . . .* (1627 [i.e., 1631]).

Which in the day of battle tire thee more
Than all the complete armor that thou wear'st.
My prayers on the adverse party fight,   200
And there the little souls of Edward's children
Whisper the spirits of thine enemies
And promise them success and victory.
Bloody thou art; bloody will be thy end.
Shame serves thy life and doth thy death attend.   205
                                                    She exits.

QUEEN ELIZABETH
Though far more cause, yet much less spirit to
    curse
Abides in me. I say amen to her.

RICHARD
Stay, madam. I must talk a word with you.

QUEEN ELIZABETH
I have no more sons of the royal blood   210
For thee to slaughter. For my daughters, Richard,
They shall be praying nuns, not weeping queens,
And therefore level not to hit their lives.

RICHARD
You have a daughter called Elizabeth,
Virtuous and fair, royal and gracious.   215

QUEEN ELIZABETH
And must she die for this? O, let her live,
And I'll corrupt her manners, stain her beauty,
Slander myself as false to Edward's bed,
Throw over her the veil of infamy.
So she may live unscarred of bleeding slaughter,   220
I will confess she was not Edward's daughter.

RICHARD
Wrong not her birth. She is a royal princess.

QUEEN ELIZABETH
To save her life, I'll say she is not so.

RICHARD
Her life is safest only in her birth.

226. **opposite:** hostile, adverse

227. **ill:** evil; **friends:** kin, relatives

228. **unavoided:** unavoidable

229. **avoided grace:** i.e., Richard, who has refused the divine grace offered to him

230. **fairer death:** i.e., death without violence

231. **fairer life:** i.e., a less blemished life

233. **cozened:** cheated (Proverbial: "Call me cousin, but cozen me not.")

235. **Whose hand soever:** i.e., whosoever's hand; **launched:** pierced

236. **indirectly:** (1) not in express terms; (2) wrongfully

240. **still use of grief:** continual grieving

243–45. **And I ... bosom:** The image she uses for her earlier "wild grief" (line 240) is of herself as a sailing ship, stripped of sails and tackling, trapped in an extremely dangerous and deadly bay, being dashed to pieces against the rocks (here, Richard's heart). **reft:** bereft, robbed

246–48. **so thrive I ... As I intend:** i.e., may I prevail ... to the extent that I intend **success:** results, consequences

251. **discovered:** uncovered, revealed

QUEEN ELIZABETH
  And only in that safety died her brothers.   225
RICHARD
  Lo, at their birth good stars were opposite.
QUEEN ELIZABETH
  No, to their lives ill friends were contrary.
RICHARD
  All unavoided is the doom of destiny.
QUEEN ELIZABETH
  True, when avoided grace makes destiny.
  My babes were destined to a fairer death   230
  If grace had blessed thee with a fairer life.
RICHARD
  You speak as if that I had slain my cousins.
QUEEN ELIZABETH
  Cousins, indeed, and by their uncle cozened
  Of comfort, kingdom, kindred, freedom, life.
  Whose hand soever launched their tender hearts,   235
  Thy head, all indirectly, gave direction.
  No doubt the murd'rous knife was dull and blunt
  Till it was whetted on thy stone-hard heart,
  To revel in the entrails of my lambs.
  But that still use of grief makes wild grief tame,   240
  My tongue should to thy ears not name my boys
  Till that my nails were anchored in thine eyes,
  And I, in such a desp'rate bay of death,
  Like a poor bark of sails and tackling reft,
  Rush all to pieces on thy rocky bosom.   245
RICHARD
  Madam, so thrive I in my enterprise
  And dangerous success of bloody wars
  As I intend more good to you and yours
  Than ever you ⟨or⟩ yours by me were harmed!
QUEEN ELIZABETH
  What good is covered with the face of heaven,   250
  To be discovered, that can do me good?

255. **type:** symbol

256. **report:** an account

257. **state:** rank

258. **demise:** transmit, convey

260. **withal:** moreover, in addition

261–62. **So . . . wrongs:** provided you will forget the wrongs   **Lethe:** the river of forgetfulness in the underworld of classical mythology

264. **process:** narrative

265. **Last . . . date:** last in the telling beyond the duration of your kindness

269, 270, 271. **from:** contrary to

272. **confound:** spoil, corrupt

RICHARD
Th' advancement of your children, gentle lady.

QUEEN ELIZABETH
Up to some scaffold, there to lose their heads.

RICHARD
Unto the dignity and height of fortune,
The high imperial type of this Earth's glory.   255

QUEEN ELIZABETH
Flatter my sorrow with report of it.
Tell me what state, what dignity, what honor,
Canst thou demise to any child of mine?

RICHARD
Even all I have—ay, and myself and all—
Will I withal endow a child of thine;   260
So in the Lethe of thy angry soul
Thou drown the sad remembrance of those wrongs
Which thou supposest I have done to thee.

QUEEN ELIZABETH
Be brief, lest that the process of thy kindness
Last longer telling than thy kindness' date.   265

RICHARD
Then know that from my soul I love thy daughter.

QUEEN ELIZABETH
My daughter's mother thinks it with her soul.

RICHARD   What do you think?

QUEEN ELIZABETH
That thou dost love my daughter from thy soul.
So from thy soul's love didst thou love her brothers, 270
And from my heart's love I do thank thee for it.

RICHARD
Be not so hasty to confound my meaning.
I mean that with my soul I love thy daughter
And do intend to make her Queen of England.

QUEEN ELIZABETH
Well then, who dost thou mean shall be her king?   275

280. **of you:** i.e., from you

281. **humor:** disposition

286. **haply:** perhaps

287. **sometime:** once

290. **purple:** i.e., crimson

291. **withal:** i.e., with it

294, 296. **mad'st away, Mad'st quick conveyance with:** i.e., killed

298. **To win:** i.e., for me successfully to woo

304. **spoil:** slaughter

RICHARD
  Even he that makes her queen. Who else should be?
QUEEN ELIZABETH
  What, thou?
RICHARD   Even so. How think you of it?
QUEEN ELIZABETH
  How canst thou woo her?
RICHARD   That ⟨would I⟩ learn of you,   280
  As one being best acquainted with her humor.
QUEEN ELIZABETH   And wilt thou learn of me?
RICHARD   Madam, with all my heart.
QUEEN ELIZABETH
  Send to her, by the man that slew her brothers,
  A pair of bleeding hearts; thereon engrave   285
  "Edward" and "York." Then haply will she weep.
  Therefore present to her—as sometime Margaret
  Did to thy father, steeped in Rutland's blood—
  A handkerchief, which say to her did drain
  The purple sap from her sweet brother's body,   290
  And bid her wipe her weeping eyes withal.
  If this inducement move her not to love,
  Send her a letter of thy noble deeds;
  Tell her thou mad'st away her uncle Clarence,
  Her uncle Rivers, ay, and for her sake   295
  Mad'st quick conveyance with her good aunt Anne.
RICHARD
  You mock me, madam. This ⟨is⟩ not the way
  To win your daughter.
QUEEN ELIZABETH   There is no other way,
  Unless thou couldst put on some other shape   300
  And not be Richard, that hath done all this.
RICHARD
  Say that I did all this for love of her.
QUEEN ELIZABETH
  Nay, then indeed she cannot choose but hate thee,
  Having bought love with such a bloody spoil.

305. **Look what:** whatever

306. **shall deal unadvisedly:** i.e., may act imprudently

307. **Which . . . repent:** i.e., for which they can later repent

311. **quicken your increase:** i.e., give life to your offspring

314. **doting . . . mother:** i.e., title of a doting mother

315. **as . . . below:** i.e., one step below being your own children

316. **metal:** substance; **very:** own

317. **pain:** labor, effort

317–18. **save . . . sorrow:** i.e., except for a night in labor endured by your daughter Elizabeth, for whom you endured the same pains **bid:** underwent, suffered (past tense of "bide")

323. **would:** wish, would like to

324. **can:** am capable of

334. **What:** interjection introducing an exclamation or question

337. **Advantaging their love:** i.e., increasing in worth the love that inspired them

RICHARD

Look what is done cannot be now amended.   305
Men shall deal unadvisedly sometimes,
Which after-hours gives leisure to repent.
If I did take the kingdom from your sons,
To make amends I'll give it to your daughter.
If I have killed the issue of your womb,   310
To quicken your increase I will beget
Mine issue of your blood upon your daughter.
A grandam's name is little less in love
Than is the doting title of a mother.
They are as children but one step below,   315
Even of your metal, of your very blood,
Of all one pain, save for a night of groans
Endured of her for whom you bid like sorrow.
Your children were vexation to your youth,
But mine shall be a comfort to your age.   320
The loss you have is but a son being king,
And by that loss your daughter is made queen.
I cannot make you what amends I would;
Therefore accept such kindness as I can.
Dorset your son, that with a fearful soul   325
Leads discontented steps in foreign soil,
This fair alliance quickly shall call home
To high promotions and great dignity.
The king that calls your beauteous daughter wife
Familiarly shall call thy Dorset brother.   330
Again shall you be mother to a king,
And all the ruins of distressful times
Repaired with double riches of content.
What, we have many goodly days to see!
The liquid drops of tears that you have shed   335
Shall come again, transformed to orient pearl,
Advantaging their love with interest
Of ten times double gain of happiness.
Go then, my mother; to thy daughter go.

347. **triumphant garlands:** the wreath of bay leaves awarded a Roman general on his return from a conquest (See below.)

349. **retail:** recount, tell

357. **Infer:** mention, argue

360. **at her hands:** from her; **King's King:** i.e., God (The church forbade marriage between uncle and niece.)

362. **vail:** abase, lower (in subjection)

365. **in force:** in effect, operative (with perhaps some wordplay on the word **force**)

"Triumphant garlands." (4.4.347)
From Giacomo Lauri, *Antiquae vrbis splendor* (1612–15).

Make bold her bashful years with your experience;   340
Prepare her ears to hear a wooer's tale;
Put in her tender heart th' aspiring flame
Of golden sovereignty; acquaint the Princess
With the sweet silent hours of marriage joys;
And when this arm of mine hath chastisèd   345
The petty rebel, dull-brained Buckingham,
Bound with triumphant garlands will I come
And lead thy daughter to a conqueror's bed,
To whom I will retail my conquest won,
And she shall be sole victoress, Caesar's Caesar.   350

QUEEN ELIZABETH
What were I best to say? Her father's brother
Would be her lord? Or shall I say her uncle?
Or he that slew her brothers and her uncles?
Under what title shall I woo for thee,
That God, the law, my honor, and her love   355
Can make seem pleasing to her tender years?

RICHARD
Infer fair England's peace by this alliance.

QUEEN ELIZABETH
Which she shall purchase with still-lasting war.

RICHARD
Tell her the King, that may command, entreats—

QUEEN ELIZABETH
That, at her hands, which the King's King forbids.   360

RICHARD
Say she shall be a high and mighty queen.

QUEEN ELIZABETH
To vail the title, as her mother doth.

RICHARD
Say I will love her everlastingly.

QUEEN ELIZABETH
But how long shall that title "ever" last?

RICHARD
Sweetly in force unto her fair life's end.   365

366. **fairly:** i.e., without foul play

368. **likes of:** i.e., likes

372. **speeds:** succeeds

375. **reasons:** arguments; **quick:** hasty (Queen Elizabeth's reply plays on the words **reasons** ["motives, grounds"], **shallow**, and **quick** ["alive"].)

380. **George, Garter:** emblems of knighthood in the Order of the Garter (This reference is anachronistic, since the **George,** an ornament bearing a figure of St. George and forming part of the insignia of the Order of the Garter, dates only from the sixteenth century. See below, and page 248.)

384. **his:** i.e., its

A garter. (4.4.380)
From Elias Ashmole, *The institution, laws & ceremonies of the . . . Order of the Garter . . .* (1672).

QUEEN ELIZABETH
But how long fairly shall her sweet life last?
RICHARD
As long as heaven and nature lengthens it.
QUEEN ELIZABETH
As long as hell and Richard likes of it.
RICHARD
Say I, her sovereign, am her subject low.
QUEEN ELIZABETH
But she, your subject, loathes such sovereignty.   370
RICHARD
Be eloquent in my behalf to her.
QUEEN ELIZABETH
An honest tale speeds best being plainly told.
RICHARD
Then plainly to her tell my loving tale.
QUEEN ELIZABETH
Plain and not honest is too harsh a style.
RICHARD
Your reasons are too shallow and too quick.   375
QUEEN ELIZABETH
O no, my reasons are too deep and dead—
Too deep and dead, poor infants, in their graves.
RICHARD
⟨Harp not on that string, madam; that is past.
QUEEN ELIZABETH
Harp on it still shall I till heart-strings break.
RICHARD⟩
Now by my George, my Garter, and my crown—   380
QUEEN ELIZABETH
Profaned, dishonored, and the third usurped.
RICHARD
I swear—
QUEEN ELIZABETH   By nothing, for this is no oath.
Thy George, profaned, hath lost his lordly honor;

385, 386. **his:** i.e., its

399. **unity:** reconciliation (between Richard's faction and the Queen's in 2.1)

405–6. **two . . . worms:** See Job 21.26: "They shall sleep both in the dust and the worms shall cover them."

409. **o'erpast:** i.e., already past

411. **Hereafter time:** i.e., future time

A George. (4.4.380)
From Elias Ashmole, *The institution, laws & ceremonies of the . . . Order of the Garter . . .* (1672).

Thy Garter, blemished, pawned his knightly virtue;   385
Thy crown, usurped, disgraced his kingly glory.
If something thou wouldst swear to be believed,
Swear then by something that thou hast not
    wronged.
RICHARD
Then, by myself—   390
QUEEN ELIZABETH   Thyself is self-misused.
RICHARD
Now, by the world—
QUEEN ELIZABETH   'Tis full of thy foul wrongs.
RICHARD
My father's death—
QUEEN ELIZABETH   Thy life hath it dishonored.   395
RICHARD
Why then, by ⟨God.⟩
QUEEN ELIZABETH   ⟨God's⟩ wrong is most of all.
If thou didst fear to break an oath with Him,
The unity the King my husband made
Thou hadst not broken, nor my brothers died.   400
If thou hadst feared to break an oath by Him,
Th' imperial metal circling now thy head
Had graced the tender temples of my child,
And both the Princes had been breathing here,
Which now, two tender bedfellows for dust,   405
Thy broken faith hath made the prey for worms.
What canst thou swear by now?
RICHARD   The time to come.
QUEEN ELIZABETH
That thou hast wrongèd in the time o'erpast;
For I myself have many tears to wash   410
Hereafter time, for time past wronged by thee.
The children live whose fathers thou hast
    slaughtered,
Ungoverned youth, to wail it ⟨in⟩ their age;

421–22. **affairs . . . arms:** battles

422. **Myself myself confound:** may I destroy myself

423. **Heaven:** may Heaven

425. **opposite:** adverse, hostile

428. **tender:** regard, esteem

436. **attorney:** advocate, pleader

440. **peevish:** foolish

441. **of:** i.e., by

". . . from the crossrow plucks the letter *G*." (1.1.59)
From Andrew W. Tuer, *History of the horn-book . . .* (1896).

The parents live whose children thou hast   415
  butchered,
Old barren plants, to wail it with their age.
Swear not by time to come, for that thou hast
Misused ere used, by times ill-used ⟨o'erpast.⟩

RICHARD
As I intend to prosper and repent,   420
So thrive I in my dangerous affairs
Of hostile arms! Myself myself confound,
Heaven and fortune bar me happy hours,
Day, yield me not thy light, nor night thy rest,
Be opposite all planets of good luck   425
To my proceeding if, with dear heart's love,
Immaculate devotion, holy thoughts,
I tender not thy beauteous princely daughter.
In her consists my happiness and thine.
Without her follows to myself and thee,   430
Herself, the land, and many a Christian soul,
Death, desolation, ruin, and decay.
It cannot be avoided but by this;
It will not be avoided but by this.
Therefore, dear mother—I must call you so—   435
Be the attorney of my love to her;
Plead what I will be, not what I have been;
Not my deserts, but what I will deserve.
Urge the necessity and state of times,
And be not peevish found in great designs.   440

QUEEN ELIZABETH
Shall I be tempted of the devil thus?

RICHARD
Ay, if the devil tempt you to do good.

QUEEN ELIZABETH
Shall I forget myself to be myself?

RICHARD
Ay, if your self's remembrance wrong yourself.

QUEEN ELIZABETH   Yet thou didst kill my children.   445

447. **nest of spicery:** perhaps an allusion to the nest of aromatic boughs and spices in which, according to ancient legend, the phoenix destroys itself and from which the new phoenix arises

448. **recomforture:** consolation

457. **Rideth:** lies at anchor

458. **doubtful:** i.e., doubt-filled

459, 460. **them, their:** references to the **puissant navy** (line 457)

461. **hull:** drift, with sails furled

463. **light-foot:** lightly treading; hence, swift; **post:** travel at full speed (i.e., by post-horses)

468. **convenient:** suitable, appropriate

469. **Salisbury:** a town southwest of London at the edge of Salisbury Plain

RICHARD
But in your daughter's womb I bury them,
Where, in that nest of spicery, they will breed
Selves of themselves, to your recomforture.
QUEEN ELIZABETH
Shall I go win my daughter to thy will?
RICHARD
And be a happy mother by the deed.   450
QUEEN ELIZABETH   I go. Write to me very shortly,
And you shall understand from me her mind.
RICHARD
Bear her my true love's kiss; and so, farewell.
                                          Queen exits.
Relenting fool and shallow, changing woman!

                  Enter Ratcliffe.

How now, what news?   455
RATCLIFFE
Most mighty sovereign, on the western coast
Rideth a puissant navy. To our shores
Throng many doubtful hollow-hearted friends,
Unarmed and unresolved to beat them back.
'Tis thought that Richmond is their admiral;   460
And there they hull, expecting but the aid
Of Buckingham to welcome them ashore.
RICHARD
Some light-foot friend post to the Duke of
    Norfolk—
Ratcliffe thyself, or Catesby. Where is he?   465
CATESBY
Here, my good lord.
RICHARD   Catesby, fly to the Duke.
CATESBY
I will, my lord, with all convenient haste.
RICHARD
⌜Ratcliffe,⌝ come hither. Post to Salisbury.

471. **villain:** rascal, scoundrel

474. **deliver:** say

475. **levy:** muster up; **straight:** straightway, immediately

476. **The greatest . . . make:** i.e., the largest army possible for him

477. **suddenly:** immediately

481. **before:** ahead, in advance

486. **Hoyday:** heyday, a sarcastic expression of delight or surprise

488. **the nearest way:** i.e., directly

492. **White-livered:** cowardly; **runagate:** renegade, fugitive, vagabond

When thou com'st thither—⌜*To Catesby.*⌝ Dull,   470
  unmindful villain,
Why stay'st thou here and go'st not to the Duke?
CATESBY
First, mighty liege, tell me your Highness' pleasure,
What from your Grace I shall deliver to him.
RICHARD
O true, good Catesby. Bid him levy straight   475
The greatest strength and power that he can make
And meet me suddenly at Salisbury.
CATESBY   I go.   *He exits.*
RATCLIFFE
What, may it please you, shall I do at Salisbury?
RICHARD
Why, what wouldst thou do there before I go?   480
RATCLIFFE
Your Highness told me I should post before.
RICHARD
My mind is changed.

                    Enter Lord Stanley.

                    Stanley, what news with you?
STANLEY
None good, my liege, to please you with the hearing,
Nor none so bad but well may be reported.   485
RICHARD
Hoyday, a riddle! Neither good nor bad.
What need'st thou run so many miles about
When thou mayst tell thy tale the nearest way?
Once more, what news?
STANLEY   Richmond is on the seas.   490
RICHARD
There let him sink, and be the seas on him!
White-livered runagate, what doth he there?
STANLEY
I know not, mighty sovereign, but by guess.

497. **chair:** throne; **sword:** sword of state; **unswayed:** i.e., without a ruler, uncontrolled

499. **York:** perhaps, the first duke of York, one of the sons of Edward III; or, perhaps, the third duke of York, father of Edward IV and of Richard; **we:** i.e., I (the royal "we")

501. **makes:** i.e., does

502. **that:** i.e., to claim the crown

504. **Welshman:** Richmond was a descendant of Owen Tudor (a Welshman) and Katherine of Valois. (See "The Line of Edward III," pages 2–3, above.)

506. **Therefore . . . not:** do not mistrust me for that reason, on that account

507. **power:** army

517. **what time:** i.e., when

RICHARD Well, as you guess?

STANLEY
  Stirred up by Dorset, Buckingham, and Morton, 495
  He makes for England, here to claim the crown.

RICHARD
  Is the chair empty? Is the sword unswayed?
  Is the King dead, the empire unpossessed?
  What heir of York is there alive but we?
  And who is England's king but great York's heir? 500
  Then tell me, what makes he upon the seas?

STANLEY
  Unless for that, my liege, I cannot guess.

RICHARD
  Unless for that he comes to be your liege,
  You cannot guess wherefore the Welshman comes.
  Thou wilt revolt and fly to him, I fear. 505

STANLEY
  No, my good lord. Therefore mistrust me not.

RICHARD
  Where is thy power, then, to beat him back?
  Where be thy tenants and thy followers?
  Are they not now upon the western shore,
  Safe-conducting the rebels from their ships? 510

STANLEY
  No, my good lord. My friends are in the north.

RICHARD
  Cold friends to me. What do they in the north
  When they should serve their sovereign in the west?

STANLEY
  They have not been commanded, mighty king.
  Pleaseth your Majesty to give me leave, 515
  I'll muster up my friends and meet your Grace
  Where and what time your Majesty shall please.

RICHARD
  Ay, thou wouldst be gone to join with Richmond,
  But I'll not trust thee.

524. **Look:** i.e., take care that

527. **Devonshire:** county in the southwest of England

528. **advertisèd:** informed

532. **Kent:** county just southeast of London

533. **competitors:** associates

534. **power:** army

536. **Out on you:** expression of impatience; **owls . . . death:** The cry of the screech owl was believed to be an omen of death.

STANLEY   Most mighty sovereign,   520
  You have no cause to hold my friendship doubtful.
  I never was nor never will be false.
RICHARD
  Go then and muster men, but leave behind
  Your son George Stanley. Look your heart be firm,
  Or else his head's assurance is but frail.   525
STANLEY
  So deal with him as I prove true to you.
                                Stanley exits.

Enter a Messenger.

⌜FIRST⌝ MESSENGER
  My gracious sovereign, now in Devonshire,
  As I by friends am well advertisèd,
  Sir Edward Courtney and the haughty prelate,
  Bishop of Exeter, his elder brother,   530
  With many more confederates are in arms.

Enter another Messenger.

⌜SECOND⌝ MESSENGER
  In Kent, my liege, the Guilfords are in arms,
  And every hour more competitors
  Flock to the rebels, and their power grows strong.

Enter another Messenger.

⌜THIRD⌝ MESSENGER
  My lord, the army of great Buckingham—   535
RICHARD
  Out on you, owls! Nothing but songs of death.
                           He striketh him.
  There, take thou that till thou bring better news.
⌜THIRD⌝ MESSENGER
  The news I have to tell your Majesty
  Is that by sudden floods and fall of waters
  Buckingham's army is dispersed and scattered,   540

543. **I . . . mercy:** I beg your pardon.
545. **well-advisèd:** cautious, prudent
549. **Yorkshire:** in the north of England
551. **Breton:** i.e., from Brittany, in the north of France
552. **Dorsetshire:** on the south coast of England
557. **Hoised:** hoisted
563. **Milford:** Milford Haven, on the coast of Wales
565. **reason:** converse

And he himself wandered away alone,
No man knows whither.

RICHARD   I cry thee mercy.
There is my purse to cure that blow of thine.
⌜*He gives money.*⌝
Hath any well-advisèd friend proclaimed   545
Reward to him that brings the traitor in?

⌜THIRD⌝ MESSENGER
Such proclamation hath been made, my lord.

Enter another Messenger.

⌜FOURTH⌝ MESSENGER
Sir Thomas Lovell and Lord Marquess Dorset,
'Tis said, my liege, in Yorkshire are in arms.
But this good comfort bring I to your Highness: 550
The Breton navy is dispersed by tempest.
Richmond, in Dorsetshire, sent out a boat
Unto the shore to ask those on the banks
If they were his assistants, yea, or no—
Who answered him they came from Buckingham   555
Upon his party. He, mistrusting them,
Hoised sail and made his course again for Brittany.

RICHARD
March on, march on, since we are up in arms,
If not to fight with foreign enemies,
Yet to beat down these rebels here at home.   560

Enter Catesby.

CATESBY
My liege, the Duke of Buckingham is taken.
That is the best news. That the Earl of Richmond
Is with a mighty power landed at Milford
Is colder ⟨tidings,⟩ yet they must be told.

RICHARD
Away towards Salisbury! While we reason here,   565
A royal battle might be won and lost.

567. **take order:** i.e., direct that

4.5 Lord Stanley sends news to Richmond, whose army is marching on London: Stanley will be unable to help because Richard is holding Stanley's son George hostage.

---

1. **Sir Christopher:** In Holinshed's *Chronicles,* this character is identified as the countess of Richmond's chaplain, Christopher Urswick. The title **Sir** was an appropriate form of address to a priest.
2. **boar:** an allusion to Richard's emblem
3. **franked up:** penned up; **in hold:** in custody, under guard
5. **present:** immediate
6. **thy lord:** i.e., Richmond
7. **Withal:** in addition
10. **Ha'rfordwest:** i.e., Haverfordwest in Pembrokeshire, Wales, just northeast of Milford Haven
11. **men of name:** i.e., titled men
14. **redoubted:** feared, dreaded
16. **name:** reputation
17. **bend their power:** turn their army
18. **by the way:** i.e., along the way; **withal:** with
19. **hie thee:** hasten
20. **resolve . . . mind:** make known to him my thinking

Someone take order Buckingham be brought
To Salisbury. The rest march on with me.
Flourish. They exit.

⌐Scene 5⌐
Enter ⌐*Stanley, Earl of* ⌐ *Derby, and Sir Christopher.*

STANLEY
    Sir Christopher, tell Richmond this from me:
    That in the sty of the most deadly boar
    My son George Stanley is franked up in hold;
    If I revolt, off goes young George's head;
    The fear of that holds off my present aid.   5
    So get thee gone. Commend me to thy lord.
    Withal, say that the Queen hath heartily consented
    He should espouse Elizabeth her daughter.
    But tell me, where is princely Richmond now?
CHRISTOPHER
    At ⟨Pembroke,⟩ or at Ha'rfordwest in Wales.   10
STANLEY   What men of name resort to him?
CHRISTOPHER
    Sir Walter Herbert, a renownèd soldier;
    Sir Gilbert Talbot, Sir William Stanley,
    Oxford, redoubted Pembroke, Sir James Blunt,
    And Rice ap Thomas, with a valiant crew,   15
    And many other of great name and worth;
    And towards London do they bend their power,
    If by the way they be not fought withal.
STANLEY, ⌐*giving Sir Christopher a paper*⌐
    Well, hie thee to thy lord. I kiss his hand.
    My letter will resolve him of my mind.   20
    Farewell.
They exit.

The Tragedy of

RICHARD III

ACT 5

5.1 Buckingham is led to execution.

------

0 SD. **Halberds:** i.e., halberdiers (See note to 1.2.0 SD.)

5. **miscarrièd:** died

7. **moody:** angry

10. **All Souls' Day:** November 2, a day observed in the Roman Catholic Church as a day of prayer for souls in purgatory

12. **doomsday:** i.e., final day

13–17. **This is ... trusted:** See Buckingham's words at 2.1.33–41.

16. **wherein:** i.e., on which

17. **By:** i.e., through, because of

ACT 5

Scene 1

*Enter Buckingham, with ⌜Sheriff and⌝ Halberds, led to
execution.*

BUCKINGHAM
Will not King Richard let me speak with him?
SHERIFF
No, my good lord. Therefore be patient.
BUCKINGHAM
Hastings and Edward's children, Grey and Rivers,
Holy King Henry and thy fair son Edward,
Vaughan, and all that have miscarrièd   5
By underhand, corrupted, foul injustice,
If that your moody, discontented souls
Do through the clouds behold this present hour,
Even for revenge mock my destruction.—
This is All Souls' Day, fellow, is it not?   10
SHERIFF   It is.
BUCKINGHAM
Why, then, All Souls' Day is my body's doomsday.
This is the day which, in King Edward's time,
I wished might fall on me when I was found
False to his children and his wife's allies.   15
This is the day wherein I wished to fall
By the false faith of him whom most I trusted.
This, this All Souls' Day to my fearful soul

19. **determined . . . wrongs:** the appointed day until which the punishment of my wrongs was delayed

20. **high All-seer:** i.e., God; **dallied:** toyed

24. **in their masters' bosoms:** i.e., on their masters

26–28. **When . . . prophetess:** See 1.3.319–20.

30. **blame . . . blame:** i.e., censure is the consequence of blameworthiness or culpability

5.2 Richmond and his army march against Richard.

---

0 SD. **Drum:** drummers; **Colors:** standard-bearer with Richmond's heraldic banner

3. **bowels:** interior

5. **father:** stepfather

6. **Lines:** i.e., written lines

7. **usurping boar:** Richard (See picture, page 270.)

9. **Swills . . . wash:** greedily devours your blood as hogwash or swill

11. **embowelled bosoms:** i.e., disemboweled bellies

13, 14. **Leicester, Tamworth:** in central England, near Bosworth, where Richmond and Richard will join battle

15. **cheerly on:** i.e., go forward heartily, with a will

Is the determined respite of my wrongs.
That high All-seer which I dallied with   20
Hath turned my feignèd prayer on my head
And given in earnest what I begged in jest.
Thus doth he force the swords of wicked men
To turn their own points in their masters' bosoms.
Thus Margaret's curse falls heavy on my neck: 25
"When he," quoth she, "shall split thy heart with
    sorrow,
Remember Margaret was a prophetess."—
Come, lead me, officers, to the block of shame.
Wrong hath but wrong, and blame the due of blame.   30
                    Buckingham exits with Officers.

Scene 2
Enter Richmond, Oxford, Blunt, Herbert, and others,
with Drum and Colors.

RICHMOND
Fellows in arms, and my most loving friends,
Bruised underneath the yoke of tyranny,
Thus far into the bowels of the land
Have we marched on without impediment,
And here receive we from our father Stanley   5
Lines of fair comfort and encouragement.
The wretched, bloody, and usurping boar,
That spoiled your summer fields and fruitful vines,
Swills your warm blood like wash, and makes his
    trough   10
In your embowelled bosoms—this foul swine
Is now even in the ⟨center⟩ of this isle,
⟨Near⟩ to the town of Leicester, as we learn.
From Tamworth thither is but one day's march.
In God's name, cheerly on, courageous friends,   15

22. **dearest:** greatest
23. **vantage:** advantage
25. **meaner creatures:** i.e., men lesser in rank

5.3 Richard and Richmond and their supporters prepare for battle. Asleep, Richard and Richmond are each visited by the ghosts of those whom Richard has killed or has had killed; the ghosts curse Richard and cheer Richmond. In the morning Richmond and Richard address their troops before battle.

---

6. **knocks:** blows

A boar destroying "summer fields
and fruitful vines." (5.2.7–8)
From Cornelis Zweerts, *K. Zweerts Zede-en Zinnebeelden
over Koning Davids Harpzangen . . .* (1707).

To reap the harvest of perpetual peace
By this one bloody trial of sharp war.

OXFORD
Every man's conscience is a thousand men
To fight against this guilty homicide.

HERBERT
I doubt not but his friends will turn to us.   20

BLUNT
He hath no friends but what are friends for fear,
Which in his dearest need will fly from him.

RICHMOND
All for our vantage. Then, in God's name, march.
True hope is swift, and flies with swallow's wings;
Kings it makes gods, and meaner creatures kings.   25

All exit.

⌜Scene 3⌝

*Enter King Richard, in arms, with Norfolk, Ratcliffe, and
the Earl of Surrey, ⌜with Soldiers.⌝*

RICHARD
Here pitch our tent, even here in Bosworth field.
                ⌜*Soldiers begin to pitch the tent.*⌝
My lord of Surrey, why look you so sad?

SURREY
My heart is ten times lighter than my looks.

RICHARD
My lord of Norfolk—

NORFOLK   Here, most gracious liege.   5

RICHARD
Norfolk, we must have knocks, ha, must we not?

NORFOLK
We must both give and take, my loving lord.

RICHARD
Up with my tent!—Here will I lie tonight.

9. **all's . . . that:** i.e., it doesn't matter

12. **battalia:** main body of troops in a battle formation; **account:** reckoning

14. **adverse:** opposing; **want:** lack

16. **vantage . . . ground:** i.e., strategic advantages provided by the field of battle

17. **direction:** instruction

21. **fiery car:** i.e., the sun god's chariot (See below.)

26. **Limit:** appoint; **several charge:** particular command

27. **part:** divide; **just:** exact; **power:** army

30. **keeps:** is staying with

The sun god's "fiery car." (5.3.20–21)
From Hyginus, *Fabularum liber* . . . (1549).

But where tomorrow? Well, all's one for that.
Who hath descried the number of the traitors?   10
NORFOLK
Six or seven thousand is their utmost power.
RICHARD
Why, our battalia trebles that account.
Besides, the King's name is a tower of strength
Which they upon the adverse faction want.—
Up with the tent!—Come, noble gentlemen,   15
Let us survey the vantage of the ground.
Call for some men of sound direction;
Let's lack no discipline, make no delay,
For, lords, tomorrow is a busy day.
                    ⌜*The tent now in place,*⌝ *they exit.*

Enter Richmond, Sir William Brandon, Oxford,
Dorset, ⌜*Herbert, Blunt, and others who set up*
                Richmond's tent.⌝

RICHMOND
The weary sun hath made a golden set,   20
And by the bright ⟨track⟩ of his fiery car
Gives token of a goodly day tomorrow.—
Sir William Brandon, you shall bear my standard.—
Give me some ink and paper in my tent;
I'll draw the form and model of our battle,   25
Limit each leader to his several charge,
And part in just proportion our small power.—
My Lord of Oxford, you, Sir William Brandon,
And ⌜you,⌝ Sir Walter Herbert, stay with me.
The Earl of Pembroke keeps his regiment.—   30
Good Captain Blunt, bear my goodnight to him,
And by the second hour in the morning
Desire the Earl to see me in my tent.
Yet one thing more, good captain, do for me.
Where is Lord Stanley quartered, do you know?   35

36. **mista'en:** mistaken; **colors:** battle ensign
41. **make:** i.e., arrange
43. **needful:** indispensable
53. **beaver:** visor on the helmet (See below.); **easier:** more loosely fitting
57. **Use . . . sentinels:** i.e., choose careful men to be **sentinels**

A helmet with the beaver closed. (5.3.53)
From Henry Peacham, *Minerua Britanna* . . . (1612).

BLUNT
  Unless I have mista'en his colors much,
  Which well I am assured I have not done,
  His regiment lies half a mile, at least,
  South from the mighty power of the King.
RICHMOND
  If without peril it be possible,   40
  Sweet Blunt, make some good means to speak with
    him,
  And give him from me this most needful note.
                                   ⌜*He gives a paper.*⌝
BLUNT
  Upon my life, my lord, I'll undertake it,
  And so God give you quiet rest tonight.   45
RICHMOND
  Good night, good Captain Blunt.   ⌜*Blunt exits.*⌝
                                   Come, gentlemen,
  Let us consult upon tomorrow's business.
  Into my tent. The dew is raw and cold.
    ⌜*Richard, Brandon, Dorset, Herbert, and Oxford*⌝
         withdraw into the tent. ⌜*The others exit.*⌝

  Enter ⌜*to his tent*⌝ *Richard, Ratcliffe, Norfolk, and
              Catesby,* ⌜*with Soldiers.*⌝

RICHARD   What is 't o'clock?   50
CATESBY
  It's suppertime, my lord. It's nine o'clock.
RICHARD
  I will not sup tonight. Give me some ink and paper.
  What, is my beaver easier than it was,
  And all my armor laid into my tent?
CATESBY
  It is, my liege, and all things are in readiness.   55
RICHARD
  Good Norfolk, hie thee to thy charge.
  Use careful watch. Choose trusty [sentinels.]

63. **pursuivant-at-arms:** junior officer who attends a herald

64. **power:** army

67–68. **Give . . . watch:** perhaps, station a sentinel by my tent; or, perhaps, provide me with a watchlight, a candle marked so that it records the time as it melts

70. **staves:** plural of *staff,* the shaft of a lance

75. **cockshut time:** i.e., twilight

79. **wont:** accustomed

82. **watch:** stand watch, be alert

An army camp at night. (5.3.67–68)
From Jacobus a. Bruck, *Emblemata . . .* (1615).

NORFOLK   I go, my lord.

RICHARD
  Stir with the lark tomorrow, gentle Norfolk.

NORFOLK   I warrant you, my lord.   [*He exits.*]   60

RICHARD   Catesby.

⌜CATESBY⌝   My lord.

RICHARD   Send out a pursuivant-at-arms
  To Stanley's regiment. Bid him bring his power
  Before sunrising, lest his son George fall   65
  Into the blind cave of eternal night.   ⌜*Catesby exits.*⌝
  ⌜*To Soldiers.*⌝ Fill me a bowl of wine. Give me a
    watch.
  Saddle white Surrey for the field tomorrow.
  Look that my staves be sound and not too heavy.—   70
  Ratcliffe.

RATCLIFFE   My lord.

RICHARD
  Sawst thou the melancholy Lord Northumberland?

RATCLIFFE
  Thomas the Earl of Surrey and himself,
  Much about cockshut time, from troop to troop   75
  Went through the army cheering up the soldiers.

RICHARD
  So, I am satisfied. Give me a bowl of wine.
  I have not that alacrity of spirit
  Nor cheer of mind that I was wont to have.
                              ⌜*Wine is brought.*⌝
  Set it down. Is ink and paper ready?   80

RATCLIFFE
  It is, my lord.

RICHARD   Bid my guard watch. Leave me.
  Ratcliffe, about the mid of night come to my tent
  And help to arm me. Leave me, I say.
              Ratcliffe exits. ⌜*Richard sleeps in his tent,*
                      which is guarded by Soldiers.⌝

87. **father-in-law:** stepfather

89. **by attorney:** as a deputy

92. **flaky darkness breaks:** i.e., the darkness begins to break up

93. **season:** time

94. **battle:** battle array

96. **mortal-staring:** i.e., deadly

97. **would:** i.e., would like to do

99. **doubtful shock of arms:** i.e., battle of uncertain outcome   **shock:** encounter

101. **being seen:** i.e., I being seen; **brother:** i.e., stepbrother; **tender:** young

103. **leisure:** i.e., short period of leisure

104. **ceremonious:** showy; formal; punctilious

108. **speed:** prosper

110. **with:** i.e., against

111. **peise:** weigh

Enter ⌐Stanley, Earl of ⌐ Derby to Richmond in his tent.

STANLEY
  Fortune and victory sit on thy helm!   85
RICHMOND
  All comfort that the dark night can afford
  Be to thy person, noble father-in-law.
  Tell me, how fares our loving mother?
STANLEY
  I, by attorney, bless thee from thy mother,
  Who prays continually for Richmond's good.   90
  So much for that. The silent hours steal on,
  And flaky darkness breaks within the east.
  In brief, for so the season bids us be,
  Prepare thy battle early in the morning,
  And put thy fortune to the arbitrament   95
  Of bloody strokes and mortal-staring war.
  I, as I may—that which I would I cannot—
  With best advantage will deceive the time
  And aid thee in this doubtful shock of arms.
  But on thy side I may not be too forward,   100
  Lest, being seen, thy brother, tender George,
  Be executed in his father's sight.
  Farewell. The leisure and the fearful time
  Cuts off the ceremonious vows of love
  And ample interchange of sweet discourse,   105
  Which so-long-sundered friends should dwell upon.
  God give us leisure for these rites of love!
  Once more, adieu. Be valiant and speed well.
RICHMOND
  Good lords, conduct him to his regiment.
  I'll strive with troubled thoughts to take a nap,   110
  Lest leaden slumber peise me down tomorrow
  When I should mount with wings of victory.
  Once more, good night, kind lords and gentlemen.

116. **Thy . . . wrath:** Compare Psalm 2.9: "Thou shalt crush them with a scepter of iron. . . ."

118. **usurping . . . adversaries:** In this figure of speech, Richard's crime in usurping the crown is displaced onto his soldiers and thence unto their helmets.

121. **watchful:** sleepless, wakeful

123. **still:** always

124. **sit heavy on:** weigh down, oppress

131. **issue:** offspring

132. **my anointed body:** At his coronation, the King is anointed with holy oil.

134. **Tower:** In Shakespeare's *Henry VI, Part 3* (5.6), Richard kills Henry VI in the Tower of London. (See picture, page 130.)

⌜*All but Richmond leave his tent and*⌝ *exit.*
⌜*Richmond kneels.*⌝

O Thou, whose captain I account myself,
Look on my forces with a gracious eye.   115
Put in their hands Thy bruising irons of wrath,
That they may crush down with a heavy fall
The usurping helmets of our adversaries.
Make us Thy ministers of chastisement,
That we may praise Thee in the victory.   120
To Thee I do commend my watchful soul,
[Ere] I let fall the windows of mine eyes.
Sleeping and waking, O, defend me still!   [*Sleeps.*]

Enter the Ghost of young Prince Edward, son [*to*] *Harry
the Sixth.*

GHOST ⌜OF EDWARD,⌝ (*to Richard*)
Let me sit heavy on thy soul tomorrow.
Think how thou ⌜stabbed'st⌝ me in my prime of   125
     youth
At Tewkesbury. Despair therefore, and die!
(*To Richmond.*) Be cheerful, Richmond, for the
     wrongèd souls
Of butchered princes fight in thy behalf.   130
King Henry's issue, Richmond, comforts thee.
⌜*He exits.*⌝

Enter the Ghost of Henry the Sixth.

GHOST ⌜OF HENRY,⌝ (*to Richard*)
When I was mortal, my anointed body
By thee was punchèd full of deadly holes.
Think on the Tower and me. Despair and die!
Harry the Sixth bids thee despair and die.   135
(*To Richmond.*) Virtuous and holy, be thou conqueror.
Harry, that prophesied thou shouldst be king,
Doth comfort thee in thy sleep. Live and flourish.
⌜*He exits.*⌝

140. **fulsome:** filling, cloying; loathsome

143. **fall:** drop

154 SD–168 SD. **Enter the Ghosts of the two young Princes. . . . He exits:** During the printing of the Third Quarto (Q3), the appearance of the Princes' ghosts was moved to follow that of Hastings' ghost. Many editors accept the Q3 arrangement on the grounds that all the other ghosts appear in the order of their deaths and that in the play Hastings was executed before the Princes were assassinated. However, Q3 has no authority as a text, and good order was not necessarily good art in Shakespeare's day.

Enter the Ghost of Clarence.

GHOST ⌜OF CLARENCE, (*to Richard*)⌝
　Let me sit heavy in thy soul tomorrow,
　I, that was washed to death with fulsome wine,   140
　Poor Clarence, by thy guile betrayed to death.
　Tomorrow in the battle think on me,
　And fall thy edgeless sword. Despair and die!
　(*To Richmond.*) Thou offspring of the house of
　　Lancaster,   145
　The wrongèd heirs of York do pray for thee.
　Good angels guard thy battle. Live and flourish.
　　　　　　　　　　　　　　　　　　　　⌜*He exits.*⌝

Enter the Ghosts of Rivers, Grey, [and] Vaughan.

⌜GHOST OF RIVERS, (*to Richard*)⌝
　Let me sit heavy in thy soul tomorrow,
　Rivers, that died at Pomfret. Despair and die!
⌜GHOST OF⌝ GREY, ⌜(*to Richard*)⌝
　Think upon Grey, and let thy soul despair!   150
⌜GHOST OF⌝ VAUGHAN, ⌜(*to Richard*)⌝
　Think upon Vaughan, and with guilty fear
　Let fall thy lance. Despair and die!
ALL, (*to Richmond*)
　Awake, and think our wrongs in Richard's bosom
　[Will] conquer him. Awake, and win the day.
　　　　　　　　　　　　　　　　　　　　⌜*They exit.*⌝

Enter the Ghosts of the two young Princes.

⌜GHOSTS OF PRINCES,⌝ (*to Richard*)
　Dream on thy cousins smothered in the Tower.   155
　Let us be lead within thy bosom, Richard,
　And weigh thee down to ruin, shame, and death.
　Thy nephews' souls bid thee despair and die.
　(*To Richmond.*) Sleep, Richmond, sleep in peace
　　and wake in joy.   160

161. **annoy:** harm, injury

179. **tyranny:** cruelty

183. **Fainting:** losing heart

184–85. **I . . . aid:** This much-debated line has not been satisfactorily explained.

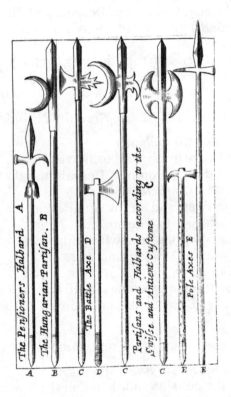

Halberds and partisans. (1.2.0; 5.1.0 SDD)
From Louis de Gaya, *A treatise of the arms* . . . (1678).

Good angels guard thee from the boar's annoy.
Live, and beget a happy race of kings.
Edward's unhappy sons do bid thee flourish.

⌜*They exit.*⌝

Enter the Ghost of Hastings.

GHOST ⌜OF HASTINGS, (*to Richard*)⌝
Bloody and guilty, guiltily awake,
And in a bloody battle end thy days.   165
Think on Lord Hastings. Despair and die!
(*To Richmond.*) Quiet, untroubled soul, awake, awake.
Arm, fight, and conquer for fair England's sake.

⌜*He exits.*⌝

Enter the Ghost of Lady Anne his wife.

⌜GHOST OF ANNE, (*to Richard*)⌝
Richard, thy wife, that wretched Anne thy wife,
That never slept a quiet hour with thee,   170
Now fills thy sleep with perturbations.
Tomorrow, in the battle, think on me,
And fall thy edgeless sword. Despair and die!
(*To Richmond.*) Thou quiet soul, sleep thou a quiet
    sleep.   175
Dream of success and happy victory.
Thy adversary's wife doth pray for thee.   ⌜*She exits.*⌝

Enter the Ghost of Buckingham.

⌜GHOST OF BUCKINGHAM, (*to Richard*)⌝
The first was I that helped thee to the crown;
The last was I that felt thy tyranny.
O, in the battle think on Buckingham,   180
And die in terror of thy guiltiness.
Dream on, dream on, of bloody deeds and death.
Fainting, despair; despairing, yield thy breath.
(*To Richmond.*) I died for hope ere I could lend
    thee aid,   185

190. **Soft:** i.e., wait a moment
197. **fly:** flee; **Great reason why:** i.e., there is an important reason to flee from myself
199. **Wherefore:** why
205. **several:** separate, different
211. **the bar:** the bar of justice
216. **Methought:** i.e., it seemed to me
217. **threat:** i.e., threaten

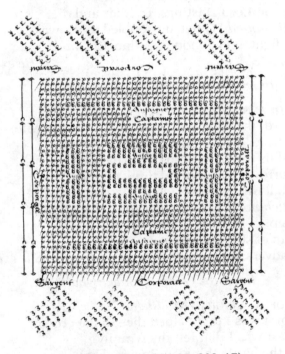

A battle formation. (5.3.25, 309–17)
From Henry Barrett, *A brief book unto private captains . . .* (1562).

But cheer thy heart, and be thou not dismayed.
God and good angels fight on Richmond's side,
And Richard [fall] in height of all his pride.
⌜*He exits.*⌝ *Richard starteth up out of a dream.*

RICHARD
Give me another horse! Bind up my wounds!
Have mercy, Jesu!—Soft, I did but dream.   190
O coward conscience, how dost thou afflict me!
The lights burn blue; it is now dead midnight.
Cold fearful drops stand on my trembling flesh.
What do I fear? Myself? There's none else by.
Richard loves Richard, that is, I [am] I.   195
Is there a murderer here? No. Yes, I am.
Then fly! What, from myself? Great reason why:
Lest I revenge. What, myself upon myself?
Alack, I love myself. Wherefore? For any good
That I myself have done unto myself?   200
O, no. Alas, I rather hate myself
For hateful deeds committed by myself.
I am a villain. Yet I lie; I am not.
Fool, of thyself speak well. Fool, do not flatter.
My conscience hath a thousand several tongues,   205
And every tongue brings in a several tale,
And every tale condemns me for a villain.
Perjury, perjury, in the highest degree;
Murder, stern murder, in the direst degree;
All several sins, all used in each degree,   210
Throng to the bar, crying all "Guilty, guilty!"
I shall despair. There is no creature loves me,
And if I die no soul will pity me.
And wherefore should they, since that I myself
Find in myself no pity to myself?   215
Methought the souls of all that I had murdered
Came to my tent, and every one did threat
Tomorrow's vengeance on the head of Richard.

220. **Zounds:** i.e., by God's wounds
228. **shadows:** illusions, phantoms, dreams
232. **proof:** proof armor, or impenetrable armor
237. **Cry mercy:** i.e., I'm sorry; **watchful:** wakeful
240. **fairest-boding:** i.e., most promising

St. George kills the fiery dragon. (5.3.285, 371–72)
From [Jacobus de Voragine], *Here begynneth the legende
named in latyn legenda aurea . . .* (1493).

Enter Ratcliffe.

RATCLIFFE My lord.
RICHARD Zounds, who is there?   220
RATCLIFFE
  Ratcliffe, my lord, 'tis I. The early village cock
  Hath twice done salutation to the morn.
  Your friends are up and buckle on their armor.
RICHARD
  O Ratcliffe, I have dreamed a fearful dream!
  What think'st thou, will our friends prove all true?   225
RATCLIFFE
  No doubt, my lord.
RICHARD   O Ratcliffe, I fear, I fear.
RATCLIFFE
  Nay, good my lord, be not afraid of shadows.
RICHARD
  By the apostle Paul, shadows tonight
  Have struck more terror to the soul of Richard   230
  Than can the substance of ten thousand soldiers
  Armed in proof and led by shallow Richmond.
  'Tis not yet near day. Come, go with me.
  Under our tents I'll play the eavesdropper
  To see if any mean to shrink from me.   235
                        [*Richard and Ratcliffe*] *exit.*

  Enter the Lords to Richmond, [*in his tent.*]

LORDS Good morrow, Richmond.
RICHMOND
  Cry mercy, lords and watchful gentlemen,
  That you have ta'en a tardy sluggard here.
A LORD How have you slept, my lord?
RICHMOND
  The sweetest sleep and fairest-boding dreams   240
  That ever entered in a drowsy head
  Have I since your departure had, my lords.

245. **cried on:** invoked

250. **direction:** instruction (to his troops)

252. **leisure:** i.e., short period of leisure

257. **except:** excluded

261. **raised:** elevated in rank; **in blood:** through bloodshed

265. **foul stone:** foul as opposed to a precious stone or gem; **foil:** thin sheet of metal placed under a gem to increase its brilliancy

266. **chair:** throne; **set:** (1) seated; (2) fixed (as a jewel on its **foil**)

269. **ward:** protect

273. **fat:** wealth (Compare Genesis 45.18: "the fat of the land.") **your . . . hire:** i.e., the hire for your efforts

Methought their souls whose bodies Richard
  murdered
Came to my tent and cried on victory.   245
I promise you, my soul is very jocund
In the remembrance of so fair a dream.
How far into the morning is it, lords?
A LORD Upon the stroke of four.
RICHMOND, ⌜*leaving the tent*⌝
Why, then 'tis time to arm and give direction.   250

     His oration to his soldiers.

More than I have said, loving countrymen,
The leisure and enforcement of the time
Forbids to dwell upon. Yet remember this:
God, and our good cause, fight upon our side.
The prayers of holy saints and wrongèd souls,   255
Like high-reared bulwarks, stand before our faces.
Richard except, those whom we fight against
Had rather have us win than him they follow.
For what is he they follow? Truly, gentlemen,
A bloody tyrant and a homicide;   260
One raised in blood, and one in blood established;
One that made means to come by what he hath,
And slaughtered those that were the means to help
  him;
A base foul stone, made precious by the foil   265
Of England's chair, where he is falsely set;
One that hath ever been God's enemy.
Then if you fight against God's enemy,
God will, in justice, ward you as his soldiers.
If you do sweat to put a tyrant down,   270
You sleep in peace, the tyrant being slain.
If you do fight against your country's foes,
Your country's fat shall pay your pains the hire.
If you do fight in safeguard of your wives,
Your wives shall welcome home the conquerors.   275

277. **quits:** i.e., repay

279. **Advance your standards:** lift up your flags

280. **For:** as for

280–81. **the ransom . . . corpse:** i.e., if I am defeated the only ransom that I will offer the enemy is my cold corpse (Usually, in medieval warfare, prior to battle noblemen settled on the price of the ransom they would pay to redeem themselves should they be captured by the enemy. See the Folger edition of *Henry V,* longer note on **ransom** [3.5.63], page 241.)

282. **gain:** profit

285. **Saint George:** traditional English war cry (St. George was adopted as England's patron saint in the time of Edward III. See picture, page 288.)

286. **as touching:** concerning

291. **Tell the clock:** i.e., count the strokes of the clock; **calendar:** almanac

294. **he:** i.e., it (the sun); **by the book:** i.e., according to the almanac

295. **braved:** adorned, made splendid

If you do free your children from the sword,
Your children's children quits it in your age.
Then, in the name of God and all these rights,
Advance your standards; draw your willing swords.
For me, the ransom of my bold attempt   280
Shall be this cold corpse on the Earth's cold face,
But if I thrive, the gain of my attempt
The least of you shall share his part thereof.
Sound drums and trumpets boldly and cheerfully.
God, and Saint George, Richmond, and victory!   285
                                   ⌜*They exit.*⌝

        Enter King Richard, Ratcliffe, ⌜*and Soldiers.*⌝

RICHARD
What said Northumberland as touching Richmond?
RATCLIFFE
That he was never trainèd up in arms.
RICHARD
He said the truth. And what said Surrey then?
RATCLIFFE
He smiled and said "The better for our purpose."
RICHARD
He was in the right, and so indeed it is.   290
                              The clock striketh.
Tell the clock there. Give me a calendar.
                    ⌜*He looks in an almanac.*⌝
Who saw the sun today?
RATCLIFFE   Not I, my lord.
RICHARD
Then he disdains to shine, for by the book
He should have braved the east an hour ago.   295
A black day will it be to somebody.
Ratcliffe!
RATCLIFFE
My lord.
RICHARD   The sun will [not] be seen today.

301. **would these dewy . . . ground:** i.e., wish the dew were off the ground

304. **sadly:** gravely, mournfully

305. **foe . . . field:** enemy display themselves on the battlefield

306. **Caparison:** put trappings on

307. **power:** army

309. **battle:** battle formation (See page 286.)

310. **foreward:** vanguard; **drawn . . . length:** i.e., stretched out in a line

311. **horse:** cavalry; **foot:** infantry

315. **directed:** i.e., deployed, positioned; **we:** i.e., I

316. **main battle:** i.e., main part of the troop formation; **puissance:** power

317. **wingèd with . . . horse:** flanked by our best cavalry

320. **direction:** i.e., battle plan (literally, order to be carried out)

322. **Jockey:** i.e., Johnny (Norfolk was named John.)

323. **Dickon:** Dick, i.e., Richard; **bought and sold:** perhaps, betrayed; or, perhaps, tricked

325. **charge:** command

The sky doth frown and lour upon our army. 300
I would these dewy tears were from the ground.
Not shine today? Why, what is that to me
More than to Richmond, for the selfsame heaven
That frowns on me looks sadly upon him.

Enter Norfolk.

NORFOLK
Arm, arm, my lord. The foe vaunts in the field. 305
RICHARD
Come, bustle, bustle. Caparison my horse.—
Call up Lord Stanley; bid him bring his power.—
I will lead forth my soldiers to the plain,
And thus my battle shall be orderèd:
My foreward shall be drawn out all in length, 310
Consisting equally of horse and foot;
Our archers shall be placèd in the midst.
John Duke of Norfolk, Thomas Earl of Surrey,
Shall have the leading of this foot and horse.
They thus directed, we will follow 315
In the main battle, whose puissance on either side
Shall be well wingèd with our chiefest horse.
This, and Saint George to [boot]!—What think'st
    thou, Norfolk?
NORFOLK
A good direction, warlike sovereign. 320
                    He sheweth him a paper.
This found I on my tent this morning.
⌜RICHARD *reads*⌝
    Jockey of Norfolk, be not so bold.
    For Dickon thy master is bought and sold.
A thing devisèd by the enemy.—
Go, gentlemen, every man unto his charge. 325
Let not our babbling dreams affright our souls.
Conscience is but a word that cowards use,
Devised at first to keep the strong in awe.

330. **Join:** i.e., join battle

332. **inferred:** i.e., said (literally, related, mentioned)

333. **cope:** meet in the shock of battle; **withal:** with

335. **lackey:** hanger-on, camp follower

336. **o'ercloyèd:** overly full, satiated

340. **restrain:** i.e., forbid your having; **distain:** stain, defile

342. **mother's cost:** The allegation that Richard's mother supported Richmond in Brittany arises from a misprint ("mother" for "brother," i.e., brother-in-law, the Duke of Burgundy) in the 1587 edition of Holinshed's *Chronicles*. See longer note, page 306.

344. **overshoes in snow:** i.e., as one feels when the snow comes in over one's shoes

346. **overweening:** arrogant, presumptuous

348. **fond:** foolish

349. **means:** i.e., means of survival

352–54. **our fathers . . . thumped:** a reference to the victories of Edward III, the Black Prince, and Henry V over the northern French in the Hundred Years' War of the fourteenth and early fifteenth centuries **bobbed:** pommeled, buffeted

355. **record:** i.e., historical record (pronounced **recòrd**)

361. **to the head:** i.e., until the arrowhead touches the bent bow

Our strong arms be our conscience, swords our law.
March on. Join bravely. Let us to it pell mell,　　　330
If not to heaven, then hand in hand to hell.

His oration to his army.

What shall I say more than I have inferred?
Remember whom you are to cope withal,
A sort of vagabonds, rascals, and runaways,
A scum of Bretons and base lackey peasants,　　　335
Whom their o'ercloyèd country vomits forth
To desperate adventures and assured destruction.
You sleeping safe, they bring to you unrest;
You having lands and blessed with beauteous wives,
They would restrain the one, distain the other.　　　340
And who doth lead them but a paltry fellow,
Long kept in Brittany at our mother's cost,
A milksop, one that never in his life
Felt so much cold as overshoes in snow?
Let's whip these stragglers o'er the seas again,　　　345
Lash hence these overweening rags of France,
These famished beggars weary of their lives,
Who, but for dreaming on this fond exploit,
For want of means, poor rats, had hanged
　　themselves.　　　350
If we be conquered, let men conquer us,
And not these bastard Bretons, whom our fathers
Have in their own land beaten, bobbed, and
　　thumped,
And in record left them the heirs of shame.　　　355
Shall these enjoy our lands, lie with our wives,
Ravish our daughters?　　　　　[*Drum afar off.*]
　　　　　　Hark, I hear their drum.
Fight, gentlemen of England.—Fight, bold
　　yeomen.—　　　360
Draw, archers; draw your arrows to the head.—

363. **Amaze the welkin:** terrify the sky

364. **power:** army

365. **deny:** refuse

372. **spleen:** angry courage (For Saint George and the dragon, see page 288.)

373. **Upon:** set upon, attack

5.4 In battle Richard has been unhorsed and faces defeat.

───────────

0 SD. **Alarum:** call to arms; **Excursions:** sorties

3. **Daring . . . danger:** perhaps, challenging whatever enemy he meets to fight to the death

Spur your proud horses hard, and ride in blood.
Amaze the welkin with your broken staves.—

[*Enter a Messenger.*]

What says Lord Stanley? Will he bring his power?
MESSENGER   My lord, he doth deny to come.   365
RICHARD   Off with his son George's head!
NORFOLK
My lord, the enemy is past the marsh.
After the battle let George Stanley die.
RICHARD
A thousand hearts are great within my bosom.
Advance our standards. Set upon our foes.   370
Our ancient word of courage, fair Saint George,
Inspire us with the spleen of fiery dragons.
Upon them! Victory sits on our helms.

They exit.

⌜Scene 4⌝
Alarum. Excursions. Enter ⌜*Norfolk, with Soldiers, and*⌝
Catesby.

CATESBY
Rescue, my lord of Norfolk, rescue, rescue!
The King enacts more wonders than a man,
Daring an opposite to every danger.
His horse is slain, and all on foot he fights,
Seeking for Richmond in the throat of death.   5
Rescue, fair lord, or else the day is lost.
⌜*Norfolk exits with Soldiers.*⌝

[*Alarums.*] *Enter Richard.*

RICHARD
A horse, a horse, my kingdom for a horse!
CATESBY
Withdraw, my lord. I'll help you to a horse.

9. **Slave:** used as a term of contempt (perhaps because Catesby has urged Richard to withdraw); **cast:** throw of the dice

10. **stand ... die:** accept the risk of one of the dice (a **die**) showing a losing number

5.5   Richmond kills Richard and is given the crown that he will wear as King Henry VII. His coming marriage to Elizabeth of York is hailed as the end of the Wars of the Roses and the beginning of a time of "smooth-faced peace."

---

4. **royalty:** crown
6. **withal:** with
12. **name:** rank, title

Richmond as Henry VII.
From John Speed, *The theatre of the empire of Great Britaine ...* (1627 [i.e., 1631]).

RICHARD
  Slave, I have set my life upon a cast,
  And I will stand the hazard of the die.   10
  I think there be six Richmonds in the field;
  Five have I slain today instead of him.
  A horse, a horse, my kingdom for a horse!
                                    ⌜*They exit.*⌝

                    ⌜Scene 5⌝
  Alarum. Enter Richard and Richmond. They fight.
  Richard is slain. Then retreat being sounded, ⌜Richmond
  exits, and Richard's body is removed.⌝ [Flourish.] Enter
  Richmond, ⌜Stanley, Earl of⌝ Derby, bearing the crown,
       with other Lords, ⌜and Soldiers.⌝

RICHMOND
  God and your arms be praised, victorious friends!
  The day is ours; the bloody dog is dead.
STANLEY, ⌜*offering him the crown*⌝
  Courageous Richmond, well hast thou acquit thee.
  Lo, here this long-usurpèd royalty
  From the dead temples of this bloody wretch   5
  Have I plucked off, to grace thy brows withal.
  Wear it, enjoy it, and make much of it.
RICHMOND
  Great God of heaven, say amen to all!
  But tell me, is young George Stanley living?
STANLEY
  He is, my lord, and safe in Leicester town,   10
  Whither, if it please you, we may now withdraw us.
RICHMOND
  What men of name are slain on either side?
[STANLEY]
  John, Duke of Norfolk, [Walter], Lord ⌜Ferrers,⌝
  Sir Robert Brakenbury, and Sir William Brandon.

18. **as . . . sacrament:** i.e., as I have vowed upon the Eucharist

19. **white rose . . . red:** the respective emblems of the families of York and Lancaster

20. **conjunction:** union (an astrological metaphor)

21. **That:** i.e., **heaven,** or, perhaps, the heavens, the stars

28. **Divided . . . division:** Editors sometimes emend the word **Divided,** but Siemon notes that the "divided house" of York and Lancaster has in fact led to multiple divisions: "faction against faction, brother against brother, generation against generation."

29. **Elizabeth:** daughter of Edward IV and Queen Elizabeth

30. **succeeders:** heirs

35. **Abate:** blunt

36. **reduce:** bring back

37. **And make:** and that would make

38. **increase:** prosperity

40. **Now:** now that; **civil wounds:** wounds made in battles among fellow countrymen; **stopped:** closed

RICHMOND
    Inter their bodies as ⌈becomes⌉ their births.   15
    Proclaim a pardon to the soldiers fled
    That in submission will return to us.
    And then, as we have ta'en the sacrament,
    We will unite the white rose and the red;
    Smile heaven upon this fair conjunction,   20
    That long have frowned upon their enmity.
    What traitor hears me and says not "Amen"?
    England hath long been mad and scarred herself:
    The brother blindly shed the brother's blood;
    The father rashly slaughtered his own son;   25
    The son, compelled, been butcher to the sire.
    All this divided York and Lancaster,
    Divided in their dire division.
    O, now let Richmond and Elizabeth,
    The true succeeders of each royal house,   30
    By God's fair ordinance conjoin together,
    And let their heirs, God, if Thy will be so,
    Enrich the time to come with smooth-faced peace,
    With smiling plenty and fair prosperous days.
    Abate the edge of traitors, gracious Lord,   35
    That would reduce these bloody days again
    And make poor England weep in streams of blood.
    Let them not live to taste this land's increase,
    That would with treason wound this fair land's peace.
    Now civil wounds are stopped, peace lives again.   40
    That she may long live here, God say amen.
                           [They exit.]

RICHARD THE IIJ,
KING OF ENGLAND,
And FRANCE,
LORD OF IRELAND, &c.

Ambition's like vnto a quenchlesse thirst:
Ambition Angels threw from Heauen to Hell,
Ambition (that infernall Hag) accurst,
Ambitiously made me aspire, rebell :
Ambition, that damned Necromanticke Spell,
Made me clime proud, with shame to tumble down,
By bloody murther I did all expell,
Whose right, or might, debard me from the Crown.
My smiles, my gifts, my fauours, or my frowne,
Were fain'd, corrupt, vile flattry, death and spite.
By cruell Tyranny I gat renowne,
Till Heau'ns iust Iudge me iustly did requite.

By blood I won, by blood I lost the throne.
Detested liu'd; dy'd ; lou'd, bewail'd of none.

"Ambition's like vnto a quenchlesse thirst . . ."
From John Taylor, *All the workes of* . . . (1630).

Longer Notes

1.1.105. **alone:** These lines also appear in subsequent quartos (the Third Quarto through the Sixth, which are merely reprints of their predecessors) and also in the First Folio, which elsewhere sometimes reproduces spurious readings that first appear in later quartos, such as the second quarto. Editors have kept these lines, in spite of their metrical deficiency, on the argument that the lines may first have appeared in copies of the First Quarto as stop-press corrections (see next paragraph), even though no copies of the First Quarto now survive with these lines in them. Because there is no evidence of anything like such extensive stop-press correction in the copies that do survive, this argument seems desperate. Because the two lines may have been introduced by the printer of the Second Quarto and retained in the Folio through an oversight, we omit them from our text.

(Stop-press corrections were corrections introduced into a printed text during the course of printing the bundle of sheets that made up a part of a book. Because paper was so expensive, the printer would not discard the sheets he had printed before noticing the need for correction. Thus, when the books were sold, some would contain the corrections in a given sheet, some not. Editors therefore must compare the various surviving copies of books printed in this period to discover such differences among them.)

1.3.139. **Poor Clarence did forsake his father Warwick:** As Shakespeare told the story of Clarence in his earlier play, *Henry VI, Part 3,* King Edward's decision to marry the Lady Grey made a laughingstock of Warwick (who was at the time negotiating a marriage between Edward and the sister of the king of France). Warwick therefore shifted his allegiance to King Henry VI. Clarence, too, was appalled by Edward's marriage, and, when Edward arranged profitable marriages for his new wife's relatives rather than for his own brothers, Clarence deserted Edward and joined Warwick and the Lancastrians, marrying one of Warwick's daughters. Later, Clarence's brotherly feelings led him to break his oath to Warwick and the Lancastrians and once again fight on Edward's side, joining his brothers Edward and Richard in the stabbing of Henry's son, Prince Edward.

2.4.1, 2. Stony Stratford, Northampton: The Archbishop is here describing the progress of Prince Edward and his escort toward London. The Folio, which we follow, might seem questionable here because it presents the Prince and his party proceeding to London by way of, first, Stony Stratford and then Northampton; Northampton is, in fact, farther from London and the court than Stony Stratford. The Folio is nevertheless correct in reproducing its source, which explains, as the play does not, that Richard forced the Prince and his entourage to backtrack. Whoever transposed these place names in the quarto so as to have the Prince proceed to London by way of first Northampton and then Stony Stratford had an accurate knowledge of geography, but not of the chronicle sources.

5.3.342. mother's cost: The play's reproduction of this misprint is one of several pieces of evidence showing that of the many versions of Sir Thomas More's "The History of King Richard the Third," Shakespeare depended primarily on that printed in Raphael Holinshed's *Chronicles of England, Scotland, and Ireland* (2nd edition, 1587). For More's position regarding Richard, see "Shakespeare's *Richard III*," page xv, above.

Textual Notes

The reading of the present text appears to the left of the square bracket. Unless otherwise noted, the reading to the left of the bracket is from **F**, the First Folio text (upon which this edition is based). Two exceptions are the passages (3.1.1–169 and 5.3.52–the end) where the present text is based on **Q**, the First Quarto of 1597. For those passages the reading to the left of the bracket is, unless otherwise noted, from **Q**. The earliest sources of readings not in **F** or **Q** are indicated as follows: **Q2** is the Second Quarto of 1598; **Q3** is the Third Quarto of 1602; **Q4** is the Fourth Quarto of 1605; **Q5** is the Fifth Quarto of 1612; **Q6** is the Sixth Quarto of 1622; **Ed.** is an earlier editor of Shakespeare, beginning with the anonymous editor(s) of the Second Folio (1632). No sources are given for emendations of punctuation or for corrections of obvious typographical errors, like turned letters that produce no known word. **SD** means stage direction; **SP** means speech prefix; **uncorr.** means the first or uncorrected state of **F** or **Q**; **corr.** means the second or corrected state of **F** or **Q**; ~ stands in place of a word already quoted before the square bracket; ʌ indicates the omission of a punctuation mark.

1.1   1.1] F; *not in* Qq, which have no act or scene divisions   1. SP RICHARD] Ed.; *omit* F, Q   13. lute] F; loue Q   17. wanton] wonton F; wanton Q   26. see] F; spie Q   32. inductions] F; inductious Q   38. upʌ] ~: F; ~, Q   40. murderer] F; murtherers Q   42. SD *Enter . . . Brakenbury*] Ed.; *Enter Clarence, and Brakenbury, guarded.* F; *Enter Clarence with a gard of men.* Q   43. day] F; dayes Q   46. appointed] F; Q *corr.;* appo nted Q *uncorr.*   48 *and hereafter to 3.1.18.* SP RICHARD] F;

309

Glo. Q   54. should be] F; shalbe Q   56. for] Q; but F
65. Hath] F; Haue Q   68. she∧] ~. F; ~, Q   69. tem-
pers] Q; tempts Q2, 4–6, F; temps Q3; this] Q   this
harsh F   71. Woodeville] Ed.; Wooduile Q; *Woodeulle*
F   75. secure] F; is securde Q   79. to her] Q; *omit* F
his] Q; her F   87. our] F; this Q   91. your] F; his Q
96. jealous] F (iealious)   105. to] F; he Q   105. alone.]
Q; alone. *Bro.* What one my Lord? | *Glo.* Her husband
knaue, wouldst thou betray me? Q2–6, F   106. do] F
only   118. else] F; *omit* Q   120. SD *Clarence*] F (*Clar.*),
Q   128. the] Q1–2; this Q3–8, F   136. eagles] F; Eagle
Q   137. prey] Q; play F   142. Saint] F (S.)   142. John]
F; Paul Q   142. that] F; this Q   146. Where] F; What Q

1.2.   0. SD F; *Enter Lady Anne with the hearse of
Harry the 6.* Q   1. SP ANNE] F; *Lady An.* Q   1. load]
F; lo Q   11. hand] F; hands Q   12. wounds] F; holes
Q   13. these] F; those Q   15. O, cursèd . . . holes] F;
Curst . . . fatall holes Q   16. Cursèd the] F; Curst be
the Q   17. F *only*   Cursèd] Cnrsed F   20. wolves, to
spiders] F; adders, spiders Q   26. F *only*   28. More]
F; As Q   29. Than . . . young] F; As . . . poore Q   32.
this] F; the Q   33. SD *Enter . . . Gloucester*] F; *Enter
Glocester.* Q 35 *and hereafter in this scene.* SP ANNE] F;
La. Q   37. Villains] F; Villaine Q   Saint] Ed.; QF (S.)
40. stand] Q; Stand'st F   42. Saint] F (S.)   62. deeds]
F; deed Q   inhuman] F, Q (inhumane)   74. nor law]
F; no law Q   77. truth] F; troth Q   80. crimes] F; euils
Q   82. a] Q; *omit* F   83. Of] F; For Q   90. shalt] F;
shouldst Q   92. That] F; Which Q   94. Then . . . slain]
F; Why then they are not dead Q   98. hands] F; hand Q
100. murd'rous] F; bloudy Q   104. That] F; Which Q
106. That . . . dream'st] F; Which . . . dreamt Q   108.
you] F (ye); yea Q   112. better] F; fitter Q   125. some-
thing] F; somewhat Q   129. wast] F; art Q   131. that]
F; which Q   133. live] F; rest Q   135. rend] Q, F (rent)
137. not . . . that] F; neuer . . . sweet Q   138. it] F; them

Q 139. sun] F (Sunne); sonne Q 145. thee] F; you Q
147. killed] F; slew Q 148. thee] F (the) 151. He] F;
Go to, he Q thee] F; you Q 155. SP RICHARD] *Rieh.* F;
Glo. Q 157. SD *spits at him.*] F; *Shee spitteth at him.*
Q 169. aspects] F; aspect Q 170–82. F *only* 184.
smoothing] F; soothing Q word] F; words Q 187.
SD F *only* 188. lip] F; lips Q it was] F; they were Q
192. breast] F; bosome Q 195. SD F *only* 196. for . . .
Henry] F; twas I that kild your husband Q 198–99.
stabbed young Edward] F; kild King Henry Q 200.
SD F; *Here she lets fall the sword.* Q 203. thy] F; the
Q 206. That] F; Tush that Q 208. This] F; That Q
214. was man] Q; man was F, Q3–6 217. shalt thou]
F; shall you Q 220. SP Q (*Glo.*); *not in* F 221. Q (*La.*);
not in F 222. my] F; this Q 225. servant] F; suppliant
Q 229. may] F; would Q you] F; thee Q 230. most]
F; more Q 231. House] F; place Q 244. SD F; *Exit.*
Q 245. SP GENTLEMAN] F (*Gent.*); *Glo.* Sirs take vp the
corse. | *Ser.* Q 246. SD F; *Exeunt. manet Gl.* Q, *1 line*
later 253. my] F; her Q 256. no friends] F; nothing
Q at all] Q; withall F, Q3–6 258. her,] ~? F 267.
abase] F; debase Q 271. halts] F; halt Q misshapen]
F; vnshapen Q 277. a] F; some Q

1.3. 0. SD *Queen Elizabeth*] Ed.; *the Queene Mother*
F; *Queene* Q *Lord Grey*] F; *Gray* Q 4. it∧ ill,] F, Q2–6;
~, ~ ∧ Q 6. with] F, Q2–6; *omit* Q 6. eyes] F; words Q
7 *and hereafter.* SP QUEEN ELIZABETH] Ed.; *Qu.* F, Q on]
F; of Q 7. me?] Q; me? | If he were dead, what would
betide on me? F 8. SP GREY] F; *Ry.* Q 9. harms] F;
harme Q 18. comes . . . Lord] F; come . . . Lords Q;
comes . . . Lords Q3–6 20 *and hereafter in this scene.*
SP STANLEY] Ed.; *Der.* F; *Dar.* Q 21. lord] F (L.); Lo:
Q 21. Derby,] ~. F 22. prayer] F; praiers Q 28. on]
F; in Q 31. SP QUEEN ELIZABETH] F (*Qu.*); *Ry.* Q 33.
Are come] F; Came Q 34. What] F, Q3–6; With Q 37.
Ay, madam] F; Madame we did Q 38, 39. Between]

F; Betwixt Q   42. height] F; highest Q   42. SD *Rich-*
ard] F; *Glocester* Q   44. is it] F; are they Q   45. That]
Thar F; That Q   48. look] F; speake Q   49. deceive]
F; dcceiue Q   54. With] F; By Q   55. SP GREY] F; *Ry.*
Q   55. who] F; whom Q   60. Grace] F; person Q   65.
on] F; of Q   68. That] F; Which Q   68. action] F;
actions Q   69. children, brothers] F; kindred, brother
Q   70. that . . . ground] F; that thereby he may gather
| The ground of your ill will and to remoue it Q   73.
Jack] Iaeke F; Iacke Q   79. we] Q; I F   83. while great
promotions] F; whilst many faire promotions Q   94.
mean] F; cause Q   96. lord, for—] F; Lord. Q   101.
desert] F; deserts Q   102. ay] F (I); yea Q   105. and] F
only   110. Of] F; With Q   110. that oft I] F; I often Q
113. so baited . . . stormèd] F; thus taunted . . . baited
Q   113. SD *1 line later* F; *placed as in* Q; *Queen*] F; *Qu.*
Q   115–30. SP QUEEN MARGARET] Q (*Qu. Mar.*); *Mar.* or
Margaret. F   115. Him] F; thee Q   118. Q *only*   119.
avouch 't] F; auouch Q   120. F *only*   122. do] F *only*
123. killed'st] F; slewest Q   125, 130, 140. ay] F (I); yea
Q   129. spent] F; spilt Q   129. own] owue F; owne Q
135. you] F; yours Q   136. this] F; now Q   147. Hie] F
(High)   147. this] F; the Q   151. sovereign] F; lawfull
Q   154. thereof] F; of it Q   157. you may] F; may you
Q   159. As] Ed.; A F, Q   164. of] F (off)   165. am] F;
being Q   172–74. F *only*   178. This] F; The Q   183.
scorns] F; scorne Q   202. Should] F; Could Q   206.
Though] F; If Q   208, 210. that] F; which Q   210. our]
F; my Q   214. death] F; losse Q   223. his] F; your Q
226. thee?] F; ~∧ Q   237. while] F; whilest Q   242.
heavy mother's] F; mothers heauy Q   244. detested—]
F; detested & c. Q   249. I . . . mercy, then] F; Then I . . .
mercy Q   did think] F; had thought Q   259. day] F;
time Q   260. this] F; that Q   275. blasts] F, Q2–6; blast
Q   279. touches] F; toucheth Q   280. Ay] F (I); Yea Q
283 *and hereafter in this scene.* SP QUEEN MARGARET] Q;

Mar. F   289. is] F; was Q   290. Peace, peace] F *corr.;*
Peвce, peace F *uncorr.;* Haue done Q   294. my hopes
by you] F; by you my hopes Q   296. that] F; my Q
297. Have done, have done] F; Haue done Q   298. kiss]
kisse F *corr.;* kissc F *uncorr.*   300. noble] F; Princely Q
302. compass] Q; eompasse F   305. think] F; belieue
Q   307. take heed] F; beware Q   310. rankle to the] F;
rackle thee to Q   321. to] F; of Q   322. yours] F; your
Q   323. SP BUCKINGHAM] F; *Hast.* Q   323. an] F; on Q
324. muse why] F; wonder Q   327. to her] F *only*   328.
SP QUEEN ELIZABETH] Q (*Qu.*); *Mar.* F   329. Yet . . . her]
F; But . . . this Q   334. thereof] F; of it Q   337. SD F
only, 3 words later in F   338. SD F *only*   340. yours] F;
you Q   340. gracious] F; noble Q   341. lords] Q (*Lo:*);
Lord F   342. I . . . me] F; we . . . vs Q   343. We wait
upon] F; Madame we will attend Q   343. SD *Exeunt all
but Gloster* F; *Exeunt man. Ri.* Q   344. begin] F; began
Q   345. abroach] abroaeh F; abroach Q   347. who
. . . cast] F; whom . . . laid Q   349. Derby, Hastings]
F; Hastings, Darby Q   350. tell them 'tis] F; say it is
Q   352. it] F; me Q   353. Dorset] F; Vaughan Q   357.
odd old . . . forth] F; old odde . . . out Q   358. SD F;
Enter Executioners Q, *1 line later*   361. thing] F; deede
Q   362, 370. SP MURDERER] Ed.; *Vil.* F; *Execu.* Q   364.
SP RICHARD] *Ric.* F *corr.;* *Riu.* F *uncorr.*   364. Well] F;
It was well Q   370. Tut, tut] F; Tush feare not Q   372.
go] F; come Q   373. fall] F; drop Q   375. straight] F
only   376–77. F *only*   377. SP MURDERERS] F (*Vil.*); *not
in* Q   377. SD Q *only*

1.4.   0. SD F *corr.; omit* F *uncorr.*   0. *and Keeper*] F;
Brokenbury Q   1, 8, 35, 43, 66, 77. SP KEEPER] F; *Brok.*
Q   3. fearful dreams, of ugly sights] F; vgly sights, of
gastly dreames Q   8. my lord? I pray you tell me] F; I
long to heare you tell it Q   9–10. Methoughts . . . Bur-
gundy] F; Me thoughts I was imbarkt for Burgundy Q
13. Thence] Q; There F, Q6   15. heavy] F; fearefulll Q

19. falling] F; stumbling Q   22. O Lord] F; Lord, Lord
Q   23. waters] Q; water F, Q6   23, 24. my] Q; mine F,
Q2–6   24. sights of ugly death] F; vgly sights of death
Q   25. Methoughts] F; Me thought Q   26. A] F; Ten
Q   29. F *only*   30. the] F; those Q   33. That] F; Which
Q   35. such] F; sueh Q   36. these] F; the Q   37–38.
F; Me thought I had, for still the enuious floud Q   39.
Stopped] F; Kept Q   40. find] F; seeke Q   42. Who]
F; Which Q   43. in] F; with Q   44. No, no] F; O no
Q   46. I] F; Who Q   47. sour] F; grim Q   51. spake]
F; cried Q   54. with] F; in Q   55. shrieked] F; squakt
Q   59. unto torment] F; to your torments Q   60.
methoughts] Q; me thought F, Q2–6   61. me] F; me
about Q   65. my] F; the Q   66. marvel] F; marueile
my Q   67. I am afraid, methinks] F; I promise you,
I am afraid Q   68. Ah keeper, keeper . . . these] F; O
Brokenbury . . . those Q   69. That . . . give] F; Which
. . . beare Q   71–74. F *only*   75. F; I pray thee gentle
keeper stay by me Q   77. SD F *only*   78. SP F *only*
78. breaks] F, Q2–6; breake Q   82. imaginations] F;
imagination Q   84. between . . . name] F; betwixt . . .
names Q   85. SD F; *The murtherers enter.* Q   86. F
only   87. SP F *only*   87. What . . . cam'st thou] F; In
Gods name what are you and how came you Q   89.
SP F; *Execu.* Q   91. What] F; Yea, are you Q   92. SP
F; *2 Exe.* Q   92. 'Tis . . . tedious] F; O sir, it is better to
be briefe then tedious Q   93. Let him see . . . and talk]
F; Shew him . . . talke Q   93. SD *Brakenbury reads*]
Ed.; *Reads* F; *He readeth it.* Q   97. from] F; of Q   98.
F; Here are the keies, there sits the Duke a sleepe Q
99. F; Ile to his Maiesty, and certifie his Grace Q   100.
to you my charge] F; my charge to you Q   101. SP F;
Exe. Q   101. You . . . 'Tis] F; Doe so, it is Q   102. Fare
. . . well] F *only*   102. SD *2 lines earlier in* F; *omit* Q
103. I] Q; we F, Q3–6   105. He'll say] F; then he will
say Q   107–8. Why . . . Day] F; When he wakes, | Why

foole he shall neuer wake till the iudgement day Q
114. warrant] F; warrant for it Q   115–16. the which
. . . me] F; which . . . vs Q   117–18. F *only*   119. I'll] F
only   120. and] F *only*   121. Nay, I . . . little] F; I . . .
while Q   122. this passionate humor of mine] F; my
holy humor Q   123. tells] F; would tel Q   125. Faith]
Q; *omit* F   129. Zounds] Q; Come F   132. O] F *only*
134. When] F; So when Q   136. 'Tis . . . matter] F *only*
138. What] F; How Q   139. it.] F; it, it is a dangerous thing Q   141. a man cannot swear] F; he cannot
sweare Q   141–42. a man cannot lie] F; he cannot lie Q
144. a man] F; one Q   146. by chance] F *only*   147. of]
F; of all Q   149. to himself] F; to | To himselfe Q   149.
liue] F; to liue Q   150. Zounds] Q *only*   151. Duke]
Dkue F; Duke Q   153. but] F *only* 155. I . . . strong-
framed] F; Tut, I . . . strong in fraud Q   156. me] F; me,
I warrant thee Q   157–58. man . . . thy] F; fellow . . .
his Q   158. fall to work] F; to this geere Q   159. on] F;
ouer Q   160. throw him into] F; we wil chop him in Q
162. and] F *only*   164. F; Harke he stirs, shall I strike Q
165. F *only*   166. SP F; 2 Q   166. we'll] F; first lets Q
168. SP F; I Q   170. SP F; 2 Q   172. SP F, Q5–6; 2 Q
174. SP F; 2 Q   176. F *only*   177. F; Tell me who are
you, wherefore come you hither? Q   178. SP F; *Am.*
Q   180. SP BOTH] F, Q (*Am.*)   180. Ay, ay] F (I, I); I Q
187. drawn . . . among] F; cald . . . from out Q   189. is
. . . doth] F; are . . . doe Q   195–96. to . . . sins] Q; for
any goodness F   200. our] F; the Q   201. vassals] F;
Vassaile Q   202. table] F; tables Q   203. Will . . . then]
F; and wilt thou then Q   205. hand] F; hands Q   207.
hurl] F; throw Q   209. sacrament] F; holy sacrament
Q   214. Unrippedst] Ed.; Vnrip'st F, Q   215. wast] F;
wert Q   217. such] F; so Q   220. He . . . you] Why sirs,
he . . . ye Q   221. that] F; this Q   222. avengèd . . . the]
F; reuenged . . . this Q   223. F *only*   225. or] F; nor Q
231. our duty . . . faults] F; the diuell . . . fault Q   232.

Provoke . . . slaughter] F; Haue brought . . . murder Q
233. If . . . do love] F; Oh if . . . loue Q 235. are] F; be
Q 237. shall] F; will Q 243, 248. SP F; *Am.* Q 245.
arm,] F; arme: | And chargd vs from his soule, to loue
each other Q 247. of] Q; on F, Q6 250–51. Come . . .
yourself] F; thou deceiu'st thy selfe Q 252. F; Tis he
hath sent vs hither now to slaughter thee Q 253–54.
he . . . | And] F; when I parted with him, | He Q 256.
SP F; 2 Q 256. when . . . you] F; now . . . thee Q 257.
Earth's] F; worlds Q 258. SP F; I Q 258. Make] F,
Q2–6; Makes Q 259. Have you . . . your souls] F; Hast
thou . . . thy soule Q 261. are you . . . your own souls]
F; art thou . . . thy owne soule Q 262. you will] F; thou
wilt Q 263. they] F; he Q 264. the] F; this Q 267–
71. F *only* 270. life?] ~, F 270. Ay] Ed.; as F 272.
No] F *only* 276. thine] F; thy Q 279. F *only* 280–82.
F; I thus, and thus: if this wil not serue, | Ile chop thee
in the malmesey But, in the next roome Q 280. SD
Stabs] F; *He stabs* Q 282. SD F *only* 283. dispatched]
F; performd Q 284. hands] F; hand Q 285. murder]
F; guilty murder done Q 285. SD F *only* 286–87.
How . . . not] F; Why doest thou not helpe me Q 288.
heavens] Q; Heauen F, Q6 288–289. you have been]
F; thou art Q 294. Well, I'll go . . . the] F; Now must
I . . . his Q 295. Till that . . . give] F; Vntill . . . take Q
296. will] F; must Q 297. then] F; here Q 297. SD F;
Exeunt. Q

    2.1 0. SD *King Edward . . . Queen Elizabeth . . .
Hastings*] Ed.; *the King . . . the Queene . . . Hastings,
Catesby* F; *Enter King, Queene, Hastings, Ryuers,
Dorcet, &c.* Q 1 *and hereafter in this scene.* SP KING
EDWARD] Ed; *King.* F, Q 1. Why] F *only* 1. have I] F;
I haue Q 5. more in] Ed.; more to F; now in Q 5. to]
F, Q *corr.*; from Q *uncorr.* 6. made] F; set Q 7. Riv-
ers and Hastings] Q; *Dorset* and *Riuers* F 9. soul] F;
heart Q 18. is . . . from] F; are . . . in Q 19. you,] F;

your Q 23. There] F; Here Q 25–26. F *only* 29. I]
F; I my Lord Q 31. wife's] F (Wiues) 34. Upon your
Grace] F; On your or yours Q 40. God] Q; heauen
F 41. love] F; zeale Q 41. SD F *only* 45. blessèd] F;
perfect Q 47. Here . . . Duke] F; here comes the noble
Duke Q 47. SD F; *Enter Glocest.* Q, *2 lines earlier* 51.
Gloucester] F; Brother Q 54. lord] F; liege Q 58.
unwittingly] Q; vnwillingly F 60. By] Q; To F 68.
and you, Lord Rivers and of Dorset] F; Lo: Riuers, and
Lord Gray of you Q 70. F *only* 78. lord . . . Highness]
F; liege . . . Maiesty Q 81. so flouted] F; thus scorned
Q 82. gentle] F; noble Q 82. SD F *only* 84. SP KING
EDWARD] F (*King*); *Ryu.* Q 87. man] F; one Q 87. the]
F; this Q 90. man] F; soule Q 91. wingèd] F, Q2–6;
wingled Q 95. and] F; but Q 95. blood] F; blond Q
97. SD *Earl of*] F *only* 98 *and hereafter in this scene.*
SP STANLEY] Ed.; *Der.* F; *Dar.* Q 100. hear me] F; grant
Q 101. say . . . requests] F; speake . . . demaundst Q
106. that tongue] F; the same Q 107. killed] F; slew Q
108. bitter] F; cruell Q 109. wrath] F; rage Q 110. at]
Q; and F 110. bade] Q; bid F 111. spoke of brotherhood? Who spoke of] F; spake of Brotherhood? who
of Q 114. at] F; by Q 119. garments . . . did give] F;
owne garments . . . gaue Q 122. plucked] F; puckt Q
125. slaughter] Slaughɪer F 133. once] onee F 133.
beg] F; pleade Q 137. SD F; *Exit.* Q 137. SD *King*]
F (*K.*) 137. SD *Queen*] Qneen F 138. fruits] F; fruit
Q 142. Come . . . go] F; But come lets in Q 144.
F *only*

2.2. 0. SD F; *Enter Dutches of Yorke, with Clarence
Children* Q 1. SP BOY] Q; *Edw.* F 1. Good . . . us] F;
Tell me good Granam Q 3. SP F; *Boy* Q 3. you] Q;
omit F 3. weep so oft] F; wring your hands Q 5. SP
F; *Gerl* Q 6. orphans, wretches] F; wretches, Orphanes
Q 7. were] F; be Q 8. both] F; much Q 11. sorrow
. . . wail] F; labour, to weepe for Q 12. you conclude

... he] F; Granam you conclude that he Q   13. mine
... it] F; my ... this Q   15. earnest] F; daily Q   16. F
only 22. to it] F *only*   24. my uncle] F; he Q   25. pitied me] F; hugd me in his arme Q   25. cheek] F, Q2–5;
checke Q   26. Bade ... on] F; And bad ... in Q   27.
a] F; his Q   28. shape] F; shapes Q   29. visor ... deep
vice] F; visard ... foule guile Q   30. ay] F; yea Q   34.
SD (*as "the Queene"*) F; *Enter the Quee.* Q   41. thy] F;
your Q   42. when ... gone] F; now ... witherd Q   43.
that want their sap] F; the sap being gone Q   47. ne'er-
changing night] F; perpetuall rest Q   48. I] Q; *omit* F
51. with] F; by Q   55. That] F; Which Q   57. left] F;
left thee Q   58. husband] F; children Q   60. hands] F;
limmes Q   61. Clarence and Edward] F; Edward and
Clarence Q   62. Thine ... but a moiety ... moan] F;
Then, ... but moity ... griefe Q   63. woes] F; plaints Q
64. Ah] F; Good Q   65. kindred] F; kindreds Q   66. SP
DAUGHTER] F; *Gerl* Q   67. widow-dolor] F; widdowes
dolours Q   69. complaints] F; laments Q   71. moon]
F; moane Q   73. dear] F; eire Q   74, 77, 80. SP CHIL-
DREN] F; *Ambo* Q   80. Were ... so dear a loss] F; Was
... a dearer losse Q   81. so ... loss] F; a dearer losse
Q   82. griefs] F; mones Q   83. is] F; are Q   84. an]
F *only*   85. weep] Q; weepes F   86–87. and ... weep]
Q1–3, 5–6; *omit* F   89. Pour] F (Power)   90. lamenta-
tion] F; lamentations Q   91–103. F *only*   103. SD F;
Enter Glocest. with others. Q   104. Sister] F; Madame
Q   106. help our] F; cure their Q   110. breast] F;
minde Q   111. Love,] ~∧ F   114. that] F; why Q   116.
heavy mutual] F; mutuall heauy Q   120. hates] F;
hearts Q   121. together] F; etogether Q   124. fet] F;
fetcht Q   126–45. F *only*   148, 159. Ludlow] Q; London F   149. sister] F; mother Q   150. this business.]
F; this waighty business? | *Ans.* With all our hearts. Q
150. SD F; *Exeunt man. Glo. Buck.* Q   152. God's] Q;
God F   152. at home] F; behinde Q   155. Prince] F;
King Q   158. as] F; like Q   159. SD F; *omit* Q

2.3. 0. SD F; *Enter two Citizens.* Q 1. Good morrow, neighbor] F; Neighbour well met Q 3. SP Hear] F; I Heare Q 4. SP FIRST CITIZEN] F (I); 2 Q 4. Yes] F; I Q 5. SP SECOND CITIZEN] F (2); I Q 5. Ill] F; Bad Q 6. giddy] F; troublous Q 7. Neighbors, God speed] F; Good morrow neighbours Q 8. F *only* 9. the] F; this Q 10. F; I It doth. Q 15. Which] F; That Q 18. Henry] F; Harry Q 19. in] F; at Q 20. No . . . wot] F; no good my friend not so Q 24. SP FIRST CITIZEN] F (I); 2 Q 24. Why, so . . . his] F; So . . . the Q 25, 26. his] F; the Q 27. emulation . . . be] F; emulation now, who shall be Q 30. sons . . . haught] F; kindred hauty Q 34. SP FIRST CITIZEN] F (I); 2 Q 34. will be] F; shalbe Q 35. are seen] F; appeare Q 37. then] F; the Q 39. makes] F; make Q 42. SP SECOND CITIZEN] F (2); I Q 42. hearts . . . fear] F; soules . . . bread Q 43. You cannot reason almost] F; Yee cannot almost reason Q 44. dread] F; feare Q 45. days] F; times Q 47. Ensuing] F *catchword,* Q; Pursuing F *text* 47. danger] F; dangers Q 48. water] F; waters Q 50. Marry, we were . . . Justices] F; We are . . . Iustice Q

2.4. 0. SD *Queen Elizabeth*] Ed.; *the Queene* F; *Enter Cardinall, Dutches of Yorke, Quee. young Yorke.* Q 1 *and hereafter in this scene.* SP ARCHBISHOP] F; *Car.* Q 1. hear] Q; heard F, Q3–6 1. Stony Stratford] F; Northhampton Q 2. And . . . tonight] F; At Stonistratford will they be to night Q 7. Has] F; Hath Q 9. good] F; young Q 12. uncle] F, Q3–6; Nnckle Q 14. do] F *only* 23. his . . . true] F; this were a true rule Q 24. SP YORK] F; *Car.* Q 24. And . . . madam] F; Why Madame, so no doubt he is Q 25. he is] F; so too Q 25. yet] F; yer Q 28. To . . . mine] F; That should haue neerer toucht his growth then he did mine Q 29. young] F; prety Q 33. been] F; heene Q 34. this] F; so Q 36. wast] F; wert Q 38. parlous] F; Q (perilous) 39. SP DUCHESS] F; *Car.* Q 40. SD F; *Enter Dorset.* Q 41. a messenger . . . news] F; your sonne, Lo: M. Dorset. | What newes

Lo: Marques Q   42 *and hereafter in this scene.* SP MES-
SENGER] F; *Dor.* Q   42. report] F; vnfolde Q   43. doth]
F; fares Q   45. news] F; newes then Q   47. And, with]
F; With Q   52. the] F; these Q   53. lord] F; Lady Q
54. ruin . . . my] F; downfall . . . our Q   56. jut] F; iet Q
57. aweless] F; lawlesse Q   58. blood] F; death Q   67.
brother to brother] F *only*   68. to] F; against Q   70.
Earth] F; death Q   72. F *only*   73. Stay, . . . go with] F;
Ile go along with Q   80. Go] F; Come Q

    3.1. 0–169. *This ed. is based on* Q, *not* F, *which
here follows* Q3 *almost exactly.* 0. SD *Richard . . .
Buckingham, the Cardinal, Catesby, and others.*] Ed.;
the Dukes of Glocester, and Buckingham, Cardinall, &c.
Q; *the Dukes of Glocester, and Buckingham, Lord Cardinall, with others.* F   2. sovereign.] Q (~,); ~∧ F   9.
Nor] Q; No F   18, 20, 25, 26, 33, 36, 38, 45, 58, 59, 71,
75, 76, 98, 102, 103, 106, 128, 139, 143, 144, 152, 154,
165. lord] Q (Lo:)   19. SP MAYOR] *Lo: M.* Q, F   24. SD
Lord Hastings] Q (*L. Hast.*)   41. in heaven] Q; *omit* F,
Q3–6   44. deep] Q; great F, Q3–6   61. SD F, Q3–6 *only,
1 line earlier*   64 *and hereafter to line* 157. SP RICHARD]
Ed.; *Glo.* Q, F   64. seems] Q; think'st F, Q3–6   79. all-
ending] Q; ending F, Q2–6   87. valor] F; valure Q   88.
this] Q; his F, Q2–6   95. SD *Hastings*] Q; *Hastings,
and* F   97. Richard] Q (*Rich.*)   97. loving] Q; Noble
F, Q3–6   98. dread] Q; deare F, Q3–6   113. cousin]
Coscn Q   122. heavy] Q; weightie F, Q2–6   125. as]
Q; as, as F, Q3   135–36. reasons! . . . uncle,] ~, . . . ~:
Q   139. will 't] Ed.; wilt Q, F   144. needs] Q; *omit*
Q2–6   152. With] Q; and with F   153. SD *A sennet. . . .
Hastings exit.*] *A Senet. Exeunt . . . Hastings, and Dor-
set.* F; *Exeunt Prin. Yor. Hast. Dors. manet, Rich. Buck.*
Q   157. parlous] Q (perillous)   170. Will not he] F;
what will he Q   173. far] F; a farre Q   174. doth stand
. . . to] F; stands . . . Vnto Q   175–76. F *only*   177. F;
if he be willing Q   178. tell] F; shew Q   180. the] F;

your Q   184 *and hereafter to 3.7.248.* SP RICHARD] F;
Glo. Q   187. lord] F; friend Q   189. go] F *only*   190.
lords] F; Lo: Q   190. can] F; may Q   193. House] F;
place Q   193. SD F, Q3–6 *only*   195. Lord] F; William
Lo: Q   196. head. Something . . . determine] F; head
man, somewhat . . . doe Q   198. all] F *only*   199. was]
F; stood Q   200. hand] F; hands Q   201. kindness] F;
willingnes Q

3.2   0. SD *the door of*] F; *Lo:* Q   1. My lord, my
lord] F; What ho my Lord Q   2. knocks] F; knockes at
the dore Q   3. One] F; A messenger Q   4. What is 't] F;
Whats Q   5. SD *2 lines earlier in* Q   6. my Lord Stan-
ley] F; thy Master Q   7. appears] F; should seeme Q
8. self] F; Lordship Q   9. What] F; And Q   10. F; And
then he sends you word Q   11. dreamt the boar had
razèd off his] F; dreamt to night the beare had raste
his Q   12. kept] F; held Q   17. you will presently] F;
presently you will Q   18. with him toward] F; into Q
21. council] F; counsels Q   23. good friend] F; seru-
ant Q   26. without] F; wanting Q   27. simple] F; fond
Q   29. pursues] F; pursues vs Q   35. I'll . . . tell] F;
My gratious Lo: Ile tell Q   35. SD *He exits.*] F, Q3–6
only   40. believe will] F; beleeue it will Q   46. Before]
F; Ere Q   48. Ay, on my life] F; Vpon my life my Lo: Q
54. my adversaries] F; mine enemies Q   60. which] F;
who Q   62. Well, Catesby, ere . . . older] F; I tell thee
Catesby. *Cat.* What my Lord? *Hast.* Ere . . . elder Q   68.
that] F; who Q   74. Come on, come on] F; What my
Lo: Q   79. you do] Q; *omit* F   80. days] F; life Q   81.
so . . . as] F; more . . . then Q   85. were] F; was Q   88.
stab] F; scab Q   90. What . . . spent] F; But come my
Lo: shall we to the tower? Q   91. Come . . . lord] F; I
go: but stay, heare you not the newes   92. Today . . .
you] F; This day those men you Q   92. talked] Q; talke
F, Q3–6   95. SD *a Pursuivant*] F; *Hastin. a Purssuant* Q
96. on] F; you Q   96. I'll . . . fellow] F; Ile follow pres-

ently Q   96. SD F, Q3–6 *only*   97. How now, sirrah]
F; Well met Hastings Q   98. your Lordship please] F;
it please your Lo: Q   99. man] F; fellow Q   100. thou
met'st me] F; I met thee Q   107. fellow . . . me] F; Hastings hold spend thou that Q   107. SD F; *He giues him
his purse.* Q   108. I . . . Honor] F; God saue your Lordship Q   108. SD *Pursuivant exits.*] F, Q3–6 *only*   109.
F *only*   110. I . . . heart] F; What Sir Iohn, you are wel
met Q   111. I . . . debt . . . last exercise] F; I am beholding to you . . . last daies exercise Q   112. you] F; you.
He whispers in his eare. Q   113. F *only*   114.   What
. . . Chamberlain] F; How now Lo: Chamberlaine, what
talking with a priest, Q   118. The] F; Those Q   119.
toward . . . Tower] F; to the tower my Lord Q   120. do,
my lord, but] F; doe, but Q   120. cannot stay there] F;
shall not stay Q   122. Nay] F; 'Tis Q   124. will you go]
F; shall we go along Q   125. F *only*

3.3   0. SD *with . . . Pomfret.*] F; *with the Lo: Riuers,
Gray, and Vaughan, prisoners* Q   0. *Pomfret.* | RIVERS] F;
prisoners. | *Ratl.* Come bring foorth the prisoners. | *Ryu.*
Q   4. bless] F; keepe Q   6–7. F *only*   11. Richard] F;
Richatd Q   12. seat] F; soule Q   13. to thee . . . blood]
F; thee vp . . . blouds Q   15. F *only*   17–19. Richard
. . . Hastings] F; Hastings . . . Richard Q   20. prayer] F;
praiers Q   21. sons] F; sonne Q   22. blood] F; blouds Q
24. F; *Rat.* Come come dispatch, the limit of your linea
is out Q   25. here] F; all Q   26. Farewell, until we meet
again in] F; And take our leaue vntill we meete in Q

3.4.   0. SD F; *Enter the Lords to Councell.* Q   1.
Now . . . peers] F; My Lords at once Q   3. speak . . .
the] F; say . . . this Q   4. Is . . . ready . . . the] F; Are . . .
fitting . . . that Q   5 *and hereafter in this scene.* SP STAN-
LEY] Ed.; *Darb.* F, Q   6. SP ELY] F; *Ryu.* Q   6. judge . . .
day] F; guesse . . . time Q   9. ELY Your . . . think] F; *Bi.*
Why you may Lo: me thinks you Q   11. We] F; Who I
my Lo? we Q   11. for] F; But for Q   13. Or . . . lord] F;

nor I no more of his Q   18. gracious] F; Graces Q   19.
honorable lords] F; noble Lo: Q   21. SD *2 lines later
in* Q   22. In happy] F; Now in good Q   23. lords] F;
L. Q   24. trust] F; hope Q   25. design] F; designes Q
27. you not] F; not you Q   27. cue] F (Q)   28. had]
F; had now Q   31. well] F; well. | *Hast.* I thanke your
Grace. *Glo.* Q   32. Ely] F; Elie. *Bish.* My Lo: | *Glo.* Q
35. ELY . . . heart] F; *Bish.* I go my Lord Q   35. SD F
only   36. of] F *only*   39. That] F; As Q   40. child . . .
worshipfully] F; sonne . . . worshipfull Q   42. yourself
. . . with] F; you hence my Lo: Ile follow Q   42. SD
Exeunt F; *Ex. Gl.* Q   44. my judgment] F; mine opinion Q   47. the . . . Gloucester] F; protector Q   49–50.
this morning] F; to day Q   52. that he bids . . . such] F;
he doth bid . . . such a Q   54. Can] F; That can Q   57.
livelihood] F; likelihood Q   59. were he, he had shown]
F; if he were, he would haue shewen Q   59. looks] F;
lookes. | *Dar.* I pray God he be not, I say. Q   59. SD
F; *Enter Glocester.* Q   60. tell me what] F; what doe Q
65. princely] F; noble Q   66. whosoe'er] F; whatsoeuer
Q   68. their evil] F; this ill Q   69. Look] F; See Q   71.
And this is] F; This is that Q   74. deed, my noble] F;
thing my gratious Q   76. Talk'st thou to me] F; Telst
thou me Q   77. I swear] F *only*   78–79. until . . . done]
F; to day I sweare | Vntill I see the same, some see it
done Q   80. rise] F; come Q   80. SD *They exit.*] *1 line
earlier in* F.   80. SD *Lovell . . . Hastings*] F; *manet Cat.
with Ha.* Q   83. raze his helm] Q; rowse our Helmes F
84. And I did scorn . . . disdain] F; But I disdaind . . .
did scorne Q   86. started] F; startled Q   88. need] F;
want Q   90. too . . . how] F; twere . . . at Q   91. Today]
F; How they Q   95. SP RATCLIFFE] F; *Cat.* Q   95. Come,
come, dispatch] F; Dispatch my Lo: Q   98. grace of
mortal] F; state of worldly Q   99. God] F; heauen Q
100. hope . . . good] F; hopes . . . faire Q   104–7. F *only*
109. who] F; that Q

3.5. 0. SD F; *Enter Duke of Glocester and Buckingham in armour.* Q 4. again begin] F; beginne againe Q 5. were] F; wert Q 6. Tut, I] F; Tut feare not me. | I Q 8. F *only* 12. At any time] F *only* 13. F *only* 14. F; Here comes the Maior Q 14. SD F; *Enter Maior.* Q *2 lines earlier* 15. F; Let me alone to entertaine him. Lo: Maior, Q 17. F; The reason we haue sent for you. Q 19. F; Harke, I heare a drumme. Q 21. innocence] Q; Innocencie F, Q2–6 21. and guard] F *only* 21. SD F; *Enter Catesby with Hast. head.* Q 22. F; *Glo.* O, O, be quiet, it is Catesby. Q 23. SP LOVELL] F; *Cat.* Q 26. creature] F; man Q 27. the] F; this Q 27. Christian.] F; christian, | Looke ye my Lo: Maior Q 33. lived ... suspects] F; laid ... suspect Q 36. imagine] F; haue imagined Q 37. Were 't] Ed.; Wert F, Q 37. that] F *only* 38. it, that the] F; it you? The Q 39. This ... plotted] F; Had this day plotted Q 41. F; What, had he so? Q 44. in] F; to Q 49. your good Graces] F; you my good Lords Q 51. SP BUCKINGHAM] F *only* 53. Yet] F; *Dut.* Yet Q 53. we not] F; not we Q 54. end] F; death Q 55. loving] F; longing Q 56. Something ... meanings] F; Somewhat ... meaning Q 57. I] F; we Q 59. treasons] F; treason Q 63. words] F; word Q 64. and] F; or Q 65. do not doubt] F; doubt you not Q 66. our] F; your Q 67. case] F; cause Q; ease Q6 69. censures ... carping world] F; carping censures ... world Q 70. Which ... intent] F; But ... intents Q 71–72. you hear ... farewell] F; we did intend, and so my Lord adue Q 72. SD *1 line later in* Q 73. Go] F *only* 75. meetest vantage] F; meet'st aduantage Q; meetest aduantage Q6 83. unto] F; to Q 85. raging] F; lustfull Q 86. lusted ... a] F; listed ... his Q 91. true] F; iust Q 95. Yet] F; But Q 96. my lord, you know] F; you know, my Lord Q 97. Doubt] F; Feare Q 99. And ... adieu] F *only* 103–4. F; About three or foure a clocke look to heare | What news Guildhall affordeth, and so my Lord farewell Q 104. SD *4 lines later in* Q 105–8. F *only* 106. Penker] Ed.; *Peuker* F 108. SD F *only* 109. go] F; in Q 111. order] F; notice Q 111. manner person] F, Q3–6; manner of person Q 112. Have . . . recourse] F; At any tyme haue recourse Q 112. SD Q; *Exeunt.* F

3.6. 0. SD *Scrivener*] F; *Scriuener with a paper in his hand.* Q 1. Here] F; This Q 3. today] F; this day Q 5. have] F *only* 6. sent] F; brought Q 8. Hastings lived] F; liued Lord Hastings Q 10. Who is] F; Why whoes Q 11. cannot see] F; sees not Q 12. who] F; whoes Q 12. bold] F; blinde Q 14. ill] F; bad Q

3.7. 0. SD F; *Enter Glocester at one doore, Buckingham at another.* Q 1. How now, how now] F; How now my Lord Q 3. say] F; and speake Q 5–6. his contract . . . France] F *only* 7. desire] F; desires Q 8. F *only* 11. F *only* 18. your] F; the Q 20. mine] Q; my F, Q3–6 20. drew . . . end] F; grew to an ende Q 23. And] F; A and Q 24. they . . . word] F *only* 26. Stared] F; Gazde Q 29. used] F; wont Q 34. spoke] F; spake Q 36. At lower] F; At the lower Q 38. F *only* 39. gentle] F; louing Q 40. cheerful] F; louing Q 41. wisdoms] Q; wisdome F, Q3–6 42. even here] F; so Q 44. speak?] F; speake? | *Buc.* No by my troth my Lo: | *Glo.* Q 46. SP BUCKINGHAM] F, Q3–6; *Glo.* Q 46. Intend] F; and intend Q 47. you spoke with but by] F; spoken withall, but with Q 49. between] F; betwixt Q 50. make] F; build Q 51. And] F *only* 51. requests] F; request Q 52. still . . . and] F; say no, but Q 53. I . . . plead] F; Feare not me, if thou canst pleade Q 55. we] F; weele Q 56. F; You shal see what I can do, get you vp to the leads. Q 56. SD *Richard exits.*] Q (*Exit.*) 56. SD *Enter . . . Citizens.*] F *only* 57. Welcome, my lord] F; Now my L. Maior Q 59. Now] Ed.; *Buck.* Now F 59. F; Here coms his seruant: how now *Catesby* what saies he. Q 60. He . . . lord] F; My Lord, he doth intreat your

grace Q   64. worldly suits] F; world- ɪy suite Q   66. SP
BUCKINGHAM] F; *Buek.* Q   66. the gracious duke] F; thy
Lord againe Q   67. aldermen] F; Cittizens Q   68. in
matter] F; and matters Q   71. F; Ile tell him what you
say my Lord Q   73. love-bed] F; day bed Q   79. virtu-
ous] F; gracious Q   80. his Grace . . . thereof] F; him-
selfe . . . thereon Q   81. not] F; neuer Q   82. defend]
F; forbid Q   83. Here . . . again] F *only*   84. Now . . .
Grace] F; how now Catesby, | What saies your Lord? Q
85. He] F; My Lo. he Q   86. come to] F; speake with
Q   88. He . . . lord] F; My Lord, he feares Q   91. we . . .
love] F; I come in perfect loue to him Q   91. perfect]
F (perfit)   92. SD *Catesby*] Q *only*   94. much] F; hard
Q   95. SD F; *Enter Rich. with two bishops a loste.* Q
96. his Grace] F; he Q   99–100. F *only*   102. ear] F;
eares Q   102. requests] F; request Q   106. I . . . to] F;
I rather do beseech you Q   108. Deferred] F; Neglect
Q   113. eye] F; eies Q   115. might] F *only*   117. On]
F; At Q   117. your] F; that Q   119. Know, then] F;
Then know Q   122. F *only* 127. The] F; This Q   127.
her] Q; his F   128. Her] Q; His F   129. F *only*   129.
Her] Ed.; His F   131. dark] F; blind Q   131. deep] F;
darke Q   133. charge] F; soueraingtie thereof Q   134.
F *only*   140. friends] F; frinds Q   142. cause] F; suite
Q   143. I . . . if] F; I know not whether Q   146–55. F
only   160. the] F; my Q   160. of] F; by Q   163. That I
would] F; As I had Q   168. were there need] F; if need
were Q   173. that] F; what Q   176. SP BUCKINGHAM] F;
Buek. Q   181. was he] F; he was Q   182. his] F; that Q
185. off] F; by Q   186. to . . . sons] F; of . . . children
Q   189. wanton] F; lustfull Q   190. his degree] F; al
his thoughts Q   193. call] F; terme Q   197. goodʌ my
lord] ~, ~ ~ F   200. forth . . . ancestry] F; out your royall stocke Q   201. times] F; time Q   204. F *only*   206.
this care] F; these cares Q   207. majesty] F; dignitie Q
214. kindred] F; kin Q   216. know, whe'er] F; whether

Q 216, 231. whe'er] F (where) 221. Zounds, I'll] Q; we will F 222. Q *only* 222. SD F *only* 223. him again, sweet prince. Accept] F; them againe, my lord, and accept Q 224. F; *Ano.* Doe, good my lord, least all the land do rew it. Q 225. Will . . . cares] F; Would . . . care Q 226. Call] F; Well, call Q 227. entreaties] F; intreates Q 228. SD F *only* 229. sage] F; you sage Q 233. foul] F; soule Q 237. doth know] F; he knowes Q 238. of this] F; thereof Q 241. royal] F; kingly Q 242. Richard] Q; King Richard F, Q3–6 242. worthy] F; royall Q 243. SP ALL] F; *M yor* Q 244. may] F; will Q 245. please, for] F; will, since Q 247. F *only* 248. work] F; taske Q 249. my] F; good Q 249. cousin] Q; Cousins F

4.1. 0. SD *Queen Elizabeth*] Ed.; *Quee. mother* Q; *Enter the Queene, Anne Duchess of Gloucester, the Duchess of Yorke, and Marquess Dorset.* F 1 *and hereafter in this scene.* SP DUCHESS] Ed.; *Duch. Yorke.* F; *Duch.* or *Du.yor.* Q 2–4. F *only* 5. Daughter] F; *Qu.* Sister Q 6–8. God . . . sister] F *only* 8. away] F; awaie so fast Q 9. SP ANNE] F; *Duch.* Q 11. gentle] F; tender Q 12. SD *the*] F *only* 15. How . . . York] F; How fares the Prince Q 16 *and hereafter.* SP BRAKEN-BURY] Ed.; *Lieu.* F, Q 16. Right . . . patience] F; Wel Madam, and in health, but by your leaue Q 17. them] F; him Q 18. strictly] F; straightlie Q 19. Who's] F; whie, whose Q 20. I] F; I crie you mercie, I Q 22. between] F; betwixt Q 23. shall bar] F; should keepe Q 25 *and hereafter in this scene.* SP ANNE] F; *Duch.glo.* or *Duch.* Q 26. bring . . . sights] F; feare not thou Q 28. No . . . so] F; I doe beseech your graces all to par-don me Q 29. and . . . me] F; I may not doe it Q 29. SD *Lieutenant exits*] F *only* 29. SD *Stanley*] F; *L. Stan-lie* Q 30. one] F; an Q 33. straight] F; go with me Q 36. asunder] F; in sunder Q 38. swoon] F; sound Q 39. F *only* 40. Be . . . cheer, mother.] Ed; Be . . .

cheare: Mother, F; Madam, haue comfort Q   41. gone]
F; hence Q   42. dogs] F; dogge Q   42. thy] F; the Q
52. hours] F; time Q   53. from] F; ftom Q   54. In . . .
way] F; To meete you on the way, and welcome you
Q   58. hatched . . . the] F; hatch . . . thc Q   60. come.
I] F; I Q   61. with] F; in Q   62. O . . . that] F; I . . . thar
Q   64. brains] F; braine Q   65. venom] F; poyson Q
67. Go, go] F; Alas Q   68. thyself] F; rhy selfe Q   69.
Why] F *only*   74. dear] F; dead Q   75. Richard's] F;
Richatds Q   80. More . . . life] F; As . . . death Q   81.
Than] F; As Q   83. Within . . . time] F; Euen in so short
a space Q   85. mine] F; my Q   86. hitherto . . . held
. . . rest] F; euer since . . . kept . . . sleepe Q   86. my] Q;
mine F, Q6   88. Did I enjoy] F; Haue *I* enioyed Q   89.
with . . . awaked] F; haue bene waked by his timerous
dreames Q   92. Poor heart, adieu . . . complaining] F;
Alas poore soule . . . complaints Q   93. with] F; from Q
95. that] F; thou Q   98. tend] F; garde Q   99. and] F
only   104–10. SD. F *only*

   4.2.   0. SD F; *The Trumpets sound. Enter Richard
crownd, Buckingham, Catesby, with other Nobles.* Q   1
and hereafter to 5.3.50. SP RICHARD] F; *King or King Ri.*
Q   2. F *only*   3. SD *Here . . . throne.*] Q *only; Sound*]
F *only*   6. glories] F; honours Q   8. let them] F; may
they Q   11. speak] F; say Q   12. loving lord] F; gracious soueraigne Q   14. lord] F; liege Q   19. wast] F;
wert Q   22. now] F *only*   26. little . . . lord] F; breath,
some little pause my lord Q   27. in this] F; herein Q
28. you . . . presently] F; your grace immediatlie Q   28.
SD *Buckingham*] *Buck.* F; *omit* Q   29. gnaws his] F;
bites the Q   33–34. High-reaching . . . circumspect.— |
Boy] F; Boy, high reaching . . . circumspect Q   35 *and
hereafter.* SP PAGE] F; *Boy* Q   37. Will] F; Would Q   38.
I] F; My lord, I Q   39. spirit] F; mind Q   44. I . . . man]
F *only*   44. boy] F; presentlie Q   46. counsels] F; counsell Q   48. Well . . . so] F *only*   48. SD *Stanley*] F; *Darby*

Q   49. Lord . . . news] F; what neewes vvith you Q   50.
SP STANLEY] F; *Darby* Q   50–52. F; My Lord, I heare the
Marques Dorset | Is fled to Richmond, in those partes
beyond the seas where he | abides. Q   53. Come. . . .
Rumor] F; Catesby. *Cat.* My Lord. | *King.* Rumor Q   54.
very grievous sick] F; sicke and like to die Q   56. poor]
F; borne Q   60. queen] F; wife Q   72. lord] F; soueraigne Q   74. Please you] F; I my Lord Q   75. then] F;
there Q   76. disturbers] F; disturbs Q   81. Hark] F
only   82. this] F; that Q   82. SD *whispers*] *he wispers
in his eare* Q   83. There is] F; Tis Q   83. it is] F, Q3–5;
is it Q   84. for it] F; too Q   85. I. . . . *Buckingham*] F;
Tis done my gracious lord. | *King.* Shal we heare from
thee *Tirrel* ere we sleep? *Enter Buc.* | *Tir.* Ye shall my
lord Q   87. request] F; demand Q   88. rest] F; passe
Q   89. the] F; that Q   90. wife's] F (Wiues)   90. son]
F; sonnes Q   90. unto] F; to Q   91. the] F; your Q   93.
Hereford] Q; Hertford F   94. Which . . . promisèd] F;
The which you promised Q   94. shall] F; should Q
97. request] F; demand Q   98. I . . . me] F; As I remember Q   101. perhaps] F; perhaps, perhaps Q   102–22.
Q *only*   102, 111. lord—] ~. Q   103–19. SP RICHARD]
Ed.; *King.* Q   105. earldom—] ~. Q   122. Why . . . no]
Q; May it please you to resolue me in my suit F   123.
Thou] F; Tut, tut, thou Q   124. And . . . thus] F; Is it
euen so Q   124. Repays . . . deep] F; rewardst . . . true
Q   125. contempt] F; deepe contempt Q

4.3.   0. SD *Tyrrel*] F; *Sir Francis Tirrell* Q   1. act] F;
deed Q   2. arch deed] F; arch-act Q   4. who] F; whom
Q   5. this piece of ruthless] Ed.; this peece of ruthfull F; this ruthles peece of Q   6. Albeit] F; Although
Q   7. Melted . . . mild] F; Melting . . . kind Q   8. two]
F (to); two Q   8. story] F; stories Q   9. O . . . the gentle] F; Lo . . . those tender Q   11. alabaster innocent]
F (Alablaster); innocent alablaster Q   13. And] F;
Which Q   15. once] Q; one F   18. When] F; Whilst Q

20. she] F; he Q   21. Hence] F; Thus Q   23. bear] F;
bring Q   23. SD *Richard*] F; *Ki. Richard* Q   24. health
. . . lord] F; haile . . . leige Q   26. gave] F, Q3–6; giue Q
28. done] F; done my Lord Q   33. where . . . truth] F;
how or in what place Q   34. SP RICHARD] F; *Tir.* Q   34.
Tyrrel] F (*Tirrel*); *Tirre!* Q   34. at] Q; and F   35. When]
F; And Q   36. thee] F (the); thee Q   38. then] F; soone
Q   39. F *only*   39. SD Q *only, 2 lines earlier*   43. this]
F; the Q   44 *and hereafter.* Breton] F (Britaine *or* Brit-
taine)   46. on] F; ore Q   47. go I] F; I go Q   47. SD
Ratcliffe] F; *Catesby* Q   48 *and hereafter in this scene.*
SP RATCLIFFE] F; *Cat. or Cates.* Q   49. Good . . . news]
F; Good newes or bad Q   50. Morton] F; *Ely* Q   54.
strength] F; armie Q   55. learned] F; heard Q   57.
leads] leds F; leades Q   60. Go] F; Come Q

4.4.   0. Scene 4] Ed.; *Scena Tertia* F   0. SD *old
Queen Margaret*] F; *Queene Margaret sola* Q   1 *and
hereafter.* SP QUEEN MARGARET] Q (*Qu. Mar.*); *Mar.* F   4.
enemies] F; adversaries Q   9. SD F; *Enter the Qu. and
the Dutchesse of Yorke* Q   10. poor] F; young Q   11.
unblown] Q; vnblowed F   18–20 *follow line 36 in* Q,
where F*'s* still and mute *reads* mute and dumbe   21–22.
F *only*   27. Dead . . . sight] F; Blind sight, dead life Q
30. F *only*   32. innocent] F; innocents Q   33. as soon] F;
aswel Q   36. we] F; *I* Q   37. reverend] F, Q (reuerent)
38. seigniory] F (signeurie); signorie Q   39. griefs] F;
woes Q   39. hand.] ~∧ F   41. Q *only*   43. husband] F;
Richard Q   47. holp'st] Q3–6; hop'st F, Q   52. blood]
F; blouds Q   53–54. F *only, there placed in reverse order
after line* 55   61. wife] F, Q2–6; wifes Q   65. killed] F;
stabd Q   66. Thy] Q; The F   68. Matched] F; Match Q
69. stabbed] F; kild Q   70. frantic] F; tragicke Q   75.
at hand, at hand] F; at hand at handes Q   78. from
hence] F; away Q   80. and] F; to Q   89. fair] F; sweete
Q   90–92. what . . . bubble] F; which thou wert a
breath, a bubble, / A signe of dignitie, a garish flagge, /

To be the aime of euerie dangerous shot Q   95. are] Q;
be F, Q3–6   95. two sons] F; children Q   96. and
kneels and says] F; to thee, and cries Q   103 *after line
104 in* Q to] F (too)   105. she] F; one Q   106. F *only*
107. *after line 103 in* Q, *where* F's she *reads* one   108.
whirled] F; whe'eld Q   110–11. wast∧ . . . art.] ~. . . . ~,
F; wert, . . . ~, Q   115. weary] Q; wearied F, Q6   115.
head] F; necke Q   118. shall] F; will Q   121. nights . . .
days] Q; night . . . day F, Q3–6   123. sweeter] F; fairer
Q   131. their clients'] F; your Client Q   132. intestate]
Q; intestine F   134. will] F; do Q   135. nothing else] F;
not at al Q   138. that] F; which Q   139. The . . .
sounds] F; *I* heare his drum Q   139. SD F; *Enter K.
Richard marching with Drummes and Trumpets.* Q
140. me in] F *only*   142. accursèd] aceursed F;
accursed Q   145. Where] Q; Where 't F   145. branded]
F; grauen Q   147. poor] F; two Q   151. the gentle] F;
kind *Hastings* Q   152. F *only*   155. SD F; *The trumpets*
Q   157. clamorous] F; clamorus Q   163. That] F;
Which Q   164–65. F *only*   166. words] F; speach Q
169. torment and in agony] F; anguish, paine and
agonie Q   178. sly, and bloody] F; bloudie, trecherous
Q   179. F *only*   181. with] F; in Q   185. eye] F; sight
Q   186. you, madam] F; your grace Q   187. F *only*
188–92. I . . . So] F; *Du.* O heare me speake for I shal
neuer see thee more. | *King.* Come, come, you art too
bitter Q   194. Ere] F; Eeare Q   196. nevermore
behold] F; neuer looke vpon Q   197. grievous] F;
heauy Q   203. victory] F; victoric Q   208. her] F; all Q
209. talk] F; speake Q   210. more] F, Q2–6; moe Q
211. slaughter.] F; murther∧ Q   220. of] F; from Q
222. a royal princess] F; of roiall bloud Q   223. say] F;
faie Q   224. safest only] F; onlie safest Q   226. birth]
F; births Q   227. ill] F; bad Q   232–45. F *only*   232.
cousins.] ~? F   235. launched] F (lanch'd)   246–47.
enterprise . . . wars] F; dangerous attempt of hostile

armes Q   249. or] Q; and F, Q6   249. by . . . harmed]
F; were by me wrongd Q   250. the] F; rhe Q   252. gen-
tle] F; mightie Q   254. Unto . . . fortune] F; No to . . .
honor Q   256. sorrow] F; sorrowes Q   259. ay] F; yea
Q   264. the] F; thc Q   265. date] F; doe Q   274. do
intend] F; meane Q   275. Well] F; Saie Q   276. else
should be] F; should be else Q   278. Even . . . it] F; I
euen I, what thinke you of it Maddame Q   280. would
I] Q; I would F, Q3–6   281. being] F; that are Q   285.
hearts;] F (:); ~∧ Q   286. will she] F; she wil Q   287.
sometime] F, Q3–6; sometimes Q   288. steeped] F; a
handkercher steept Q   289–90. F *only*   291. wipe] F;
drie Q   291. withal] F; therewith Q   292. move] F;
force Q   293. letter . . . deeds] F; storie . . . acts Q
295. ay] F; yea Q   297. You . . . madam] F; Come,
come, you mocke me Q   297. is] Q *only*   302–56. F
only   338. Of ten times] Ed.; Oftentimes F   359. Tell
her . . . that] F; Saie that . . . which Q   362. vail] F;
waile Q   365. life's] F, Q (liues)   367, 368. As] F; So Q
368. and] F *corr.;* end F *uncorr.*   369. low] F; loue Q
373. plainly . . . tell] F; in plaine termes tell her Q   375.
Your] F; Madame, your Q   375. ²too] F (to); too Q
377. graves] F; graue Q   378–79. Q; 379–78 F   382.
swear—] ~. F; sweare by nothing Q   384–86. Thy] F;
The Q   384. lordly] F; holie Q   386. glory] F; dignitie
Q   387. wouldst] F; wilt Q   390–91. F; *after line 395 in*
Q, *reading* "King. Then by my selfe. | Qu. Thy selfe, thy
selfe misusest."   392–93. F; *after line 389 in* Q   395. it]
F; that Q   396. God] Q; Heauen F   397. God's] Q; Hea-
nens F   398. didst fear . . . with] F; hadst feard . . . by
Q   399. husband] F; brother Q   400. Thou . . . died] F;
Had not bene broken, nor my brother slaine Q   402.
head] F; brow Q   405. bedfellows] F; plaie-fellowes Q
406. the] F; a Q   407. F *only*   408. The] F; By the Q
409. the] F *only*   411. past . . . thee] F; by the past
wrongd Q   412. fathers] F; parents Q   414. in] Q; with

F, Q5–6   417. barren] F; withered Q   419. times ill-
used] F; time misused Q   419. o'erpast] Q; repast
F   421. affairs] F; attempt Q   423. F *only*   426.
proceeding . . . dear] F; proceedings . . . pure Q   430.
myself and thee] F; this land and me Q   431. Herself,
the land] F; To thee her selfe Q   432. Death] F; Sad Q
434. by] F, Q2–6; *omit* Q   435. dear] F; good Q 438.
my] F; by Q   440. peevish found] F; pieuish, fond Q
442. you] F; thee Q   445. Yet] F; But Q   446. daughter's] daughtcrs F; daughters Q   446. bury] F, Q3; buried Q   446. them,] ~. F; ~, Q   447. will] F; shall Q
448. recomforture] F; recomfiture Q   452. F *only*
453. and so] F *only*   453. SD *Queen*] Ed.; Q. F, *which
prints SD 1 line earlier; Exit.* Q, *placed here*   454. SD *1
line later in* F; *Enter Rat.* Q, *placed here*   455. F *only*
456. Most mighty] F; My gracious Q   457. our shores]
F; the shore Q   466. good] F *only*   467. Catesby] F
only   468–69. CATESBY . . . hither] F *only*   469. Rat-
cliffe] Ed; *Catesby* F   469. to] F; thou to Q   470.
thither] F; there Q   472. stay'st . . . here] F; standst . . .
still Q   473. liege . . . pleasure] F; Soueraigne, let me
know your minde Q   474. to him] F; them Q   476.
that] F *only*   477. suddenly] F; presentlie Q   478. SD.
F *only*   479. may . . . I] F; is it your highnes pleasure, I
shall Q   482. changed] F; changd sir, my minde is
changd Q   482. SD F; *Enter Darbie* Q, *1 line later*   483.
Stanley] F; How now Q   484 *and hereafter in this scene.*
SP STANLEY] F; *Dar.* Q   484. None ʌ good,] Ed.; ~, ~ʌ F;
~ʌ ~ʌ Q   484. liege] F; Lord Q   485. well . . . reported]
F; it may well be told Q   487. What need'st . . . miles]
F; Why doest . . . mile Q   488. the nearest] F; a neerer
Q   494. Well . . . guess] F; Well sir, . . . guesse, as you
guesse Q   495. Morton] F; Elie Q   496. here] F; there
Q   501. makes] F; doeth Q   501. seas] F; sea Q   506.
my good lord] F; mightie liege Q   508. be] F; are Q
512. me] F; Richard Q   514. king] F; soueraigne Q

515. Pleaseth] F; Please it Q   518. Ay] F; I, I Q   519.
But I'll . . . thee] F; *I* will . . . you Sir Q   523. Go . . .
but] F; Well, go muster men, but heare you Q   524.
heart] F; faith Q   526. SD *Stanley exits.*] F *only*   529.
Edward] F; William Q   530. elder brother] F; brother
there Q   532. In . . . liege] F; My Liege, in Kent Q   534.
the . . . strong] F; their aide, and still their power
increaseth Q   535. great] F; the Duke of Q   535. Buckingham—] ~. F   536. SD *1 line earlier in* Q   537. There
. . . bring] F; Take that vntill thou bring me Q   538.
The . . . Majesty] F; Your grace mistakes, the newes *I*
bring is good Q   539. Is . . . floods . . . waters] F; My
newes is . . . floud . . . water Q   540. Buckingham's] F;
The Duke of Buckinghams Q   541. wandered away
alone] F; fled Q   543. I . . . thee mercy] F; O I . . . you
mercie, I did mistake Q   544. There . . . thine] F; Ratcliffe reward him, for the blow I gaue him Q   545. pro-
claimed] F; giuen out Q   546. Reward to . . . the traitor
in] F; Rewardes for . . . in Buckingham Q   547. lord] F;
liege Q   549. in Yorkshire] F *only*   549. are] F; are vp
Q   550. But . . . Highness] F; Yet . . . grace Q   551. by
tempest] F *only*   552. Dorsetshire] F; Dorshire Q   553.
Unto the shore, to . . . those . . . banks] F; to . . . them.
. . . shore Q   557. his course again] F; away Q   564.
tidings, yet] Q; Newes, but yet F; newes, yet Q6   568.
SD *Flourish*] F *only*

   4.5.   0. Scene 5] Ed.; *Scena Quarta* F   0. SD *Enter*]
F; *Entee* Q   0. SD *and*] F *only*   1 *and hereafter in this
scene.* SP STANLEY] Ed.; *Der.* F; *Dar.* Q   2. the . . . deadly]
F; this . . . bloudie Q   4. off] F *corr.;* oft F *uncorr.*   5.
holds off] F; with holdes Q   6. So . . . gone] F *only*
6–8. Commend . . . daughter] F; *after "lord" in line 19 in*
Q, *reading* commend me to him, | Tell him, the Queene
hath hartelie consented, | He shall . . . daughter Q   10.
Pembroke] Q; Penbroke F   10. Ha'rfordwest] Ed.;
Hertford West F; Harford-west Q   12. SP CHRISTOPHER]

F; *S. Christ.* Q   15. And Rice ap] F; Rice vp Q   16. And . . . other of great name] F; With . . . moe of noble fame Q   17. do they . . . power] F; they doe . . . course Q   19. Well . . . hand] F; Retourne vnto thy Lord, commend me to him Q   20. My letter] F; These letters Q

5.1.   0. SD *This ed.; Enter Buckingham with Halberds, led to Execution.* F; *Enter Buckingham to execution.* Q   2 *and hereafter in this scene.* SP SHERIFF] F; *Rat.* Q   2. good] F *only*   3. Grey and Rivers] F; Riuers, Gray Q   10. fellow] F; fellowes Q   11. is] F; is my Lord Q   13. which] F; that Q   15. and] F; or Q   15. wife's] F, Q (wiues)   17. whom . . . trusted] F; I trusted most Q   20. which] F; that Q   24. in] F; on Q   24. bosoms] F; bosome Q   25. Thus . . . falls . . . neck] F; Now . . . is fallen vpon my head Q   25. neck] F *corr.* (necke); neeke F *uncorr.*   26. quoth] F; quorh Q   29. lead me, officers] F; sirs, conuey me Q   30. SD *This ed.; Exeunt Buckingham with Officers.* F; *omit* Q

5.2.   0. SD F; *Enter Richmond with drums and trumpets* Q   12. Is] F; Lies Q   12. center] Q; Centry F   13. Near] Q; Ne're F   18. SP OXFORD] F; I *Lo.* Q   18. men] F; swordes Q   19. this guilty] F; that bloudie Q   20. SP HERBERT] F; 2 *Lo.* Q   20. turn] F; flie Q   21. SP BLUNT] F; 3 *Lo.* Q   21. what] F; who Q   22. dearest . . . fly] F; greatest . . . shrinke Q   25. makes] F; make Q   25. SD F; *Exit.* Q

5.3.   0. SD F; *Enter King Richard, Norffolke, Ratcliffe, Catesbie, with others.* Q   1. tent] F; tentes Q   2. My . . . sad] F; Whie, how now Catesbie, whie lookst thou so bad Q   3. SP SURREY] F; *Cat.* Q   4. F; Norffolke, come hether Q   5. F *only*   7. loving] F; gracious Q   8. tent] F; tent there Q   10. traitors] F; foe Q   11. utmost] F, Q *corr.;* greatest Q *uncorr.*   11. power] F; number Q   12. battalia] F; battalion Q   14. faction] F; partie Q   14. want] F *corr.;* went F *uncorr.*   15. the . . . noble] F; my tent there, valiant Q   16. ground] F; field

Q   18. lack] F; want Q   19. SD *Sir William . . . tent*] F
(*which reads "and Dorset"*); *with the Lordes, &c.* Q   21.
track] Q; Tract F   22. token] F; signall Q   23. Sir . . .
you] F; Where is Sir . . . he Q   24–27. F; *after line 46
in* Q, *reading* strength *for* power   28–29. F *only*   29.
you] Ed.; your F   30. keeps] F; keepe Q   34. captain
. . . me] F; Blunt before thou goest Q   35. do you] F;
doest thou Q   41–42. F; Good captaine Blunt beare
my good night to him Q   43. note] F; scrowle Q   45.
F *only*   46. F; Farewell good Blunt Q   47. gentlemen]
F *only*   49. my] F; our Q   49. dew] F; aire Q   49. 1st
SD F *only, reading "They withdraw. . . ."*   49. 2nd SD
F; *Enter king Richard, Norff. Ratcliffe Catesbie, &c.* Q
50. is 't] F; is Q   51. F; It is sixe of clocke, full supper
time Q   52–end of play. Q *is the basis of this edition*
52, 77, 220–369. SP RICHARD] Ed.; *King.* Q, F   56 *and
hereafter (with exceptions noted in the preceding note).*
SP RICHARD] F; *King.* Q (192 *King Ri.*)   57. sentinels]
F; centinell Q   60. SD F *only*   61. Catesby] Q; *Ratcliffe*
F   62. SP CATESBY] Ed.; *Rat.* Q, F   73. thou] Q; *omit*
F   73. Lord] Q (Lo.)   85 *and hereafter in this scene.* SP
STANLEY] Ed.; *Darby* Q, F   85. sit] Q (set); sit F, Q2–6
86. SP RICHMOND] Ed.; *Rich.* Q, F   88. loving] Q; Noble
F, Q3–6   91. that.] ~∧ Q   99. doubtful] doubful Q;
doubtfull F   106. sundered] Q (sundried)   109. SP
RICHMOND] Ed.; *Rich.* Q; *Riehm.* F   110. thoughts] Q;
noise F   113. SD *Exunt.* Q; *Exeunt. Manet Richmond.* F
120. the] Q; thy F, Q3–5   122. Ere] F; Eare Q   123. 1st
SD F *only*   123. 2nd SD *young*] Q; *omit* F, Q3–6   123.
2nd SD *to*] F, Q2–6; *omit* Q   123. 2nd SD *Harry*] Q;
Henry F, Q2–6   123. 2nd SD *Sixth*] F, Q3–6; *sixt, to Ri.*
Q   124. SD *to Richard*] Q, F (*to Ri.*)   125. stabbed'st]
Ed.; stabst Q, F   128. SD *To Richmond.*] Q (*To Rich.*);
Ghost to Richm. F   132. SD *to Richard*] Q (*to Ri.*); *omit*
F   133. deadly] Q; *omit* F, Q2–6   136, 144. SD *To Rich-
mond.*] Q (*To Rich.*); F (*To Richm.*)   138. thy] Q; *omit* F

138. sleep.] ~∧ Q   139. sit] Q (set); sit F   147. battle.]
~∧ Q   148. SP GHOST OF RIVERS] Ed.; *King.* Q; *Riu.* F,
Q3–6   153. SD *Richmond*] Ed.; *Ri.* Q; *Richm.* F   154.
Will] F, Q2–6; Wel Q   154. SD–163. *Enter . . .* flourish.]
Q; *placed after line 168 in* F   155. GHOSTS *. . . to Rich-
ard*] Ed.; *Ghost to Ri.* Q; *Ghosts* F   156. lead] Q; laid
F, Q2–6   158. souls bid] Q; soule bids F   159. SD *To
Richmond.*] Q (*To Rich.*); *Ghosts to Richm.* F   163. SD
Hastings] Q; *Lord Hastings* F   167. SD *To Richmond.*]
Ed.; *To Rich.* Q; *Hast. to Rich.* F   168. England's] F;
Engiands Q   168. SD *Lady*] Q *only*   169. SD, 178 SD.
GHOST *. . . Richard*] Ed.; *Ghost to Rich.* F; *omit* Q   171.
perturbations] F; preturbations Q   173. sword.] Ed.;
~∧ Q   174. SD, 184 SD. *To Richmond.*] Ed.; *To Rich.*
Q; *Ghost to Rich.* F   178. SP Ed.; *Ghost* F   188. fall]
F; fals Q   188. SD *starteth up*] Q; *starts* F   188. SD *a*]
Q; *his* F   189. SP RICHARD] F; *King Ri.* Q   192. now] Q;
not F, Q2–6   194. What∧ . . . fear?] Q; ~? . . . ~∧ F   195.
am] F, Q2–6; and Q   203. villain] Q; Vlllaine F   208.
Perjury, perjury] Q; Periurie F, Q3–6   211. Throng] Q;
Throng all F, Q3–6   213. will] Q; shall F, Q3–6   214.
And] Q; Nay F   220. Zounds] Q; *omit* F   224–26. Q;
omit F   233. day.] ~∧ Q   234. eavesdropper] Ed.; ease
dropper Q, F   235. see] Q; heare F, Q3–6   235. 1st SD
Richard and Ratcliffe] F *only*   235. 2nd SD *in his tent*]
F (*sitting in his Tent*); *omit* Q   236. SP LORDS] Q3–6; *Lo.*
Q; *Richm.* F   237 *and hereafter throughout this scene.*
SP RICHMOND] Ed.; *Rich.* Q, F   239. SP A LORD] Ed.;
Lo. Q; *Lords.* F   242. departure] F; depature Q   246.
soul] Q; heart F   249. SP A LORD] Ed.; *Lo.* Q, F   257.
Richard∧ except,] ~, ~∧ Q; (~ ~) F   265. foil] Q; soile
F, Q3–6   269. in] F; ln Q   270. sweat] Q; sweare F,
Q3–6   285. SD *Ratcliffe, and Soldiers*] Ed.; *Rat. &c.* Q;
Ratcliffe, and Catesby. F   290. SD *The*] Q *only*   296–97.
somebody. | Ratcliffe] F; some bodie Rat. Q   299. not]
F; nor Q   310. out all] Q *only*   314. this] Q; the F, Q3–6

315. follow] Q; fllow F   316. main] matne Q; maine F
318. boot] F, Q3–6; bootes Q   320. SD Q *only*   324. SP
A] Ed.; *King.* A Q, F   325. unto] Q; to F   327. Conscience is but a] Q; For Conscience is a F; Conscience
is a Q3–6   329. conscience,] F; ~ ∧ Q   331. SD Q *only*
334. rascals] rascols Q; rascals F   338. to you] Q; you
to F, Q2–6   339. wives] Q (wifes); wiues F   343. milk-
sop] Q (milkesopt)   355. in] Q; on F, Q3–6   357. SD
F *only*   359. Fight] Q; Right F, Q3–6   359. bold] Q;
boldly F, Q2–6   363. SD F *only*   373. them!] them ∧
Q; them, F   373. helms] Q; helpes F, Q3, 5–6   373. SD
Q *only*

5.4.   6. SD *Alarums*] F *only*

5.5.   0. SD *Alarum*] Q; *Alatum* F   0. SD *Then. . . .*
Flourish] *then retrait being sounded* Q; *Retreat, and*
Flourish F   0. SD *with other*] Q; *with diuers other* F   0.
SD *and Soldiers*] &c. Q   1 *and hereafter throughout this*
scene. SP RICHMOND] F (*Richm.*); *Ri.* or *Rich.* Q   3 *and*
hereafter. SP STANLEY] Ed.; *Dar.* Q; *Der.* F   4. this . . .
royalty] Q; these . . . Royalties F; this . . . royalties Q2–6
4. royalty ∧] ~. Q   7. enjoy it] Q; *omit* F, Q3–6   11. if
it please you, we may now] Q; (if you please) we may F
13. SP STANLEY] F (*Der.*); *omit* Q   13. Walter] F; *Water*
Q   13. Ferrers] Ed.; *Ferris* Q, F   14. Brakenbury] Ed.;
Brookenbury Q; Brokenbury F   15. becomes] Ed.;
become Q, F   32. their] Q; thy F, Q3–6   41. SD F *only*

Richard III:
A Modern Perspective

Phyllis Rackin

From the standpoint of Tudor history, the most important event in *Richard III* is the conclusion, and the most important character is Richmond. The victory of Queen Elizabeth's grandfather at Bosworth Field and his marriage to Elizabeth of York ended the Wars of the Roses and established the Tudor dynasty.[1] On Shakespeare's stage, however, the future Henry VII was a pallid figure with a minimal part, and he was not even mentioned on the title page of the first published edition, which identified the play as *The Tragedy of Richard the third, Containing, His treacherous Plots against his brother Clarence: the pittiefull murther of his iunocent nephewes: his tyrannicall vsurpation: with the whole course of his detested life, and most deserued death.* The monstrous villain of Tudor history became the star of Shakespeare's play. Almost always onstage, he dominates the dramatic action in a role that has attracted leading actors from Shakespeare's time to our own. The most memorable scene in the play, moreover, is Richard's courtship of Anne Neville, which had no relevance, either in history or in Shakespeare's play, to his plot to win the throne. Richmond's marriage to Elizabeth of York was the foundation of the Tudor dynasty, but we see nothing of their courtship or wedding, and the bride-to-be never even appears on Shakespeare's stage.

Shakespeare's portrait of Richard as a moral and physical monster has been discredited by modern his-

torians, but it had ample precedents in Tudor historiography. A new dynasty whose founder had won his
crown in battle, the Tudors fostered official histories
that vilified Richard in order to authenticate their own
claim to the throne. That Richard would be remembered as a monster during the reign of the Tudors is
easily understandable; what is perhaps more difficult
to understand is his popularity during that same period
as a subject for theatrical representation.[2] A Latin play
Richardus Tertius, written by Thomas Legge and performed at Cambridge in 1579, was repeatedly copied
in manuscript and much admired during the period.
An anonymous play entitled *The True Tragedy of Richard III*, published in 1594, continued to be performed
well into the seventeenth century. Shakespeare's *Richard III* was one of his most popular plays, the subject
of numerous contemporary references and an excep-
tionally large number of early reprints.[3]

This contradiction between Richard's villainous
role in Tudor historiography and his popularity on
the Tudor stage points to the very different functions
served by historical writing and theatrical performance
in Shakespeare's time. History was an honorable
institution, respected as a source of practical wisdom
and moral edification. Sir Thomas Elyot, the English
humanist, made it the center of his educational pro-
gram: "Surely if a noble man do thus seriously and dili-
gently rede histories," he wrote, "I dare affirme there
is no studie or science for him of equal commoditie
and pleasure, havynge regarde to every tyme and age."[4]
As Elyot's title—*The Boke Named the Gouernour*—
suggests, the projected audience for history came from
the upper reaches of the social hierarchy. So did its subjects. Having a history, in fact, was equivalent to having
a place in the status system. As the prefatory letter to
Hall's *Union* explained, "what diversitie is betwene a

noble prince & a poore begger . . . if after their death there be left of them no remembrance or token." Just as the Tudor monarchs fostered histories that justified their claim to the throne, Tudor subjects provided a thriving business for the heralds who constructed coats of arms to represent real or fabricated genealogies that would authorize their status as gentlemen.

Written during a time of rapid cultural change, Tudor history looked to the past to stabilize a hierarchical status system based on heredity, a system threatened by the unprecedented social mobility produced by an increasingly commercial economy. The commercial theater was a recent innovation, associated with many of the disturbing changes that threatened to destabilize the social order. The official status system was based on inheritance, which determined the place each person should occupy. But playhouses were open to anyone who could afford the low price of admission, permitting the common rabble to rub shoulders in the audience with their betters (and sometimes pick their pockets) because the playgoers could sit or stand in whatever part of the theater they had paid to enter instead of occupying places that were dictated by their ranks in the social hierarchy. Sumptuary laws dictated the sort of apparel that could be worn by people of different social positions, but the common players who impersonated kings and nobles were costumed in the cast-off clothes of aristocrats, and the stories they enacted allowed common subjects in the audience to spy on the private lives of their betters, pass judgment on their character and statecraft, and enjoy the spectacle of the sufferings of nobles and the deposition and murder of kings. Since women were not allowed to appear on the English stage, female parts were acted by boys dressed in women's clothing; but, as the pious were quick to point out, this practice violated bibli-

cal injunctions against cross-dressing and threatened
to evoke illicit lust among the playgoers. Sex, in fact,
figured prominently in denunciations of the theater.
Prostitutes and procurers, it was claimed, turned the
playhouses into "a generall market of bawdrie," and
even the virtuous were in danger: "the pure chastitie
bothe of single and maried persons, men and women"
was so quickly corrupted that "such as happilie came
chaste unto showes, returne adulterers from plaies."[5]

Antitheatrical tracts denounced the dangerous
allure of playhouses, "the springs of many vices, and
the stumbling-blocks of godliness and virtue," where
audiences were seduced to every sort of "ungodly
desires," crimes, and treason.[6] "If you will learne
to . . . blaspheme both Heaven and Earth," wrote Philip
Stubbes, "if you will learn to rebel against Princes, to
commit treasons . . . if you will learne to contemne GOD
and al his lawes, to care nither for heaven nor hel, and
to commit al kinde of sinne and mischeef, you need to
goe to no other schoole, for all these good Examples
may you see painted before your eyes in . . . playes."[7]
This is an extreme—although certainly not unique—
example of antitheatrical invective, and the theater had
its defenders as well. If opponents of the stage argued
that playgoing incited personal vice and political sub-
version, its defenders could argue just the opposite.
Representations of moral virtue and heroic patriotism
could provide uplifting models for their audiences,
and dramatizations of criminal actions punished by
divine providence could serve as cautionary examples.
According to Thomas Nashe, reenactments of the valiant deeds of heroic forefathers would inspire the men
in the theater audience with patriotic sentiment and
martial valor. According to Thomas Heywood, the
spectacle of rebels and traitors punished would inspire
obedience to the crown.[8]

Both Nashe and Heywood used the example of the English history play to argue that playgoing could make the lessons of history accessible to the ignorant and unlearned. One of those lessons, according to the first English treatise on historiography, was to provide "notable examples" of God's "wrath, and revenge towardes the wicked, as also his pittie and clemencie towardes the good," for "though things many times doe succeede according to the discourse of man's reason: yet man's wisedome is oftentymes greatlye deceyved" because "nothing is done by chaunce, but all things by [God's] foresight, counsell, and divine providence."[9] *Richard III* seems admirably calculated to teach this lesson. Richard "greatlye deceyves" himself and the other characters, but prophecies, prophetic dreams, and curses that take effect all suggest that supernatural forces are at work in the events that Richard believes are completely under his control. The play begins with Richard's clever manipulations and self-congratulatory soliloquies as he arranges his brother Clarence's death, but Clarence's prophetic dream and death's-door recognition remind the audience that Clarence's impending doom is actually God's punishment for the crimes he committed in the time of Henry VI. The play ends with Richmond's victory, heralded by prophetic dreams and heavenly imagery that clearly identify him as God's agent, just as the many references to Richard's diabolical nature define his own place within the providential scheme.

Most members of the audience that entered Shakespeare's theater were probably well aware of Richard's villainous role in Tudor history, but the character they encountered on Shakespeare's stage threatens to subvert the providential moral of his story by the sheer energy and dramatic force of his characterization. The images of theatrical dissembling traditionally associated with

Richard's character are reinforced in Shakespeare's representation by allusions to the seductive player described in the antitheatrical tracts. In *3 Henry VI* Richard has a long soliloquy in which he identifies himself as a villain in exactly the same terms that Renaissance writers typically used to describe actors:

> Why, I can smile, and murder whiles I smile,
> And cry "Content" to that which grieves my heart,
> And wet my cheeks with artificial tears,
> And frame my face to all occasions. . . .
> I can add colors to the chameleon,
> Change shapes with Proteus for advantages,
> And set the murderous Machiavel to school.
>
> (3.2.184–95)

In Shakespeare's time, the "chameleon player" was a standard epithet for actors, and allusions to Proteus the shape-shifter appeared not only in admiring descriptions of leading actors like Richard Burbage (who perhaps played Richard's part)[10] but also in condemnations of actors and other upstarts who refused to abide in the social place to which God had assigned them. In Richard's self-description, moreover, the reference to Proteus slides inexorably into a reference to the Machiavel, a far more sinister symbol of unprincipled hypocrisy, who was also associated with Proteus in contemporary thought.[11]

In *Richard III*, Richard's identity as a master performer becomes the structural principle of the dramatic action. The play begins with a long soliloquy in which Richard announces his chosen dramatic role ("to prove a villain"), and the early scenes are punctuated by more soliloquies in which he not only describes his motivations but also presents himself as the contriver of the entire drama. "Plots have I laid, inductions dangerous," he says, identifying his plots with the plots of the action to come. Like the tragic playwright himself, Richard takes an amoral, artistic delight in cleverly arranging the ruin of the other characters. Richard's power on Shakespeare's stage is not simply or even primarily the product of his role in the represented historical action. It derives mainly from his theatrical presence—the wit and energy that allow him to monopolize the audience's attention and the ability to transcend the frame of historical representation that allows him to address the audience directly without the knowledge of the other characters. In the early scenes of the play, it is always Richard who has the last word (along with the first). He comes to the front of the stage to share his wicked plots with the audience, steps back into the upstage frame of dramatic representation to execute them upon the other characters, and then returns to the forestage to boast to the audience about the efficacy of his performance. Confiding in the audience, flaunting his witty wickedness, and gloating at the weakness and ignorance of the other characters, he draws the playgoers into complicity with his wicked schemes.

By defining his villainy as a theatrical tour de force, Richard invites the playgoers to evaluate his actions simply as theatrical performances. Significantly, the most striking instance of this maneuver occurs in his soliloquy at the end of the scene when he seduces Anne. "Was ever woman in this humor wooed?" he asks the audience. "Was ever woman in this humor won?"

> What, I that killed her husband and his father,
> To take her in her heart's extremest hate,
> With curses in her mouth, tears in her eyes,
> The bleeding witness of my hatred by . . . ? . . .
> Hath she forgot already that brave prince,

Edward, her lord, whom I some three months since
Stabbed in my angry mood at Tewkesbury?
A sweeter and a lovelier gentleman,
Framed in the prodigality of nature,
Young, valiant, wise, and, no doubt, right royal,
The spacious world cannot again afford.
And will she yet abase her eyes on me,
That cropped the golden prime of this sweet prince
And made her widow to a woeful bed?
On me, whose all not equals Edward's moiety?

                                        (1.2.247–70)

This soliloquy, which ends the scene, is thirty-eight lines long, reminding the audience of the historical wrongs that should have made Anne reject his suit, flaunting the theatrical power that made her forget the past. Here, and throughout the first act of the play, Richard performs a similar seduction upon the audience. For the audience as for Anne, the seduction requires the suspension of moral judgment and historical memory, since the demonic role that Richard had been assigned in Tudor history was well known; but the sheer theatrical energy of his performance supersedes the moral weight of the historical tradition.

The conflation of the historical seduction represented onstage with the theatrical seduction of the present audience and of Richard with the actor who played his part is implicit in a well-known anecdote associated with the play from the beginning of the seventeenth century. In March 1602, John Manningham wrote in his diary,

Upon a tyme when Burbidge played Rich. 3. there was a citizen greue [i.e., grew] soe farr in liking wth him, that before shee went from the play shee appointed him to come that night unto hir by the name of Ri: the 3. Shakespeare overhearing their conclusion,

went before, was intertained, and at his game ere
Burbidge came. Then message being brought that
Rich. the 3ᵈ was at the dore, Shakespeare caused
returne to be made [i.e., sent an answer] that William the Conquerour was before Rich. the 3.[12]

Although Shakespeare triumphs at Burbage's expense,
the anecdote clearly suggests that, even in Shakespeare's time, the theatrical power of Richard's part
was identified with erotic conquest. Richard's perverse seduction of Anne over the coffin that contains
the body of Henry VI is, as I stated earlier, irrelevant
to the historical plot (Richard merely mentions that
he has a "secret close intent"), but it works onstage as
the most compelling demonstration of that power. The
scene also serves as an anticipation of another wooing
scene near the end of the play when Richard attempts
to persuade his brother's widowed queen to give him
her daughter Elizabeth in marriage. Richard's motiva-
tion for this second courtship, and the reason for its
inclusion in the play, are absolutely clear: as the daughter of a king, Elizabeth, unlike Anne Neville, plays a
crucial role in the contention for the crown. But there
is no more basis in Shakespeare's chronicle sources for
this courtship scene than there was for the earlier one.
It is worth noting that Shakespeare does not dramatize
Richmond's courtship of the Queen's daughter: all we
get is the laconic announcement in a later scene that
"the Queen hath heartily consented / He [Richmond]
should espouse Elizabeth her daughter" (4.5.7–8) and
Richmond's reiteration at the end of the play that the
marriage will take place. What matters from the point
of view of the dramatic action is Richard's loss rather
than Richmond's victory, a loss that is dramatized in
the implicit contrast between the two scenes.

In both cases Richard encounters a woman who
insists on recalling the historical record of his vil-

lainy, in both he attempts to blot it out with an out-
rageous erotic conquest, and in both he thinks he has
prevailed; but the structure of the two scenes is significantly different. Richard dominated the action of the
earlier scene, interrupting Anne as she went to bury
the murdered king, sending her offstage at the end so
he could gloat to the audience in a long soliloquy. In
Act 4, scene 4, by contrast, Richard does not appear
onstage until line 140, and now it is Richard himself
who is interrupted: attempting to cross the stage in
a martial procession, he is "intercepted" by a chorus
of outraged women and forced, unwillingly, to hear
their reproaches and curses. The ending of the scene
offers an even more striking demonstration of Richard's inability to control—or even to anticipate—the
course of the dramatic action. When Elizabeth leaves
the stage, he exclaims, "Relenting fool and shallow,
changing woman!" apparently prepared to deliver one
of his characteristic, gloating soliloquies. This time,
however, he has no leisure to continue his address to
the audience or to exult about the victory he thinks he
has won because he is immediately interrupted by Ratcliffe, who brings the news that Richmond has arrived
on the west coast of England with a powerful navy.
The scene ends in disarray with the rapid entrances of
no less than four additional messengers and Richard's
confused and agitated responses to their reports about
the offstage progress of Richmond's invasion.

   Richmond arrives like a deus ex machina to save
the suffering country from Richard's tyrannical rule.
Characterized simply as Richard's antithesis, he has no
real theatrical presence. On Shakespeare's stage Margaret is a much more powerful antagonist than Richmond because she opposes Richard's amoral theatrical
appeal by reminding the audience of the providential
moral of the historical action. Railing at the Yorkists,
she recalls the crimes committed during the time of

Henry VI that justify their present sufferings. Leading the other women in a litany of lamentation, she identifies Richard's role in the providential drama as the agent of divine vengeance and foretells his destruction.

Although Margaret appears in only two scenes, the other characters' recollections of her curses and prophecies sustain her status as Richard's competitor for control and interpretation of the dramatic action. At the beginning of Act 4, scene 4, it is Margaret and not Richard who addresses the audience, defining the previous action in theatrical terms as a "dire induction" [i.e., prologue] and identifying the generic form of the drama when she confides her hopes that the conclusion will be just as "tragical." From the point of view of Richmond and England, of course, the play has a happy conclusion when Richmond kills the tyrant and invites the playgoers as well as the actors onstage to join him in a prayer for a peaceful and prosperous future that will be theirs as well as his own. Nonetheless, whoever wrote the title that appeared on the early printed editions regarded the play as "The Tragedy of King Richard III," and modern critics have echoed that judgment in their descriptions of the many ways in which Shakespeare's characterization of Richard anticipates his practice in the later tragedies. The comforting pieties of Richmond's final prayer probably elicited more enthusiasm in Shakespeare's time than they do today, but even then the attraction that drew audiences to the playhouse was not the victory of the virtuous Richmond but the dangerous theatrical vitality of Richard III.

---

1. Edward Hall's chronicle history, one of the main sources for Shakespeare's English history plays, was actually entitled *The Union of the two noble and illustre famelies of Lancastre and Yorke, beeyng long in con-*

tinual discension for the croune of this noble realme,
with all the actes done in bothe the tymes of the princes,
bothe of the one linage and of the other, beginnyng at the
tyme of Kyng Henry the fowerth, the first aucthor of this
devision, and so successively proceadyng to the reigne
of . . . Kyng Henry the Eight, the undubitate flower and
very heire of both the said linages (London, 1548). As
Hall explained, Henry VIII was the "undubitate" heir
to the English crown because he was the product of the
union between "Kyng Henry the seventh and the lady
Elizabeth his moste worthy Quene, the one beeyng
indubitate heire of the hous of Lancastre, and the other
of Yorke" (*Union*, p. 1).

2. Hugh M. Richmond, *Shakespeare in Performance: King Richard III* (Manchester and New York: Manchester University Press, 1989), pp. 25–30.

3. E. A. J. Honigmann, introduction to *King Richard the Third* (Harmondsworth, Middlesex: Penguin Books, 1968), p. 7. See also "An Introduction to This Text," above, p. liii.

4. *The Boke Named the Governour,* edited from the edition of 1531 by Henry H. S. Croft (London: Kegan Paul, Trench, 1883), 1:91.

5. Stephen Gosson, *The School of Abuse* (1579); John Northbrooke, *A Treatise wherein Dicing, Dauncing, Vaine playes, or Enterluds . . . are reproved* (1577); and Anthony Munday, *A Second and Third Blast of Retrait from Plaies and Theaters* (1580), all quoted by Ann Jennalie Cook in "'Bargaines of Incontinencie': Bawdy Behavior in the Playhouses," *Shakespeare Studies* 10 (1977): 271–90, esp. pp. 272–74.

6. George Whetstone (1584) and Gervase Babington (1583), reprinted in E. K. Chambers, *The Elizabethan Stage* (Oxford: Clarendon Press, 1923), 4:227, 225.

7. *The Anatomie of Abuses* (London, 1583), in Chambers, *Elizabethan Stage*, 4:224.

8. Nashe's defense of plays appeared in *Pierce Penilesse his Supplication to the Devil* (1592), Heywood's in *An Apology for Actors* (1612). It is worth noting that both Nashe and Heywood wrote plays for the commercial theater.

9. Thomas Blundeville, *The true order and Methode of wryting and reading Hystories* (London, 1574) F3–F3^v.

10. For a good summary of Elizabethan descriptions of actors, including Burbage, see Louis Adrian Montrose, "The Purpose of Playing: Reflections on a Shakespearean Anthropology," *Helios*, n.s. 7.2 (1980): 56–57. On the image of Proteus as applied to actors, see Jonas Barish, *The Antitheatrical Prejudice* (Berkeley: University of California Press, 1981), pp. 99–107.

11. The Machiavel was a stock character on the English stage who embodied the ruthless ambition, atheism, and deceptiveness that were associated in popular thought with the Florentine political philosopher Niccolò Machiavelli.

12. Manningham's *Diary* (British Museum, Harleian MS. 5353, fol. 29^v), reprinted in *The Riverside Shakespeare*, ed. G. Blakemore Evans et al. (Boston: Houghton Mifflin, 1974), p. 1836.

Further Reading

In addition to the following books and articles,
see *www.folger.edu/shakespeare* and
www.folger.edu/online-resources.

Richard III

Anderson, Judith H. *Biographical Truth: The Representation of Historical Persons in Tudor-Stuart Writing.* New Haven: Yale University Press, 1984.

Following a discussion of Sir Thomas More's *History of King Richard III* as a mix of history and biography (Chap. 6), Anderson turns her attention to the "metamorphosis of biographical truth to fiction" in Shakespeare's play (Chap. 7). Shakespeare's protagonist is "both more real as a psychological entity and more imaginary . . . more clearly and consistently a type . . . more insistently a symbol . . . more self-conscious about his own shape . . . and more consciously a player of roles and a shaper of his own identity."

Baldwin, David. *Richard III.* Stroud, Gloucestershire: Amberley Publishing, 2013.

Baldwin's full biography of Richard III views him as neither "a villain [nor] a man unjustifiably vilified throughout history": "Somewhere behind all the conflicting arguments stands a real man who had both qualities and failings." In addition to a prologue ("Conflicting Opinions") and an epilogue ("The Discovery of King Richard's Grave"—a recounting of the 2013 archaeological excavation in Leicester that unearthed Richard's skeletal remains), the volume includes fifteen chapters, most of which are arranged in minutely chronological order by year, sometimes by months of a particular year: "'Richard Liveth Yet,' 1452–1461"; "The King's Brother, 1461–1469"; "The Years of Crisis, 1469–1471"; "Warwick's Heir, 1471–1475"; "War and Peace, 1475–1482"; "'The King is Dead,' April–June 1483"; "'Long Live the King!' July 1483"; "Conspiracy and Rebellion, July–November 1483"; "Regaining the Initiative, 1484"; "Cultivating the Bishops, 1484"; "The Two Elizabeths [Elizabeth Woodville (Edward IV's queen) and Elizabeth of York], February–March 1485"; "The Gathering Storm, April–June 1485"; and "Bosworth Field, August 1485." Chapter 8 ("Richard 'Crookback'?") takes up the historical accuracy of Richard's reported physical disfigurement, while Chapter 15 deals with his legacy and the legend that has attached to him. Baldwin contends that only a close examination of the episodes in Richard's life both before and after he became king can help us determine "if the Richard who seized the Crown was the same Richard who had played a leading, and generally commendable, role in the politics of the late 1460s, 1470s and early 1480s, or if his character had changed over time." In short, "we need to see him in the round."

Baldwin, William, ed. *A Myrroure for Magistrates* (1559, 1563, 1571, 1574, 1575, 1578, 1587). Reprinted as *The Mirror for Magistrates*. Ed. Lily B. Campbell. Huntington Library Publications. Cambridge: Cambridge University Press, 1938. Reprint, New York: Barnes & Noble, 1970.

The *Mirror* (which went through several editions between 1559 and 1587) is an anthology of verse monologues recounting the downfall of public figures from antiquity and English history. Their lives serve as moral exempla on the vicissitudes of Fortune and on the price paid for lives of villainy and misplaced trust in the vanities of the world. The "tragic" stories having relevance for *Richard III* are those of Clarence, Hastings, Shore's wife, Edward IV, Rivers, Buckingham, and Richard.

Carroll, William. "'The Form of Law': Ritual and Succession in *Richard III.*" In *True Rites and Maimed Rites: Ritual and Anti-Ritual in Shakespeare and His Age*, ed. Linda Woodbridge and Edward Berry, pp. 203–19. Urbana: University of Illinois Press, 1992.

For Carroll, Richard's failure to achieve emotional maturity through rites of passage is only one example of the general failure of legal and cultural ritual in the play as a whole (e.g., the "farce" of Hastings's indictment, rumors of illegitimacy, the perversion of courtship traditions, and the violated rites of execution and burial). The only "form of law" Richard supports absolutely is that of hereditary succession; ironically, however, he cannot retain that "form" nor can the audience fully accept Richmond's confident and ceremonial reaffirmation of lineal succession at the end because Richard "has contaminated everything." The play reflects uncertainties in the 1590s surrounding the issue of who will succeed Elizabeth I as England's monarch.

Charnes, Linda. "Belaboring the Obvious: Reading the Monstrous Body in *King Richard III.*" In *Notorious Identity: Materializing the Subject in Shakespeare*, pp. 20–69. Cambridge, Mass.: Harvard University Press, 1993.

Charnes discusses the ideological foundations of "notorious identity" (the pathological form of fame) in *Richard III, Troilus and Cressida,* and *Antony and Cleopatra* and explores how Shakespeare is less interested in "reproducing cultural mythography" than in demonstrating what is involved in the "experience of being reiterated," that process through which each "notorious" figure confronts the determinant power of an infamous name as he or she self-fashions a new identity. The chapter on Richard examines his desire, efforts, and ultimate failure to break out of a "prior textual history" that inscribes him as monstrous object in order to construct himself as "something undisclosed," i.e., as a subject of his own making. Charnes deals with the courtship of Lady Anne (1.2) at some length.

Clemen, Wolfgang. *A Commentary on Shakespeare's Richard III*. Tr. Jean Bonheim. London: Methuen, 1968.
Clemen provides a detailed analysis that examines the structure of each scene, its position in the plot and its overall dramatic significance, the grouping and function(s) of characters, the treatment of time and space, techniques of dialogue, stylistic devices, rhetorical strategies, image clusters and iterative words, meter and versification. Types of irony and ambiguity and patterns of anticipation and foreboding receive special emphasis.

Colley, Scott. *Richard's Himself Again: A Stage History of Richard III*. Westport, Conn.: Greenwood Press, 1992.
Colley provides a comprehensive account of the play's stage history in Great Britain and North America from 1690 to the early 1990s, focusing primarily on leading interpreters of the title role. The first chapter's overview of problems involved in staging *Richard III* (e.g., its length, the tendency by actors and directors to allow Richard too much focus, numerous set pieces, and difficulties in "balancing the earthly and cosmic dramas inherent in [the] design") illustrates that there is "something about the play that forces one to alter it."

The ghost of Cibber's conception and later the curse of Olivier's film (a "drastically simplified" version that followed from "a deliberate misreading") have haunted the play's stage history. Three modern Richards, however, have succeeded in breathing new life into the role in productions that were also box office successes: the "pint-sized" Richard of Ian Holm (1963–64), the "surrealist Napoleon" of Ramaz Chkhikvadze (1979), and the "acrobatic cripple" of Antony Sher (1984–85). A "coda" deals with more recent Richards, most notably Ian McKellen's.

Connolly, Annaliese, ed. *Richard III: A Critical Reader.* Arden Early Modern Drama Guides. London: Bloomsbury Arden Shakespeare, 2013.

The eight essays gathered in this volume provide a comprehensive survey of major issues in the contemporary study of *Richard III*. The first three essays address, respectively, *Richard*'s critical reception from the eighteenth-century Samuel Johnson to postmodern readings in the twenty-first century (Peter J. Smith, "The Critical Backstory"), the play's performance history from Shakespeare's day to more recent revivals by Laurence Olivier and Ian McKellen (Kate Wilkinson, "*Richard III* on Stage"), and key themes and mass media adaptations in the current critical and performance environment of *Richard III* (Nina Levine, "The State of the Art"). Levine identifies disability studies, trauma theory, and childhood studies as examples of new approaches posing a challenge to the "various historicisms" that have dominated critical readings of the play for the past thirty years. Essays four through seven are grouped under the heading "New Directions" to indicate their "cutting edge analysis": "Audience Engagement and the Genres of *Richard III*" (Brian Walsh), "Tyranny and the State of Exception in Shakespeare's *Richard III*" (Rebecca Lemon), "'Some tardy cripple': Timing Disability in *Richard III*" (David Houston Wood), and "'Put[ting] on Some *Other* Shape': *Richard III* as an Arab V.I.P." (Adele Lee). David Cadman's guide to resources available for the teaching and study of the play—critical editions, online resources, genealogies of the two competing houses of York and Lancaster, and an annotated bibliography—concludes the collection. Connolly's introduction is divided into five parts: Finding Richard, Tragedy and History, Shakespeare and the Wars of the Roses, Reconsidering *Richard III* and the Tudor Myth, and Guide (to the essays that follow). Describing Richard as "this chameleon king," the editor claims that his "bustling" villainy and "conspiratorial relationship with the audience" will forever complicate a stable reading of the character. Two motifs that run throughout the volume are (1) a sense of the play's "startling resonances with the present" and (2) "the critical re-evaluation of the Tudor Myth," long held as an "an interpretative model" for the play. The recent discovery of Richard's remains in an excavated car park in Leicester "foregrounds the tension between myth and fact and feeds into Shakespeare's own dramatization of the manipulation of history."

Garber, Marjorie. "Descanting on Deformity: Richard III and the Shape of History." In *Shakespeare's Ghost Writers: Literature as Uncanny Causality*, pp. 28–51. New York: Methuen, 1987.

Garber is interested in the ways Shakespeare "has come to haunt our culture . . . whether in literature, history, psychoanalysis, philosophy, or politics." In the chapter on *Richard III* her subject is the "dramatization of the power of deformity inherent in both tragedy and history." The Tudor image of the monster king was for Shakespeare not a "given" but a "presupposition" in service of the question, "was [Richard's] villainy the result of his deformity?" The same process of "ideological and polemical distortion" operating in the creation of Richard and his self-conscious rhetoric of deformity is at work in the play's misshaping of history itself: Richard's twisted body "encodes the whole strategy of history as a necessary deforming and unforming—with the object of reforming—the past."

Hassell, Chris. *Songs of Death: Performance, Interpretation, and the Text of Richard III.* Lincoln: University of Nebraska Press, 1987.

An initial comparison and contrast of the 1955 Olivier film with the 1982 BBC-TV videotape (both readily available) and an epilogue on Antony Sher's interpretation of Richard in the 1984–85 RSC season frame this examination of interpretive and textual cruxes. Making considerable use of historical and literary sources, military manuals, and theological commentary, Hassel urges a providential reading of the play that views the portrayal of Richmond as positive, the play's Queen Elizabeth as a worthy opponent of Richard, and the presumably gulled citizenry as being prudent and cautious.

Hodgdon, Barbara. " 'The Coming on of Time': *Richard III.*" In *The End Crowns All: Closure and Contradiction in Shakespeare's History*, pp. 100–126. Princeton: Princeton University Press, 1991.

Combining performance criticism (mostly of RSC productions) with study of the Quarto and Folio variants, Hodgdon explores the multiplicities of meaning in Acts 4 and 5 of *Richard III.* The play's movement toward closure consists of two parts, the narrative strategy of each carrying implications for gender and power: the first part condenses around the Princes' murder and aligns reader/spectator allegiance primarily with Richard's female victims; the second part, with an almost exclusively male focus, centers on the explicit doubling or pairing of Richard and Richmond structurally and verbally.

Kendall, Paul Murray, ed. *Richard III: The Great Debate*. New York: W. W. Norton, 1965. Reissued 1992.

In one volume Kendall brings together two major documents central to the "great debate" over the true character of the historical Richard III: Sir Thomas More's *History of King Richard III* (c. 1513) and Horace Walpole's *Historic Doubts on the Life and Reign of King Richard III* (1768). More presents Richard as monster and devil incarnate; Walpole casts Richard as the tragic victim of Tudor bias. The More text (Shakespeare's primary source as reproduced in the chronicles of Hall and Holinshed) has been modernized for spelling and punctuation.

Leggatt, Alexander. "Richard III." In *Shakespeare's Political Drama: The History Plays and the Roman Plays*, pp. 32–53. London: Routledge, 1988.

In *Richard III* Leggatt observes a new element being introduced into Shakespeare's dramaturgy: "the audience's conscious awareness of its own reactions as an important part of the drama." While Richard appears to take the audience into his confidence as coconspirators in the opening soliloquy, the play is filled with warning signs that such seeming rapport is deceptive. Richard slips out of focus at the moment of his highest achievement; ironically, the public role of king that he has relentlessly sought is the one role he (as the consummate solitary) "cannot effectively" perform. Soon he develops a fear of the language he once was master of, finally yielding the play to Richmond, whose treatment of the audience as fellow members of the English community stands in marked contrast to Richard's feigned collaboration.

Machiavelli, Niccolò. *The Prince* (1513). Trans. and ed. Robert M. Adams. 2nd ed. New York: W. W. Norton, 1992.

In this famous political treatise, Machiavelli draws upon his experience as a member of the Florentine government in order to present his conception of the kind of strong leader and tactics required to impose political order for the good of the unified Italy he envisioned. Because Machiavelli separates politics from ethics and is more concerned with ends than with means, his name has become identified with all that is cynical and even diabolical in state affairs. In Shakespeare's England, this exaggeratedly negative reputation gave rise to the conventional villain known as the Machiavel, of which Richard is an example.

Magnusson, Lynne A. "Grammatical Theatricality in *Richard III*: Schoolroom Queens and Godly Optatives." *Shakespeare Quarterly* 64 (2013): 32–43.

Magnusson argues that *Richard III*'s "verbal inventiveness . . . arises out of a deeply embedded grammatical culture renewed in England with the reestablishment and spread of grammar schools in the course of the Reformation and specifically with the development of Lily's *Grammar* . . . as the one grammar text for the realm." The focus of the essay is the play's "distinctive language of female passion" (i.e., the women's curses and lamentations) and "heightened attention" to the optative mood of desiring or wishing. As a schoolboy in Stratford engaged in the daily translating of Latin constructions into English, Shakespeare would have been exposed to Lily's "showy" and "Godly" mistranslation of the optative mood, whereby internal situations of wishing became occasions of "oratorical declamation," and secular constructions such as "I pray" / "Would I" became "I pray God" / "Would God." The explicit introduction of God as the agent needed to bring about the speaker's desire dominates the cursing that is the primary speech act in 1.3; Queen Margaret's "God I pray Him / That none of you may live his natural age" (lines 222–23) illustrates "optative cursing" as not "merely invective but potentially effectual." *Richard III*—"a grammatical play, framed upon a virtuoso set of grammatical variations"—demonstrates how Shakespeare used Lily's mediated optative mood to "create . . . a heightened language for passionate utterance" and "to explore an alternative form of potency in his female characters." Moreover, the incorporation of the deity "into the performative speech acts of human wishes" opens up "the God-question attaching itself to the play's larger trajectory": Are the forces shaping events driven by divine will, or by human action? Shakespeare's well-learned and creatively supplemented use of the optative mood in *Richard III* suggests to Magnusson "an effective structure for an apparently providential tragedy."

McDonald, Russ. "*Richard III* and the Tropes of Treachery." *Philological Quarterly* 68 (1989): 465–83.

In *Richard III* McDonald detects an increasing skepticism about the linguistic medium that will develop in Shakespeare's later plays into a fully tragic conception of the instability of language. The key rhetorical pattern in *Richard III* involves a stronger speaker wresting verbal power away from one who is weaker, usually by appropriating and then reapplying the word, phrase, or metrical form of the latter. That Shakespeare's concerns about the reliability of language developed faster than his suspicions about the role of Providence in the political world can be seen in the depiction of the dull and flat Richmond: "The historical victor is a rhetorical loser."

Mooney, Michael E. "Language, Staging, and 'Affect': *Figurenposition* in *Richard III.*" In *Shakespeare's Dramatic Transactions*, pp. 23–49. Durham, N.C.: Duke University Press, 1990.

Mooney applies Robert Weimann's (*Shakespeare and the Popular Tradition*) term *Figurenposition* (figural positioning) and his distinctions between *platea* (a neutral, undifferentiated downstage playing area) and *locus* (an illusionistic, localized upstage site) to a study of Richard's shifting relationship with the audience, arguing that what changes between the first and second courtship scenes is not Richard's character but the way the character is portrayed and the consequent shift in audience response.

Pearlman, E. "The Invention of Richard of Gloucester." *Shakespeare Quarterly* 43 (1992): 410–29.

Pearlman traces Richard's genesis through *2* and *3 Henry VI*, seeing the character as an experimental work in progress who undergoes a radical metamorphosis in the major soliloquy that begins "Ay, Edward will use women honorably" (*3H6*, 3.2.126–97). In that speech Shakespeare fuses the symbolic (Richard as Vice) with the realistic (Richard's consciousness of his deformity as the causation of his villainy) and reveals for the first time the dissimulating, "ironic, leering, self-conscious, and devilish" character familiar to audiences of *Richard III*.

Prescott, Paul. *The Shakespeare Handbooks: Richard III*. Basingstoke: Palgrave Macmillan, 2006.

Prescott's performance-oriented handbook consists of six chapters: (1) The Texts and Early Performances, (2) The Play's Sources and Cultural Contexts, (3) Commentary, (4) Key Productions and Performances, (5) The Play on Screen, and (6) Critical Assessments. The core of the book is a scene-by-scene commentary that encourages readers to "envisage the words . . . unfurling in performance," thereby opening up the "environment for which [the play was] written and [offering] an experience as close as possible to an audience's progressive experience of a production." Prescott argues for a date of composition "sometime in 1592," with a first performance soon after; as to whether the 1597 Quarto or the 1623 Folio text "more faithfully represents Shakespeare's play as it was performed in his lifetime," he advocates "a healthy agnosticism as the best frame of mind" for those "seeking a way to an ideal text of *Richard III*." The chapter on sources and contexts provides excerpts from Sir Thomas More's *The History of King Richard III*, Edward Hall's *The Union of the Two Noble and Illustre Families of Lancaster and York*, *The Mirror for Magistrates*, an anonymous verse tribute to Elizabeth in honor of her coronation in 1559, and Francis Bacon's essay "Of Deformity" (which, though written years after Shakespeare wrote *Richard III*, sheds light on "orthodox attitudes to disability and deformity in early modern England"). As part of the dramatic context, Prescott discusses earlier plays on Richard (e.g., Thomas Legge's *Ricardus Tertius*) and the influence of Seneca, medieval drama (most notably the Vice character), Thomas Kyd, and Christopher Marlowe. Stage productions and performances singled out for special mention include those of Colley Cibber (1699), Edmund Kean (1814), Henry Irving (1877 and 1896), Laurence Olivier (1944), and Ian McKellen (1990); several appropriations of Shakespeare's play (e.g., Bertolt Brecht's *The Resistible Rise of Arturo Ui* [1941]) illustrate its "fruitful alternative afterlife." The chapter on cinematic revivals examines two silent films

(Sir Frank Benson's [1910] and James Keane's, with Frederick B. Warde as Richard [1912]), Laurence Olivier's transfer of his Old Vic performance to the screen (1955), Jane Howell's BBC TV *Richard III* (1983), Richard Loncraine's reworking of Richard Eyre's 1990 stage production, both starring Ian McKellen (1995), and Al Pacino's "streetwise" *Looking for Richard* (1996). Prescott organizes his assessment of critical studies under the following headings: "Before the Romantics," "Among the Romantics," "Freud and Shaw," "Tillyard, Kott and the Nightmare of History," "Beyond Tillyard," "Psychoanalytic and Feminist Studies," and "New and Old Histories." In the past half-century, the politics of historiography has replaced individual psychology as the dominant concern in *Richard III* criticism. Prescott's account of critical responses concludes that "the meanings of Shakespeare's text will admit no absolute, definitive interpretation, only provisional degrees of probability and plausibility." An annotated bibliography keyed to chapter headings rounds out the volume.

Rackin, Phyllis. "Engendering the Tragic Audience: The Case of *Richard III.*" *Studies in the Literary Imagination* 26 (1993): 47–66.

Rackin notes gendered differences between history and tragedy with respect to subjects (e.g., the marginalization of women in history plays) and emotional responses evoked from audiences (e.g., history's celebration of the masculine virtues of courage and patriotism versus tragedy's association with "womanish weeping" and the "feminine passions of pity and fear"). Rackin then "delineate[s] the ways the reconstruction of history as tragedy in *Richard III* transvalued the representations of women on Shakespeare's stage and transformed the gendered relationship between actors and audience in the playhouse," specifically placing the theater audience in a passive, feminine position.

Saccio, Peter. "Richard the Third: The Last Planta-genet." In *Shakespeare's English Kings: History, Chronicle, and Drama,* pp. 157–86. 2nd ed. New York: Oxford University Press, 2000.

The three-part chapter on *Richard III* covers the reign of Edward IV, the intrigues and strategies practiced by Richard during the nominal reign of Edward V, and the victory of Richmond at Bosworth Field, which heralded the Tudor dynasty. An examination of the historical record of Richard's life and reign reveals a figure somewhere between the extreme images of "Richard the Monster and Richard the Good."

Schwyzer, Philip. "Trophies, Traces, Relics, and Props: The Untimely Objects of *Richard III." Shakespeare Quarterly* 63 (2012): 297–327.

Through the lens of "object biography," Schwyzer traces "the afterlives of objects associated with the reign and person of Richard III" (e.g., his prayer book, crown, dagger, bed, and armor) to explore their "second afterlife" as "haunted properties" in Shakespeare's play. The opening soliloquy makes clear the dramatic text's deep engagement "with the problem of things that have outlived their time, yet linger on both to bear witness to the past and to offer themselves for employment in the present." Of all the play's theatrical properties, Richard's "bruisèd" armor (1.1.6) "provide[s] the most complex and provocative example of how *Richard III* interrogates its own objects" as "material palimpsests in which past meanings and functions co-exist with those of the present." Schwyzer considers at length the implications of the phrase "rotten armor" in the stage direction that opens 3.5. Identifying this piece of armor as a "brigander"—i.e., a leather vest with metal rings, worn by foot soldiers in the fifteenth and early sixteenth centuries but out of date by the 1590s—Schwyzer finds the adjective "appropriate to leather that is decaying, crumbling to pieces," to armor, in other words, that is not only old but that looks its age. In performances of historical drama on the early modern stage, the use of such garments (purchased for their economic and symbolic value, presumably having been worn by past generations of soldiers) "contributed to the blurring of the boundary between the present and the past, and hence between the players and the persons they presented." In the context of 3.5, "[r]ather than allowing the audience to believe that they are seeing the past as it really was," the armor "becomes an emblem of theatricality and deceit," reminding us "of the way the past generally survives in the present—as remnant, as residue, as rubbish." By "thematiz[ing certain objects] . . . at once as theatrical props and as objects with histories," the play "invites us to consider how much and how little separates the dramatic property from the genuine article, and in doing so to gauge the proximity and the distance between Shakespeare's era and Richard's own."

Spivack, Bernard. "The Hybrid Image in Shakespeare." In *Shakespeare and the Allegory of Evil*, pp. 379–414. New York: Columbia University Press, 1958.

Spivack locates the source of Richard's theatrical power in the Vice character of the medieval morality drama. From such a conventional type Richard derives his "bravura," self-mocking humor, penchant for disguise and dissimulation, habit of "verbal equivocation," and intimate relationship with the audience. Richard is a hybrid in consisting of two realities: one naturalistic (and in this case historical) and the other symbolic. Both are "enclosed by the single name of Richard," but it is only as the Vice figure that he is intelligible.

Shakespeare's Language

Abbott, E. A. *A Shakespearian Grammar.* New York: Haskell House, 1972.

This compact reference book, first published in 1870, helps with many difficulties in Shakespeare's language. It systematically accounts for a host of differences between Shakespeare's usage and sentence structure and our own.

Blake, Norman. *Shakespeare's Language: An Introduction.* New York: St. Martin's Press, 1983.

This general introduction to Elizabethan English discusses various aspects of the language of Shakespeare and his contemporaries, offering possible meanings for hundreds of ambiguous constructions.

Dobson, E. J. *English Pronunciation, 1500–1700.* 2 vols. Oxford: Clarendon Press, 1968.

This long and technical work includes chapters on spelling (and its reformation), phonetics, stressed vowels, and consonants in early modern English.

Hope, Jonathan. *Shakespeare's Grammar.* London: Arden Shakespeare, 2003.

Commissioned as a replacement for Abbott's *Shakespearian Grammar*, Hope's book is organized in terms of the two basic parts of speech, the noun and the verb. After extensive analysis of the noun phrase and the verb phrase come briefer discussions of subjects and agents, objects, complements, and adverbials.

Houston, John. *Shakespearean Sentences: A Study in Style and Syntax.* Baton Rouge: Louisiana State University Press, 1988.

Houston studies Shakespeare's stylistic choices, considering matters such as sentence length and the relative positions of subject, verb, and direct object. Examining plays throughout the canon in a roughly chronological, developmental order, he analyzes how sentence structure is used in setting tone, in characterization, and for other dramatic purposes.

Onions, C. T. *A Shakespeare Glossary.* Oxford: Clarendon Press, 1986.

This revised edition updates Onions's standard, selective glossary of words and phrases in Shakespeare's plays that are now obsolete, archaic, or obscure.

Robinson, Randal. *Unlocking Shakespeare's Language: Help for the Teacher and Student.* Urbana, Ill.: National Council of Teachers of English and the ERIC Clearinghouse on Reading and Communication Skills, 1989.

Specifically designed for the high-school and undergraduate college teacher and student, Robinson's book addresses the problems that most often hinder present-day readers of Shakespeare. Through work with his own students, Robinson found that many readers today are particularly puzzled by such stylistic characteristics as subject-verb inversion, interrupted structures, and compression. He shows how our own colloquial language contains comparable structures, and thus helps students recognize such structures when they find them in Shakespeare's plays. This book supplies worksheets—with examples from major plays—to illuminate and remedy such problems as unusual sequences of words and the separation of related parts of sentences.

Williams, Gordon. *A Dictionary of Sexual Language and Imagery in Shakespearean and Stuart Literature.* 3 vols. London: Athlone Press, 1994.

Williams provides a comprehensive list of words to which Shakespeare, his contemporaries, and later Stuart writers gave sexual meanings. He supports his identification of these meanings by extensive quotations.

Shakespeare's Life

Baldwin, T. W. *William Shakspere's Petty School.* Urbana: University of Illinois Press, 1943.

Baldwin here investigates the theory and practice of the petty school, the first level of education in Elizabethan England. He focuses on that educational system primarily as it is reflected in Shakespeare's art.

Baldwin, T. W. *William Shakspere's Small Latine and Lesse Greeke.* 2 vols. Urbana: University of Illinois Press, 1944.

Baldwin attacks the view that Shakespeare was an uneducated genius—a view that had been dominant among Shakespeareans since the eighteenth century. Instead, Baldwin shows, the educational system of Shakespeare's time would have given the playwright a strong background in the classics, and there is much in the plays that shows how Shakespeare benefited from such an education.

Beier, A. L., and Roger Finlay, eds. *London 1500–1700: The Making of the Metropolis.* New York: Longman, 1986.

Focusing on the economic and social history of early modern London, these collected essays probe aspects of metropolitan life, including "Population and Disease," "Commerce and Manufacture," and "Society and Change."

Chambers, E. K. *William Shakespeare: A Study of Facts and Problems.* 2 vols. Oxford: Clarendon Press, 1930.

Analyzing in great detail the scant historical data, Chambers's complex, scholarly study considers the nature of the texts in which Shakespeare's work is preserved.

Cressy, David. *Education in Tudor and Stuart England.* London: Edward Arnold, 1975.

This volume collects sixteenth-, seventeenth-, and early eighteenth-century documents detailing aspects of formal education in England, such as the curriculum, the control and organization of education, and the education of women.

Duncan-Jones, Katherine. *Shakespeare: An Ungentle Life.* London: Arden Shakespeare, 2010.

This biography, first published in 2001 under the title *Ungentle Shakespeare: Scenes from His Life,* sets out to look into the documents from Shakespeare's personal life—especially legal and financial records—and it finds there a man very different from the one portrayed in more traditional biographies. He is "ungentle" in being born to a lower social class and in being a bit ruthless and more than a bit stingy. As the author notes, "three topics were formerly taboo both in polite society and in Shakespearean biography: social class, sex and money. I have been indelicate enough to give a good deal of attention to all three." She examines "Shakespeare's uphill struggle to achieve, or purchase, 'gentle' status." She finds that "Shakespeare was strongly interested in intense relationships with well-born young men." And she shows that he was "reluctant to divert much, if any, of his considerable wealth towards charitable, neighbourly, or altruistic ends." She insists that his plays and poems are "great, and enduring," and that it is in them "that the best of him is to be found."

Dutton, Richard. *William Shakespeare: A Literary Life.* New York: St. Martin's Press, 1989.

Not a biography in the traditional sense, Dutton's very readable work nevertheless "follows the contours of Shakespeare's life" as it examines Shakespeare's career as playwright and poet, with consideration of his patrons, theatrical associations, and audience.

Honan, Park. *Shakespeare: A Life.* New York: Oxford University Press, 1998.

Honan's accessible biography focuses on the various contexts of Shakespeare's life—physical, social, political, and cultural—to place the dramatist within a lucidly described world. The biography includes detailed examinations of, for example, Stratford schooling, theatrical politics of 1590s London, and the careers of Shakespeare's associates. The author draws on a wealth of established knowledge and on interesting new research into local records and documents; he also engages in speculation about, for example, the possibilities that Shakespeare was a tutor in a Catholic household in the north of England in the 1580s and that he acted particular roles in his own plays, areas that reflect new, but unproven and debatable, data—though Honan is usually careful to note where a particular narrative "has not been capable of proof or disproof."

Potter, Lois. *The Life of William Shakespeare: A Critical Biography.* Malden, Mass.: Wiley-Blackwell, 2012.

This critical biography of Shakespeare takes the playwright from cradle to grave, paying primary attention to his literary and theatrical milieu. The chapters "follow a chronological sequence," each focusing on a handful of years in the playwright's life. In the chapters that cover his playwriting years (5–17), each chapter focuses on events in Stratford-upon-Avon and in London (especially in the commercial theaters) while giving equal space to discussions of the plays and/or poems Shakespeare wrote during those years. Filled with information from Shakespeare's literary and theatrical worlds, the biography also shares frequent insights into how modern productions of a given play can shed light on the play, especially in scenes that Shakespeare's text presents ambiguously.

Schoenbaum, S. *William Shakespeare: A Compact Documentary Life.* New York: Oxford University Press, 1977.

Schoenbaum's evidence-based biography of Shakespeare is a compact version of his magisterial folio-size *Shakespeare: A Documentary Life* (New York: Oxford University Press, 1975). Schoenbaum structures his readable "compact" narrative around the documents that still exist which chronicle Shakespeare's familial, theatrical, legal, and financial existence. These documents, along with those discovered since the 1970s, form the basis of almost all Shakespeare biographies written since Schoenbaum's books appeared.

Shakespeare's Theater

Bentley, G. E. *The Profession of Player in Shakespeare's Time, 1590–1642.* Princeton: Princeton University Press, 1984.

Bentley readably sets forth a wealth of evidence about performance in Shakespeare's time, with special attention to the relations between player and company, and the business of casting, managing, and touring.

Berry, Herbert. *Shakespeare's Playhouses*. New York: AMS Press, 1987.
   Berry's six essays collected here discuss (with illustrations) varying aspects of the four playhouses in which Shakespeare had a financial stake: the Theatre in Shoreditch, the Blackfriars, and the first and second Globe.

Berry, Herbert, William Ingram, and Glynne Wickham, eds. *English Professional Theatre, 1530–1660*. Cambridge: Cambridge University Press, 2000.
   Wickham presents the government documents designed to control professional players, their plays, and playing places. Ingram handles the professional actors, giving as representative a life of the actor Augustine Phillips, and discussing, among other topics, patrons, acting companies, costumes, props, playbooks, provincial playing, and child actors. Berry treats the twenty-three different London playhouses from 1560 to 1660 for which there are records, including four inns.

Cook, Ann Jennalie. *The Privileged Playgoers of Shakespeare's London*. Princeton: Princeton University Press, 1981.
   Cook's work argues, on the basis of sociological, economic, and documentary evidence, that Shakespeare's audience—and the audience for English Renaissance drama generally—consisted mainly of the "privileged."

Dutton, Richard, ed. *The Oxford Handbook of Early Modern Theatre*. Oxford: Oxford University Press, 2011.
   Dutton divides his study of the theatrical indus-

try of Shakespeare's time into the following sections: "Theatre Companies," "London Playhouses," "Other Playing Spaces," "Social Practices," and "Evidence of Theatrical Practices." Each of these sections is further subdivided, with subdivisions assigned to individual experts. W. R. Streitberger treats the "Adult Playing Companies to 1583"; Sally-Beth MacLean those from 1583 to 1593; Roslyn L. Knutson, 1593–1603; Tom Rutter, 1603–1613; James J. Marino, 1613–1625; and Martin Butler, the "Adult and Boy Playing Companies 1625–1642." Michael Shapiro is responsible for the "Early (Pre-1590) Boy Companies and Their Acting Venues," while Mary Bly writes of "The Boy Companies 1599–1613." David Kathman handles "Inn-Yard Playhouses"; Gabriel Egan, "The Theatre in Shoreditch 1576–1599"; Andrew Gurr, "Why the Globe Is Famous"; Ralph Alan Cohen, "The Most Convenient Place: The Second Blackfriars Theater and Its Appeal"; Mark Bayer, "The Red Bull Playhouse"; and Frances Teague, "The Phoenix and the Cockpit-in-Court Playhouses." Turning to "Other Playing Spaces," Suzanne Westfall describes how " 'He who pays the piper calls the tune': Household Entertainments"; Alan H. Nelson, "The Universities and the Inns of Court"; Peter Greenfield, "Touring"; John H. Astington, "Court Theatre"; and Anne Lancashire, "London Street Theater." For "Social Practices," Alan Somerset writes of "Not Just Sir Oliver Owlet: From Patrons to 'Patronage' of Early Modern Theatre," Dutton himself of "The Court, the Master of the Revels, and the Players," S. P. Cerasano of "Theater Entrepreneurs and Theatrical Economics," Ian W. Archer of "The City of London and the Theatre," David Kathman of "Players, Livery Companies, and Apprentices," Kathleen E. McLuskie of "Materiality and the Market: The Lady Elizabeth's Men and the Challenge of Theatre History," Heather Hirschfeld of " 'For the author's credit': Issues of Authorship in English Renaissance Drama," and Natasha Korda of "Women in the Theater." On "Theatrical Practices," Jacalyn Royce discusses "Early Modern Naturalistic Acting: The Role of the Globe in the Development of Personation"; Tiffany Stern, "Actors' Parts"; Alan Dessen, "Stage Directions and the Theater Historian"; R. B. Graves, "Lighting"; Lucy Munro, "Music and Sound"; Dutton himself, "Properties"; Thomas Postlewait, "Eyewitnesses to History: Visual Evidence for Theater in Early Modern England"; and Eva Griffith, "Christopher Beeston: His Property and Properties."

Greg, W. W. *Dramatic Documents from the Elizabethan Playhouses.* 2 vols. Oxford: Clarendon Press, 1931.

Greg itemizes and briefly describes almost all the play manuscripts that survive from the period 1590 to around 1660, including, among other things, players' parts. His second volume offers facsimiles of selected manuscripts.

Harbage, Alfred. *Shakespeare's Audience.* New York: Columbia University Press, 1941.

Harbage investigates the fragmentary surviving evidence to interpret the size, composition, and behavior of Shakespeare's audience.

Keenan, Siobhan. *Acting Companies and Their Plays in Shakespeare's London.* London: Bloomsbury Arden Shakespeare, 2014.

Keenan "explores how the needs, practices, resources and pressures on acting companies and playwrights informed not only the performance and publication of contemporary dramas but playwrights' writing practices." Each chapter focuses on one important factor that influenced Renaissance playwrights and players. The initial focus is on how "the nature and composition of the acting companies" influenced the playwrights who wrote for them. Then, using "the Diary of theatre manager Philip Henslowe and manuscript playbooks showing signs of theatrical use," Keenan examines the relations between acting companies and playwrights. Other influences include "the physical design and facilities of London's outdoor and indoor theatrical spaces" and the diverse audiences for plays, including royal and noble patrons.

Shapiro, Michael. *Children of the Revels: The Boy Companies of Shakespeare's Time and Their Plays.* New York: Columbia University Press, 1977.

Shapiro chronicles the history of the amateur and quasi-professional child companies that flourished in London at the end of Elizabeth's reign and the beginning of James's.

The Publication of Shakespeare's Plays

Blayney, Peter W. M. *The First Folio of Shakespeare.* Hanover, Md.: Folger, 1991.

Blayney's accessible account of the printing and later life of the First Folio—an amply illustrated catalogue to a 1991 Folger Shakespeare Library exhibition—analyzes the mechanical production of the First Folio, describing how the Folio was made, by whom and for whom, how much it cost, and its ups and downs (or, rather, downs and ups) since its printing in 1623.

Hinman, Charlton. *The Norton Facsimile: The First Folio of Shakespeare.* 2nd ed. New York: W. W. Norton, 1996.

This facsimile presents a photographic reproduction of an "ideal" copy of the First Folio of Shakespeare; Hinman attempts to represent each page in its most fully corrected state. This second edition includes an important new introduction by Peter W. M. Blayney.

Hinman, Charlton. *The Printing and Proof-Reading of the First Folio of Shakespeare.* 2 vols. Oxford: Clarendon Press, 1963.

In the most arduous study of a single book ever undertaken, Hinman attempts to reconstruct how the Shakespeare First Folio of 1623 was set into type and run off the press, sheet by sheet. He also provides almost all the known variations in readings from copy to copy.

Werstine, Paul. *Early Modern Playhouse Manuscripts and the Editing of Shakespeare.* Cambridge: Cambridge University Press, 2012.

Werstine examines in detail nearly two dozen texts associated with the playhouses in and around Shakespeare's time, conducting the examination against the background of the two idealized forms of manuscript that have governed the editing of Shakespeare from the twentieth into the twenty-first century—Shakespeare's so-called foul papers and the so-called promptbooks of his plays. By comparing the two extant texts of John Fletcher's *Bonduca*, one in manuscript and the other printed in 1647, Werstine shows that the term "foul papers" that is found in a note in the *Bonduca* manuscript does not refer, as editors have believed, to a species of messy authorial manuscript but is instead simply a designation for a manuscript, whatever its features, that has served as the copy from which another manuscript has been made. By surveying twenty-one texts with theatrical markup, he demonstrates that the playhouses used a wide variety of different kinds of manuscripts and printed texts but did not use the highly regularized promptbooks of the eighteenth-century theaters and later. His presentation of the peculiarities of playhouse texts provides an empirical basis for inferring the nature of the manuscripts that lie behind printed Shakespeare plays.

Key to
Famous Lines and Phrases

Now is the winter of our discontent
Made glorious summer by this son of York . . .

[*Richard*—1.1.1–2]

O, wonderful, when devils tell the truth!

[*Anne*—1.2.77]

Was ever woman in this humor wooed?
Was ever woman in this humor won?

[*Richard*—1.2.247–48]

A sweeter and a lovelier gentleman,
Framed in the prodigality of nature, . . .
The spacious world cannot again afford.

[*Richard*—1.2.263–66]

I do mistake my person all this while!
Upon my life, she finds, although I cannot,
Myself to be a marv'lous proper man.
I'll be at charges for a looking glass
And entertain a score or two of tailors. . . .
Shine out, fair sun, till I have bought a glass,
That I may see my shadow as I pass.

[*Richard*—1.2.273–84]

Cannot a plain man live and think no harm,
But thus his simple truth must be abused
With silken, sly, insinuating Jacks?
                              [*Richard*—1.3.52–54]

        The world is grown so bad
That wrens make prey where eagles dare not perch.
Since every Jack became a gentleman,
There's many a gentle person made a Jack.
                              [*Richard*—1.3.71–74]

The first that there did greet my stranger-soul
Was my great father-in-law, renownèd Warwick,
Who spake aloud "What scourge for perjury
Can this dark monarchy afford false Clarence?"
And so he vanished. Then came wand'ring by
A shadow like an angel, with bright hair
Dabbled in blood, and he shrieked out aloud
"Clarence is come—false, fleeting, perjured Clarence,
That stabbed me in the field by Tewkesbury."
                              [*Clarence*—1.4.49–58]

O momentary grace of mortal men,
Which we more hunt for than the grace of God!
Who builds his hope in air of your good looks
Lives like a drunken sailor on a mast,
Ready with every nod to tumble down
Into the fatal bowels of the deep.
                              [*Hastings*—3.4.98–103]

                    . . . I am in
So far in blood that sin will pluck on sin.
                              [*Richard*—4.2.66–67]

Harp not on that string . . .   [*Richard*—4.4.378]

O coward conscience, how dost thou afflict me!
[*Richard*—5.3.191]

A horse, a horse, my kingdom for a horse!
[*Richard*—5.4.7]

. . . I have set my life upon a cast,
And I will stand the hazard of the die.
[*Richard*—5.4.9–10]